MANAGEMENT DEVELOPMENT

MANAGEMENT DEVELOPMENT

Advances in Practice and Theory

Edited by

Charles Cox and John Beck

Department of Management Sciences
The University of Manchester Institute
of Science and Technology

JOHN WILEY & SONS
Chichester · New York · Brisbane · Toronto · Singapore

Library of Congress Cataloging in Publication Data:

Main entry under title:
Management Development.
   Includes indexes.
   1. Management – Study and teaching – Addresses, essays,
lectures.   I. Cox, Charles.   II. Beck, John Edward.
HD30.4.M348   1984   658.4′07124   84-5274
ISBN 0 471 90388 4

British Library Cataloguing in Publication Data:

Management development.
   1. Management – Congresses
   2. Executives, Training of – Congresses
   I. Cox, Charles   II. Beck, John
   658.4′07124   HD29

   ISBN 0 471 90388 4

Typeset by Oxford Verbatim Limited
Printed in Great Britain by St Edmundsbury Press, Suffolk

Acknowledgement

The editors take this opportunity to record their appreciation of all the work done by Mrs Rene Parsonage in typing, collating, and checking the manuscript.

Contributors

JOHN BECK   *Department of Management Sciences, University of Manchester Institute of Science and Technology*

JOHN BESSANT   *Department of Business Studies, Brighton Polytechnic*

RICHARD BOOT   *Centre for the Study of Management Learning, University of Lancaster*

CHARLES COX   *Department of Management Sciences, University of Manchester Institute of Science and Technology*

S. FINEMAN   *Centre for the Study of Organisational Change and Development, University of Bath*

TONY FRASER   *Roffey Park, Management College*

A. BAKR IBRAHIM   *Management Department, Concordia University, Montreal*

ANDREW N. JONES   *Independent Consultant*

ANDREW KAKABADSE   *Cranfield School of Management*

JOE KELLY   *Management Department, Concordia University, Montreal*

SANDRA LANGRISH   *Department of Adult Education, University of Manchester*

RONNIE LESSEM   *The City University Business School*

GEORGE LESTER   *Manchester Business School*

IAIN L. MANGHAM   *Centre for the Study of Organisational Change and Development, University of Bath*

CHARLES
MARGERISON
University of Queensland Business School

A. J. McLEAN
Centre for the Study of Organisational Change and Development, University of Bath

C. F. MOLANDER
Management Centre, University of Bradford

CHRISTOPHER
PARKER
Cranfield School of Management

MICHAEL
REYNOLDS
Centre for the Study of Management Learning, University of Lancaster

T. RICKARDS
Manchester Business School

MIKE SMITH
Department of Management Sciences, University of Manchester Institute of Science and Technology

ROGER STUART
Centre for the Study of Management Learning, University of Lancaster

R. J. TALBOT
Department of Management Sciences, University of Manchester Institute of Science and Technology

PAUL TEMPORAL
T. J. Smith & Nephew Ltd

D. WALTON
Lancashire County Council

Contents

ix

Preface

This book is a follow-up to a previous volume (Beck and Cox, 1980) in which we assembled a collection of papers identifying and discussing a number of trends in management education. Here we are presenting a further series of papers which fill some gaps in the earlier book and develop some new themes. We have also, this time, selected papers which are more practice oriented, with consequently less emphasis on the development of theories of management learning.

Margerison, in Chapter 1, provides a good general introduction to the book as a whole. He traces many of the strands which have become woven into the fabric of management education and goes on to speculate on future development. He suggests that there will be an increasing emphasis on pragmatism and on an *existential* approach. Within this framework the main themes which seem to us to be significant are as follows.

1. *Organizational Politics*. There is a growing realization in many organizations that the emphasis on *openness* and *authenticity* as a solution to organizational problems that was advocated by so many social scientists in the 1960s and 1970s has not proved effective. More and more the trend in both thinking and practice is towards accepting politics as an inevitable part of organizational life. Thus, to be effective the manager must learn to cope with organizational politics. This thinking is reflected in both Chapter 2 (Parker and Kakabadse) and Chapter 3 (Beck and Cox).

2. *Assessment Centres*. There is an increasing use of assessment centres, both for selection and identification of training needs. The use of the assessment centre has wide implications for training. Kelly and Ibraham (Chapter 4) look at one possible application for developing decision-making skills.

3. *Women in Management*. The under-representation of women at all levels of management has received widespread attention, and much effort has been expended in many different ways to increase equality of opportunity in this, as well as other fields. Smith and Langrish (Chapter 5) present one approach to increasing the managerial potential of women.

4. *Managerial Obsolescence*. One thing which is very clear is that during the next decade managers are increasingly going to have to cope with technological innovation, particularly in the use of computers and information technology. Managers will also have to learn to adapt to a continually changing and relatively turbulent environment. One consequence of all this is that managers' skills could become quite quickly out of date. Jones (Chapter 6) discusses some research on managerial obsolescence and its prevention.

5. *Creativity*. One response to low levels of innovation and competitiveness in British industry has been to emphasize the need for greater creativity in management. As a result there has been an enormous increase in the number of courses and programmes aimed at developing both organizational and individual creativity. Talbot and Rickards (Chapter 7) and Bessant and Lester (Chapter 8) describe approaches to such training. Mangham (Chapter 9) takes a wider view of managerial creativity, looking for lessons from the management of creative endeavour in the theatre.

6. *Management's Responsibility for Training*. The view that the ultimate responsibility for training rests with line management has long been part of the accepted wisdom of training departments. Progress in making this a reality has been relatively slow. In Chapter 10 Molander and Walton describe an initiative aimed at developing line managers into management development advisers, in which role they take over much of the traditional responsibilities of management development specialists.

7. *Self-Development*. A logical extension of placing responsibility for development with line management is that, ultimately, development is the responsibility of the individual. A number of papers are, therefore, concerned with self-development and learning from experience. Temporal (Chapter 11) and Fineman and McLean (Chapter 12) are both concerned with the problems of organizing self-development programmes. Stuart (Chapter 13) is concerned with facilitating a manager's day-to-day learning and Boot and Reynolds (Chapter 14) contribute some ideas on experiential learning. One widely used approach to self-development via experience is *action learning*. Lessem (Chapter 15) provides an evaluative survey and synthesis of this field. The paper by Fraser (Chapter 16) on the use of *gestalt techniques*, with its heavy emphasis on personal responsibility, also belongs with this group.

There are many ways in which a collection of papers such as this could be organized. What we have aimed to do is to group similar papers under the headings listed above, in order to give a framework and cohesion to the book. However, each paper is a separate entity and other sequences and groupings would be just as logical. There is, also, no intention that this should be a complete manual or handbook for management development. Rather, we see it as a source for inspiration and ideas to be dipped into as suits the reader. We hope that such a reader will find it as stimulating and thought-provoking as we have in its compilation.

REFERENCE

Beck, J. and Cox, C. (Eds.) (1980) *Advances in Management Education*, Wiley, Chichester.

Management Development: Advances in Practice and Theory
Edited by C. Cox and J. Beck
© 1984 John Wiley & Sons Ltd

CHAPTER 1

Existential Management Development

Charles Margerison

INTRODUCTION

Management education is now an industry in its own right. Millions of pounds are spent each year in various management education and development activities. However, it is still argued that this sum does not compare on a pro rata basis with that spent on other forms of training. Nevertheless, the situation has changed dramatically from the early 1960s when the Franks Report proposed that management education be taken seriously. Over the last decade and a half both industry and academia, not to mention the consulting businesses, have put considerable effort into improving the level of managerial competence. It is important to review where we have been and where we are going. During this period we have had a golden opportunity to explore new ways of training and development. For professionals in the field, it has been an exciting time where the rewards for success have been great. In the next decade we must, therefore, look to the way management education will develop and the demands made upon the management teachers.

Essentially, management educators must become market orientated. The clients have far more power than the students of old. They are no longer subordinates but equals in a learning partnership. They have the power to vote with their money where they wish to place their educational custom. Their experience and immediate job requirements make them more forceful judges of performance. Management education, therefore, has to be a marketable commodity meeting the same standards that managers who participate will demand for their own products. All this is a long way from the production-centred concept of education where the teacher has a virtual monopoly in deciding what is best for the student. Their power rests heavily upon the pass/fail reward system of the examination. Their superiority lies in the fact that their knowledge, although limited, is assumed to exceed that of their students. This approach has long been criticized by industrialists who have

1

demanded a far more effective approach to education. As Lord Leverhulme, the founder of the Unilever organization, wrote over 50 years ago: 'What we want is not more book learning but more practical training and education. It is well known that nothing is so fatal to thought as continuous reading' (Leverhulme, 1918).

The industrialists were not alone in their criticism of the educational approaches being taken. A number of educationists had already raised concern in the nineteenth century about the static form of education, emphasizing memory and repetition. Noticeably, the work of Rousseau, Pestalozzi, and Froebel had put forward radically different approaches emphasizing the value of experience and building upon the individual's interest. However, it was probably John Dewey (1963) who, through his 'Pedagogic Creed' and other writings, had most influence. He wrote: 'The only true education comes through the stimulation of the child's (student's) powers by the demands of the social situation in which he finds himself.'

It is, therefore, somewhat disconcerting to find that this kind of philosophy had not been introduced into management education when the Franks Report came to be written. The traditional lecture and tutorial approach still dominated. The exceptions seem to be the practical exercises given in such training programmes associated with the professions, such as accountancy, or the case studies which had been tried and tested at Harvard and exported as a major innovation in management teaching. Indeed, with one or two notable exceptions, such as the works of Barnard (1938), Jaques (1951), Brown (1960), and Dalton (1959) there was little effort to find out exactly what managers did. Detailed diary-keeping by Horne and Lupton (1965) and Stewart (1967) helped provide a sounder framework upon which to build and gradually practical research began to provide a foundation for management education.

MANAGEMENT EDUCATION AND ORGANIZATIONAL CHANGE

Over the last decade, therefore, there have been a number of attempts to link management education with organizational change. A whole new range of methods and ideas has been introduced to help managers not just with the technical aspect of their work but with the behavioural and organizational problems also. Management education has moved more towards involvement with the real-life experiences of its clients. It is useful, therefore, to review some of the developments that we have seen as a basis for considering what the next steps during the forthcoming decade are going to be.

Group Dynamics

The T groups organized by the Tavistock Institute in the United Kingdom, and the National Training Laboratories in the United States were an early attempt to move towards a greater involvement of the participants. Despite its early popularity the research conducted by Oshry and Harrison (1966) showed that there were really very few positive long-term effects from this approach once the person had returned to his organizational role. Nevertheless, such training events made the distinct move from education as a product to education as a process. Participants were encouraged to learn by reflecting on their own experience and gaining feedback on their behaviour from others. Critics argued that it was a pooling of ignorance. Advocates argued that it was an opportunity for people to learn about themselves. The important point is that it stimulated and encouraged other non-traditional forms of educational endeavour.

Many of these came to fruition in what came to be called the 'encounter movement' and we have had a succession of innovations in this field including such things as Gestalt groups, bio-energetic workshops, and others. It would be true to say that the process consultation approaches, which underlie much of the original group dynamics work, have been positively used in industry. There is now a greater awareness of the importance of group management and team building, and process consultation as a method has become increasingly used. The original experiments in group dynamics continue to have an application but need to be structured much more to the problems and tasks associated with people in their work roles. An important point is the increasing acceptance of feelings as an issue for discussion and the use of the group method in the facilitation of change.

Experiential Exercises

Another important innovation which gathered momentum during the 1960s was the development of simulations of business problems in the form of micro exercises. The aim again was to get away from conventional teaching towards some form of experience. The exercises developed were, therefore, a half-way house between the world of knowledge and the world of practise. Through these exercises people were given the opportunity to behave and learn in controlled conditions. Examples of the exercises developed were those produced by Bass *et al*. (1968) and Kolb *et al*. (1979). The value of such exercises is that they enable people to become active and to try out new behaviours in situations of relatively low risk. However, the problem-solving situations that have been created rarely match the complexity of real life. Participants therefore get the opportunity to model new behaviours and try out new problem-solving processes, but without the threats and dangers normally present. The central issue for management educators is the transfer of training associated with such activities.

Leadership Programmes

Some of the most interesting and innovative advances in management education have come through the development work based upon the original Ohio State leadership studies (Fleishman, 1973). Essentially, this research highlighted the importance of two major elements concerned with initiating structure and supportive factors. This was adapted by Blake and Mouton (1961) into a major leadership programme which proved to be a tremendous commercial success. A high proportion of the time on the programme was given to group work, where participants had the opportunity to engage in competitive tasks, case study analysis, and gather personal feedback both on specially constructed tests and from other participants. It was an amalgamation of many methods of education combined into an opportunity for self-learning and exploration. Participants felt that they learnt from interaction rather than being taught.

This was followed by other similar initiatives based upon the same research. For example, Reddin (1970) and later Hersey and Blanchard (1972) were to also develop similar educational methods with a slight refinement of the theoretical base. The important point about these initiatives was they provided an opportunity for managers to reflect on their own style within the context of structured exercises. The educational designs were a major move forward in so far as they helped managers link their personal experience to well-tested concepts through simple but practical experiential exercises.

Problem-solving and Decision-making Methods

Alongside these moves came other important innovations. A number of people developed educational programmes to deal with the key issues of problem-solving and decision-making. One of the most commercially successful but least tested of these was that developed by Coverdale (1968). In essence he had a very straightforward approach to planning and doing, but actually scored by his inventive educational designs which got people to work on real tasks, which could be done in short periods of time. He emphasized learning by doing in groups, so that people reflected on their activity, identified factors of success, and then repeated the work until improvements were manifest. A more mechanistic approach to problem-solving was developed by Kepner and Tregoe (1965) and this provided useful educational experience for those particularly concerned with operating problems. At a different level, there have been a number of initiatives to enable managers to develop their creative skills and the work of Gordon (1961) illustrated some of the key approaches which again extended the educational methods available.

Role Playing

A lot of the developments that occurred were based upon new conceptual insights and providing opportunities for people to work together on a group basis. However, the developments in role playing were primarily opportunities for people to practise what they preached. The work of Maier (1963) provided the foundation for much subsequent work and his research has formed the basis of considerable work in the field. Indeed, Maier's concern for the totally integrated process of progressive educational initiatives linked to solid research endeavour leading to further improvement, is a model for management educators. His early work has subsequently been developed into much of the work that goes on in role modelling and more recently in the practical work that has been done in performance appraisal programmes, sales training, and negotiation training. Such work over the last decade has received a great boost from the availability of technological aids such as tape recorders and TV video recorders. This work is really only at its early stages and still has much to offer.

Self-assessment

The work of the management educator has been considerably helped by the introduction of reliable tests and the process of giving feedback. The development and wider use of psychological tests has been an increasing feature of management education. There are a wide number of applications, but the work of Cattell and Eber (1964) in particular has had a considerable impact. There have been other adaptations of similar work, which was not originally designed for management education, such as that by Kirton (1977) and Myers (1976). These and other instruments have provided an opportunity for educators to help managers reflect upon their own approach to work and life. It has been a very powerful form of intervention and one which will continue to grow. It reflects a trend which I shall refer to later in this paper.

In addition to psychological tests there has been a major movement towards other forms of self-assessment. Perhaps the most notable of these was stimulated by the work of Kelly (1980) on the Repertory Grid. This was taken up particularly by Bannister and Fransella (1971). The result has been an increasing use of personal feedback based upon self-perceptions without the use of formal tests. Again management educators have been able to introduce such data and therefore facilitate more of a process than a product orientation into their work.

Surveys

Alongside the above developments have come equally interesting and useful developments in organizational surveys. The work of Likert (1967) and his colleagues Bowers and Franklin (1977) established a considerable body of research and instrumentation which has increasingly been used by management educators. At a different level the work of Hackman and Oldman (1980) has encouraged many educators to work with managers using the Job Description Survey to generate data on their work which could then be used as an integral part of the learning and development process. The use of such surveys is increasing in industry generally and we are likely to see wider use of these in the management education process in the years to come.

Action Learning

Beyond the formal techniques and tests has developed a whole range of activities which are based upon a very pragmatic approach. The action learning approach as outlined by Revans (1980) challenges the traditional educational approaches to its very roots. He argues for structured and varied experience rather than formal static tuition and illustrates how it can work with a variety of applied examples ranging from hospitals through to initiatives in developing countries. There has been little evaluation of such work, but the descriptions such as those provided by Casey and Pearce (1977) and Boddy (1980) give an insight into the dynamic way in which the management educator can work on real-life problems to fulfil both learning needs and the achievement of objectives. The research conducted by Wieland and Leigh (1971) on action learning programmes in hospitals indicated that it is difficult to measure specific improvements, but there was a feeling amongst the doctors, nurses and administrators that 'The achievements were primarily in terms of problem solving. Later research shows "good evidence of improvement." ' (Wieland 1981)

While the term 'action learning' has gained a general coinage there have been numerous other well-planned activities within the overall framework. For example, the work of Hague (1979a, 1979b), also the work of Ashton (1974) and his colleagues and their work on project-based management development, illustrate another strand of the action-orientated approach to management education. The linking of the world of work and ongoing education is, therefore, possible in a practical way and we shall see major developments in this field in the future.

Self-development

It has been argued that successful managers are not only self-starters but are experts in self-development. They may not always take the formal route but they have a happy knack of finding out what they need to know in order to progress. Increasingly, therefore, management educators have been examining ways in which self-development can be facilitated through the provision of resources and guidelines. Again the work of Hague (1974) has indicated provocative ideas on how managers can integrate education and work simultaneously. On a wider basis, Pedler, Burgoyne, and Boydell (1978) produced resources for 39 activities upon which managers concerned with self-development could concentrate. In addition, Pedler (1979) surveyed the range of research and resources and indicated the considerable contributions that are now being made to advance the self-development approach.

Joint Development Activities (JDAs)

This is a collective term covering a wide range of activities. A characteristic feature has been the working together of people mainly from business organizations in conjunction with management educators on specific development activities. The initial concept is largely associated with the work of Morris and Burgoyne (1973). The essence of JDAs, according to a retrospective review by Morris (1980), was the development of resourceful managers based upon developing projects focused on organizational opportunities. There is, therefore, an interesting overlap between action learning and self-development work and the JDA approach. However, as Morris has indicated, perhaps the key difference is that the JDA activities took off from 'A particular state of affairs within each enterprise, set out what seemed agreed to be an important state of affairs and made detailed proposals on how to move from one to the other. The reports, which in the research model are the focus of activity, were only one aspect of a complicated set of activities and relationships.'

There have, of course, been many other developments on the principle of academic organizations working together with business organizations. At Cranfield a major innovation has been the establishment of management development through consortia. As Margerison and New (1980) have illustrated, a business school can help bring together people who have a similar job in the same industry in order to compare and share experience and learn both from each other as well as the more formal methods. In addition, many business schools now have close working relationships with organizations in which the curriculum is specially designed to meet the particular needs and requirements of a company's markets, technology, culture and philosophy. All this makes considerable demands upon the management educator to have a wider approach than that of the traditional teacher. The future developments along these lines will further change the role of the management educator and require a role which involves both action research and action learning.

Self-cases

More recently there has been a move to get people to use themselves as case examples. This has been particularly prevalent in the teaching of organizational behaviour where people have been asked to take their own role as the major focus for analysis and development. In this context, a considerable amount of work has gone into helping people understand their own personality in the context of their role. Work is currently taking place on the issue of transitions both through life and between roles (Lewis and Parker, 1980). This is an important advance since it moves away from special knowledge as the centre point to personal development and example as the key issue for consideration.

THE NEXT DECADE IN MANAGEMENT EDUCATION

It is clear that we have come a long way in the last 10–15 years in the way we organize and communicate the elements of management education. Clearly, the fundamental routes are still there in so far as we teach the basic disciplines underlying management and the functions within which they are applied. However, the methods we use are increasingly dynamic rather than static, process-orientated rather than product-centred, and learner-related rather than teacher-dominated. We need, therefore, to consider the way in which the profession of management education will advance within the next decade.

We have developed our educational methods to a high level of sophistication. Now we need to relate them to the people in organizations, not just on formal programmes. The key problem is one of educational transfer. The work of Vandenput (1973) indicates that the organization has a specific influence upon the transfer of training and furthermore in his study this 'seems to be inhibitive rather than facilitative'.

It is this issue that management education has to face with its clients over and above any specific techniques or technology. We will have to develop an existential philosophy of management education. I envisage therefore that management education will have to develop a pragmatic philosophy which can be important in guiding the methodology and technology that we use.

I believe the methods will follow the philosophy and the philosophy will be determined by the clients. Essentially, they are making it clear that they want education more closely related to the problems and opportunities that they face and be integrated into their normal working activities.

Management education will, therefore, be increasingly less concerned with subject-matter and more concerned with people's existence and how they interact using the knowledge available to solve the existing problems and opportunities. As McQuarrie (1973) states, existentialism is concerned with 'Man's constant movement beyond where he is at any given time'. This is certainly a characteristic feature of any managerial activity in so far as the effort and energy expended is to build more effective organizations and affect improvements in products and service. However, it is not only a movement beyond *where* we are but beyond *what* we are. It is here that we see the basis of management education as an integral part of personal growth.

This links closely to the elements in existential thought which emphasizes the uniqueness of each person and enhancing the way in which we relate to each other. As we have found over the years, the technology of organizations often reduces both of these factors through the increasing division of labour. The original job enrichment work and, more recently, the emphasis on quality control circles, have been positive attempts to manage this dilemma and help restore personal identity and a sense of community within the work place. The role of management educators as researchers, communicators, and facilitators of these ideas have been influential in bringing about a number of changes.

The existential philosophy is essentially that we cannot stand outside to make such improvements but must work from the inside. The work of Argyris (1964, 1974, 1976) is an interesting example of this approach in action. He wrote: 'The individual must value themselves and aspire to experience an increasing sense of competence. The second requirement is an organisation that provides opportunities for work in which the individual is able to define his immediate goals, define his own paths to these goals, relate these to the goals of the organisation, evaluate his own effectiveness and constantly increase the degree of challenge in work.' The subsequent work of Argyris has provided a number of examples in which he has worked as a management educator alongside people in industry using his own particular values and methods, which although he does not call existential, have such ideas at the centre.

While this approach is not new, as evidenced by the work of Jaques (1951), it does indicate a further development. The description and articulation of such approaches has gathered ground and close links between the management educator and organization development practitioners was clearly made evident in the works of Beckhard (1969) and Schein (1969). The closer links that educators are developing with problem-solving will, therefore, be the dominant approach in management education in the next decade. It is not purely a philosophical movement which is finding favour. On the other side, management educators are recognizing that many of their traditional teaching skills are now redundant. The advent of the micro-computer and the floppy disc containing set lessons and instant feedback threaten the traditional role as never before. Add to this the video machine and the infinitely repeatable high class message then the teacher – chalk, talk, and standard lecture – will increasingly become almost totally redundant. Beyond technological change we must redesign our tuition and rewards structures. Organization structure must reflect the philosophic shift.

The Open University has been a considerable success with the educators' emphasis primarily reserved for design and coaching. Higher degrees are increasingly going to be obtained through such distance teaching and practical opportunities are already emerging in a number of far-sighted universities to provide flexible structures for students who are simultaneously executives and wish to integrate their work and their learning; as Wills (1983) has shown through the development of the International Management Centre.

The management educator must also therefore increasingly be concerned with phenomenology. Already Peters (1978) has indicated the importance of symbols, patterns, and settings as key elements in managerial action. He emphasizes that much action is a function not simply of knowledge and skill but the way in which executives structure their world in terms of the time they allow for meetings, how the seating configuration is set out, and the cues and clues given to people through interaction.

The management educator, therefore, needs to work at a level beyond mere technique and skill to show the organizational relevance and power of the techniques. A good example is that provided by Hopwood (1974) in his study of the impact of accountants and accounting methods on colleagues at work. He examines the existential patterns of interaction that facilitate and inhibit real progress. Increasingly we therefore need to be involved in working through the applications of our disciplines. Some may argue therefore, that the role of the future management educator is that of a consultant rather than a teacher. My view is that increasingly the management educator will have to see things through in a more integrated way than at present and, therefore, will be engaged in both consultative research and consultative education.

The Educational Architect Role

However, I consider that rather than being a solution-centred product-dispensing consultant, the management educator of tomorrow will spend far more time as an educational architect. His task will be to assess the requirements of the executive client and advise on the most appropriate methods, techniques, and processes in a collaborative working relationship. However, like all architects he must leave it to the executive client at the end of the day to decide ultimately how the methods, techniques, and processes are implemented. It is here that we are touching on a clear issue of management education ethics and the limitations of the role.

My own work suggests that there will, in fact, be four major aspects to the management educator's role in the future. Each one of these will involve close association with the existence of the client and understanding his purpose.

Finding out. The first element will be research and finding out through a variety of means the requirements, needs, views, and political realities of the client.

Design. The second will be to work with the client to design, develop, and produce whatever resources are required to improve the situation.

Implementation. The third will be to help, where required, the client to operate and implement the new approaches.

Review. The fourth is to reinforce and follow-up in a supportive and integrative way to ensure that the learning has been applied.

In this way we shall be definitely working from the inside to the outside, rather than imposing what we think is good upon the client. In doing so, we will be adopting both an intellectual and pragmatic approach to management education.

Our own experience indicates clearly that this is the kind of relationship that clients increasingly wish to have with management educators. We have to think of our work more in professional terms. To this end it is useful to look at the way in which other professions relate with their clients. There is a great deal to be gained from studying the nature of the relationship between the medical practitioner and the patient, the accountant and his client, the lawyer and his client. In each case there is a close relationship between theory and practice. However, each of these professions has established clear principles to govern the form of interaction and has been accused of becoming in some cases too bureaucratic and remote from those they serve.

The same danger besets management education as it enters the 1980s. We can seek to establish some detached purity by separating our work out from the real day-to-day activities of people in business by doing esoteric studies removed from the actual world in which people make a living. Too many of the laboratory studies and the simulations have gone down this route.

The alternative is to work more closely with the existence of the people who work in organizations and to share the purpose of improving this existence. In this sense the management educator cannot be value free. It is important, therefore, that management educators understand their purpose and work with people in the spirit of partnership.

That said, we have to be careful how far management education and educationists become subservient. This is always the danger. It is here that the politics of management development need to be brought out into the open. The essence of a successful professional relationship is one of partnership and we need to be able to establish principles as for other professions on the way in which we can relate meaningfully with our clients. Argyris (1970), for example, has already illustrated his normative views on intervention and the ethical implications. Likewise others have made reference to their own experience, as shown in the experiences of management educators working as consultants (Lippitt, 1975; Sinha, 1979).

Therefore, in conclusion I would suggest that we will see the following changes during the 1980s beginning to gather pace.

From Teaching to Resourcing

The role of the teacher will decline considerably as the mini computer becomes widely available. There will be little requirement for the mass lecture in an age when everyone will have their own access to interactive self-learning devices. Teachers must, therefore, change their role and become more skilled in personal consulting and counselling. Equally, they must be able to work in the wider sense as resources providing information, working through current problems, and applying their knowledge on a real-time basis.

From Programmes to Contracts

Increasingly, we will see more intra-organizational assessments based upon problems and opportunities. This contrasts with the existing product orientation where management educationists put out a range of holiday-type brochures full of the latest educational offerings. While there will always be a place for these, they will decline in importance in relation to tailor-made activities based upon thorough research and design.

From Individual to Group Orientation

The traditional emphasis has been on training and developing individuals. During the 1980s we shall see a considerable emphasis upon the development of teams and their relationship with other teams. People have to work together as a group and increasingly they will want to learn together as a group. Such activities demand flexible educational structures and teachers capable of acting as consultative resources.

From Standard Cases to Real Cases

The case method has served us well. However, people will increasingly become less enamoured with the case written 10 years ago. They will want to deal with their present case and apply their learning to current issues. Again, this will demand a considerable change in the role of the management educator into real-time learning and teaching.

From Delegating to Developing

Increasingly we shall see line managers taking far more responsibility for the training and educational function. Already there are major signs that managers are prepared to act within their organizations as developers of others. This will be further facilitated by the provision of distance teaching resources. Moreover, this will further help the real process of management development, since it is well known that nobody learns as much as the person who has to teach.

From Top-down Appraisal to Bottom-up Appraisal

We shall also see considerable changes in the way in which people are reviewed. The appraisal process is now well established but increasingly needs to be based upon more of a problem-solving approach, as I outlined a number of years ago (Margerison, 1976). We shall, therefore, see people being asked to take more responsibility for their own appraisals and in addition we shall see innovations such as team appraisal (Margerison, 1983).

From Product Centred to Marketing Centred Orientation

Perhaps the biggest change will be the overall philosophy and attitudinal change that will take place. Educators are no longer living in a market where the producer is king. This is certainly true of management education where the number of suppliers has grown rapidly. It will continue to grow rapidly. The result is that management educators must be much more market orientated. Evidence is already emerging on the way in which this will affect our operations. For example, the degree structures are being radically altered. There are many different ways of gaining an MBA. Increasingly, Masters degrees are being opened up on a part-time basis to people who wish to integrate their organizational work with concurrent research links with management educators. In addition, there are a number of schemes available for part-time tuition and innovative ways in which industrial organizations are linking with academic organizations to enable managers to further their qualifications as an integral process of their work. In one sense these innovations are not new in so far as there have always been such experiments, particularly in the United States and also in the United Kingdom. However, what we will witness is a major expansion and development of these facilities.

From Inputs to Outputs

Management education, like all education, has for too long stressed inputs. We have tried to pump into people new knowledge and skills. Clearly, at the appreciation phase of any new area becoming professionalized, there is a need to do this. However, we now need to concentrate more upon outputs rather than inputs. In this context we need to get the managers to learn by producing outputs. This is what they are, in effect, paid for on a day-to-day basis. We should thus try to organize learning on a similar basis. This will involve trying to relate knowledge and skills far more to projects and tasks which have a purpose rather than teaching them as ends in themselves.

From Fixed to Continuing Education

We are moving very fast towards a concept of continuing education. Management education is a vital and integral part of this. The notion of acquiring an education early in life which can fit you for the whole of your career, is no longer adequate. The world is changing so fast that we need to structure learning opportunities so that people can join in on a flexible basis and adapt to new requirements. Therefore, we shall see tremendous structural changes to accommodate the concept of life-long learning and the notion that someone is a perpetual student may not be seen as a negative thing providing they are applying their learning as they go.

SUMMARY

The 1980s will, therefore, see the acceleration of many changes in management education. However, the major change will be the way in which we see the task before us. I believe that this will be determined far more by what I have called an existential approach to management education. In this the educator needs to see himself as a part of the existence of those whom he wishes to influence. It is about understanding through association rather than through detached analysis. It is about an involvement in the problems and opportunities. However, it is an existential approach with a difference in that it does involve the management educator not just taking things as they come but having a pro-active approach responding to real issues. To this end, management education during the 1980s is in search of a relevant philosophy to guide its practice.

It was Thomas Kuhn (1970) who suggested that major advances in science had little to do with scientific experimentation but more to do with the conception of a new paradigm. In essence, it requires people to look at the world in a new way such as Copernicus did in order that we can move forward. Only then can the process of validation have any particular meaning. I would argue the same is true in management education. We are limited by our paradigms. The time has come to review our approach and look at radical alternatives. Otherwise we shall become the servants of our traditional conceptions of teaching and learning and not take the major opportunities which are now available. Recently, a number of people have reviewed the changes in management education over the last 10–15 years. The work of Nancy Foy (1979) suggests that we have gone off in many directions some of which, as we would expect, have led into blind alleys.

What emerges, therefore, is that we have many new techniques for organization structures, new courses and methodologies, but no overall dominating paradigm. Perhaps it is too much to ask. Maybe it is through diversity that we begin to fulfil a more useful approach to developing managers. Every profession has to go through a period of experimentation before settling upon a model that governs the best practice. The scientific revolution in medicine, for example, took a long time to evolve but even now there are many who will question the exclusive validity of this particular paradigm with the calls for alternative medicine.

However, within the field of management, we are still struggling towards our dominating paradigm. Newbigging (1980) has stressed that one of the problems associated with advances in the area are the divisions that we put into our educational system which mirror the class differences in society. He argues: 'The values are elitist, academic and professional.' Not only that, he emphasizes the term 'management' is a catch-all phrase which does not help us define what we are doing. This stands in contrast to the German and French concepts which have been much more specific in identifying the relationship between technical specialism and its relationship to the management of enterprises. His paradigm emphasizes the need for a much closer link in the building of managerial competence based upon sound technical backgrounds. He indicates that 'The so called classic or liberal education . . . have all promoted a middle class, professional ethic which continues to maintain a dubious distinction from the world of work. The development of U.K. management education has reinforced the idea of the manager as a separate profession.' It can be argued, therefore, that this creates more of a concern with career than it does with the development of an effective product and organization. To this end, it has also been suggested by Wills (1980) that we are far too narrow in our concepts of what are required. He emphasizes the need for continuing life-long learning and that management educationists should work more closely with technologists to achieve this. The separation of technological education from management education again produces an artificial divide.

All this suggests that we must look much more closely at the real demands of industry, commerce, and the public organizations. It is the challenges they have to face which should determine the forms of education and development that we produce. In essence we have to get in touch with the political realities as well as the commercial realities. My own approach is to try and work with groups of people in the context of organizational problems and opportunities. This is in contrast to the traditional mode of emphasizing individual development. It is not a question of whether one is right and the other is wrong. It is a question of balance and so far there has been too much emphasis on individual development. The reality of organizational life is that people have to work in groups on a task basis. It is here that we need more effort.

In this context, Lupton (1980) has developed a number of interesting views on what the business school of the future needs to do. He sees the growth of more part-time management education, the development of an open business school, and an extension of the action research and joint development activities. Clearly, we need new structures which enable people to move easily between our educational resource centres and their organizations where they produce products and services. Already we can begin to see such changes emerging with part-time MBA courses, opportunities for MScs to be conducted while occupying an organizational role, and, of course, the innovations in continuing executive education programmes with consortia, projects, and a variety of other mechanisms.

All this I believe indicates a much more political awareness and involvement in the real issues by educationists. However, it must not stop there. Management education tends to be limited to those who have the designation 'manager'. However, we must not forget those who manage but do not have the title. To make real progress, we need a paradigm which brings in the way we work with trade unions who at present prefer a separate approach to the development of their own style.

In short, management education is fragmented, not sufficiently politically based, too product orientated, and individualistically centred. We must evolve a paradigm which will help us tackle these issues. I believe that one way in which we the educationists can move towards this is to be far more involved in the existence of the players on the commercial, industrial, and public pitches of managerial endeavour. Only by working with them more closely can we hope to produce a contribution which will be relevant to the real issues. We must move from theories and techniques to practice.

REFERENCES

Argyris, C. (1964) *Integrating the Individual and the Organization*, Wiley.
Argyris, C. (1970) *Intervention Theory and Method*, Addison & Wesley.
Argyris, C. (1974) *Behind the Front Page*, Jossey-Bass.
Argyris, C. (1976) *Increasing Leadership Effectiveness*, Wiley.
Ashton, D. (1974) The trainer's role in project based management development, *Journal of European Industrial Training*, **3**, 3.
Bannister, D. and Fransella, F. (1971) *Enquiring Man*, Penguin Books.
Barnard, C. (1938) *The Functions of the Executive*, Harvard University Press.
Bass, B. M., Vaughan, J. A., and Cox, C. J. (1968) A programme of exercises for management and organisational psychology, ERGOM.
Beckhard, R. (1969) *Organisation Development*, Addison Wesley.
Blake, R. and Mouton, J. (1961) *The Managerial Grid*, Gulf Publishing.
Boddy, D. (1980) Some issues in the design of action learning programmes, in: *Advances in Management Education*, Edited by J. Beck and C. Cox, Wiley.
Bowers, D. G. and Franklin, J. L. (1977) *Survey Guided Development – Data Based Organizational Change*, University Associates.
Brown, W. (1960) *Explorations in Management*, Heinemann.
Casey, D. and Pearce, D. (1977) *More than Management Development*, Gower.
Cattell, R. and Eber, H. (1964) *Handbook for the 16 Personality Factor Questionnaire*, Institute for Personality and Ability Testing.
Coverdale, R. (1968) *Thought – A Framework for Teamwork*, Training Partnerships, London.
Dalton, M. (1959) *Men who Manage*, Wiley.
Dewey, J. (1963) *Experience and Education*, Collier Macmillan.
Fleishman, E. (1973) Twenty years of consideration and structure, in: *Current Developments in the Study of Leadership*, Edited by E. A. Fleishman and J. G. Hunt, Southern Illinois University Press.
Foy, N. (1979) Management education – Current action and future trends, *Journal of European Industrial Training* (Monograph), **3**, 2.
Gordon, W. J. J. (1961) *Synectics*, Harper & Rowe.
Hackman, J. and Oldman, G. (1980) *Work Redesign*, Addison Wesley.

Hague, H. (1979a) *Helping Managers to Help Themselves*, Context.

Hague, H. (1979b) *Management Training for Real*, Context.

Hague, H. (1974) *Executive Self Development*, Macmillan.

Hersey, P. and Blanchard, K. (1972) *Management of Organization Behaviour*, Prentice-Hall.

Hopwood, A. (1974) *Accounting and Human Behaviour*, Accountancy Age Books.

Horne, J. and Lupton, T. (1965) The work activities of middle managers: An exploratory study, *Journal of Management Studies*, **1**, 21.

Jaques, E. (1951) *The Changing Culture of the Factory*, Tavistock.

Kelly, G. (1980) *The Psychology of Personal Constructs*, Norton.

Kepner, C. and Tregoe, B. (1965) *The Rational Manager*, McGraw-Hill.

Kirton, M. (1977) *Kirton Adaptation/Innovation Inventory*, N.F.E.R.

Kolb, D., Robin, I. M., and McIntyre, J. M. (1979) *Organizational Psychology: An Experiential Approach*, 3rd Edition, Prentice-Hall.

Kuhn, T. (1970) *The Structure of Scientific Revolutions*, 2nd Edition, University of Chicago Press.

Leverhulme, Lord (1918) *The Six-Hour Day*, Allen and Unwin.

Lewis, R. and Parker, C. (1980) *Moving Up . . . How to Handle Transitions to Senior Levels Successfully*, MODRC Working Paper, Cranfield School of Management.

Likert, R. (1967) *The Human Organization*, McGraw-Hill.

Lippitt, G. (1975) *The Role of the Training Director as an Internal Consultant*, MCB Publications.

Lupton, T. (1980) *Business Schools in the 80s and Beyond*, Manchester Business School and Centre for Business Research, Working Paper No. 49.

Maier, N. (1963) *Problem Solving Discussions and Conferences*, McGraw-Hill.

Margerison, C. (1976) A constructive approach to appraisal, *Personnel Management*, **July 1976**.

Margerison, C. (1983) *Team Appraisal. Leadership and Organisation Development Journal*, 4, 2.

Margerison, C. and New, C. (1980) Management development by inter-company consortium, *Personnel Management*, **November 1980**.

McQuarrie, J. (1973) *Existentialism*, Pelican Books.

Morris, J. (1980) Joint development activities from practice to theory, Chapter 8 in: *Advances in Management Education*, Edited by J. Beck and C. Cox, Wiley.

Morris, J., and Burgoyne, J. (1973) *Developing Resourceful Managers*, Institute of Personnel Management.

Myers, I. (1976) *Myers–Briggs – Introduction to Type*, Centre for Applications of Psychological Type.

Newbigging, E. (1980) Management development: Panacea, placebo or punk, *The Business Graduate*, **X**, II.

Oshry, B. and Harrison, R. (1966) Transfer from here and now to there and then: Changes in organizational problem diagnosis stemming from T group training, *Journal of Applied Behavioural Science*, **2**.

Pedler, M. (1979) *Self Development Bibliography*, MCB Publications.

Pedler, M., Burgoyne, J., and Boydell, T. (1978) *A Manager's Guide to Self Development*, McGraw-Hill.

Peters, T. J. (1978) Symbols, patterns and settings: An optimistic case for getting things done. *Organizational Dynamics*, **Autumn 1978**.

Reddin, W. (1970) *Managerial Effectiveness*, McGraw-Hill.

Revans, R. (1980) *Action Learning*, Blond and Briggs.

Schein, E. (1969) *Process Consultation*, Addison Wesley.

Sinha, D. (1979) *Consulting and Consulting Styles*, Penguin Books.
Stewart, R. (1967) *Managers and Their Jobs*, Macmillan.
Vandenput, A. E. (1973) The transfer of training, *Journal of European Training*, **2**, 3.
Wieland, G. (1981) *Improving Health Care Management. Part IV*, Health Administrative Press, Ann Arbor.
Wieland, G. and Leigh, H. (1971) *Changing Hospitals*, Tavistock.
Wills, G. S. C. (1980) Cobblers in the business schools, *The Business Graduate*, **X**, II.
Wills, G. S. C. (1983) Management Development through Action, *The Journal of Management Development* 2, 1.

Management Development: Advances in Practice and Theory
Edited by C. Cox and J. Beck
© 1984 John Wiley & Sons Ltd

CHAPTER 2

The Undiscovered Dimension of Management Education: Politics in Organizations

Andrew Kakabadse and Christopher Parker

INTRODUCTION

Analysing organizations in terms of political behaviour is not new in the organization psychology field. Over 20 years ago, well-known theorists such as French (1956), Burns (1961), and March (1962), indicated that the political aspects of life in organizations require substantial exploration. It is only recently that further study into the field has been conducted (McClelland, and Burnham, 1976; Pettigrew, 1977; Schein, 1977; Porter *et al.*, 1981), but without any noticeable impact in the area of management education.

In this paper we assume that the reality of organizational life must be mirrored in management education practice. Hence, in order to make any training event a worthwhile experience, we explore some of the practices commonly utilized in management education; examine the different interpretations and definitions of politics in organizations; indicate why management education practitioners have not taken into account the political reality of organizational life in their work; offer a model of political behaviour; and suggest ways of developing management education practice to take account of politics in organizations.

PHILOSOPHY OF MANAGEMENT EDUCATION

Consider certain commonly applied management education techniques, such as case studies; simulated exercises; data feedback/behavioural training approaches; and learning in project team exercises. What really is achieved? Fundamentally, management education practice is either geared towards de-

19

veloping the participant's work-related experience in a management education event, and/or to stimulating the learning of knowledge that is 'acceptable' and 'applicable' to the place of work. How is this done?

Managers are expected to bring with them pertinent issues for general debate. Management education tutors are expected to develop their inputs around some of the participants' agendas. As part of the process, managers are placed into situations where they have to examine their way of operating. Self-analysis is achieved through check lists, questionnaires, managerial style indicators, and CCTV. Learning takes place in groups through interpersonal consultation and practise in preference to didactic exposition. Furthermore, learning is increasingly being seen as something spread over a life-time as opposed to the more traditional view of gaining education, then acquiring full-time employment. Modular-based learning is likely to be as popular as qualification-based learning, for individuals can learn under controlled conditions, attempt to implement in the workplace, learn again, and once more attempt implementation. Such operations attempt to provide continuous reinforcement, utilizing skills, logical deduction, and assimilation through active participation and realistic experience.

Successful self-oriented learning depends on the extent to which each individual's experience can be utilized in management training situations. Obviously, there are certain practical problems, e.g. on certain programmes everyone's experience cannot be fully examined. Yet, whether fully examined or not, the key to 'successful' management training hinges on *what* inputs are planned for each programme and *how* each participant's experiences have been utilized and developed.

By adopting a 'what and how' analysis, certain interesting questions emerge. For example: How effective is any one form of management training to any other or even how effective is management training in general? How applicable and practicable is management training (i.e. to what extent can knowledge or insight gained in one setting be transferred to another setting)? How beneficial will individuals find any one or other form of management training? These questions relate to performance measures, i.e. to what extent will this organization/group/individual benefit in a specific or even general sense, from any one or other form of management education? Hence, how is success measured? Basically, success is measured by generating commonly shared and acceptable performance oriented criteria that determine so-called successful or unsuccessful training events. For example, a successful in-company general management programme of 3–4 weeks' duration would probably be considered successful if the majority of the participants indicate their satisfaction with the programme (a shared view which has developed over the duration of the programme) and further, because each participant's boss indicated that X has come back an interesting and stimulating man (perhaps interesting to the boss without being a threat to his status, position, and authority). *Success relates to acceptable and shared group norms and to a dominant hierarchical philosophy of downward influence.*

Our view is that management educationists, participants on training programme, and decision-makers in client organizations who invest in management education, strive for the same objective – to achieve *shared meaning*. Shared meaning relates to the norms, attitudes, personal values, views of the world, and feelings about situations that are a common experience for the individuals concerned in that situation.

For example, consider a sentiment participants may bring with them to training programmes: 'I am a manager, please help me manage better.' A search process then begins, attempting to satisfy the individual and often the supporting organization's needs, with a training event that is satisfactory both in format and content to the requirements of the clients. The first common value shared by all parties is that 'managers have the right to manage'. Hence, managers should be exposed to qualitative and quantitative data that will lead to improved performance. Once onto a training event, strong pressures exist for additional forms of shared meaning to be accepted by the participant – work in groups; be open; share information; ask questions; debate issues, etc. Whether involved in a T group or multi-subject general management programme, disclosure of information about self, or self in relation to others, or to the use of techniques or aids (from computers to marketing techniques), is a strong pressure brought to bear on participants. Get involved, take part, make a contribution, support your study/reference group, are influences that any participant on any training event cannot ignore. Such influences are instrumental in developing a strong sense of shared meaning. The underlying dynamic, whether involved in project group work or individual introspective counselling, is to achieve 'best fit' – come to terms with the environment around you – work through and with other people. In fact, the platitudes are almost endless.

Not that the dominant philosophy of achieving shared meaning is unique to management education. Related areas of organization development and organization behaviour, in the 1960s and 1970s, were dominated by theories propounding shared meaning. In the Organization Development field, there has emerged an espoused philosophy of care, trust, and affection for the individual and, by implication, for the organization as a whole (Argyris, 1964; Fiedler, 1967). Similarly, in the Organization Behaviour field, strong emphasis has been given to identifying the commonly shared norms that seem to drive organizations in a particular way. For example, the organization climate studies (Pervin, 1967; Litwin and Stringer, 1968; Payne and Phehey, 1971; Georgiades, 1972; Pritchard and Karasick, 1973); the Aston-type studies on organization structure (Pugh, 1966; Hage and Aiken, 1967, 1969; Pugh *et al.*, 1968; Pugh and Hickson, 1976); identifying the commonly shared characteristics of motivation/demotivation (Carpenter, 1971; Mumford, 1970); and the search for the 'perfect' work organization (Jaques, 1976). These and other studies have been a dominant influence in driving researchers to attempt to identify the commonly shared and accepted criteria that gives both people and organizations, identity.

Notions of shared meaning are at times valuable. The 'pulling together' philosophy, especially in recession, is necessary and vital. But, so often shared meaning becomes compulsive and enforced. Furthermore, what happens to the idiosyncratic, creative people? History shows that creativity stems from the idiosyncratic, the mutant gene, the persistent lone voice. So often the creative conflict necessary for progress is personalized and the very necessary rebel is 'cast out'.

Studies of shared meaning and their underlying philosophy hold firm under conditions of collaboration. However, as Herman (1974) points out, anger, hate, coercion, and aggression are as usual as love, peacefulness, and compassion. Living and interacting with other people has as much to do with *unshared meaning* as it has to do with *shared meaning*. Any management training event which generates data from participants about situations where trust and acceptance of the other are impossible objectives to pursue, is likely to be poorly utilized by trainers, if they have no model for interpreting such stimuli. What is required is a model of thinking, feeling, and behaving that takes account of the values and behaviours that are as much unshared as shared. Traditionally, politics has been seen as concentrating on negative interactions between people (i.e. concentrating on unshared meaning). In fact, the *political process* in organizations relates to both shared and unshared meaning. Politics is about influencing other people. It is the outcomes of this influence process which are perceived as either negative or positive.

Our concern is to bridge the gap between individual motivation, group norms and identities, and the pressures brought to bear on individuals to adopt acceptable behaviours. We do this by relating politics to the longer-term preferred work strategies that individuals adopt. Preferred work strategies are related to the personal values and the norms of behaviour with which people identify. By linking the longer-term strategies or plans each individual has developed, it is possible to map out the degree of shared and unshared meaning in a situation. Hence, politics in organizations takes into account shared and unshared meaning and is portrayed by the influencing skills of key actors in achieving their objectives through others. In effect, what we describe in the next section is a motivational model of human behaviour; identifying the similarities and differences between people by trying to understand why people think, feel, and behave in the way they do.

COGNITIVE MAPS AND POLITICAL ACTIVITY

A wealth of evidence exists in the psychological literature that individual behaviour is driven by cognitive maps. Bartlett (1932) and Neisser (1977) suggest we operate on cognitive schema. Kelly (1955), and later Slater (1976), have developed the Repertory Grid to test this notion. Piaget (1978) and Brunner (1972, 1981) offer similar arguments in the field of developmental psychology. Bandura (1977) and Mischel (1977) suggest that people use symbolic processes to represent events and to communicate with others. Goffman (1974) suggests that 'frames' of individual reference are created through subjective interpretation of social interaction. Tolman (1924) has suggested that we structure our experience to form 'purposive maps' which drive behaviour, and Broadbent (1977) has suggested that subjective maps may be structured on a hierarchical basis forming global and local schema.

Salancik and Pfeffer (1978) have offered 'a social information processing model' to describe how salient 'purposive maps' can be developed, which in turn drive behaviour. We assert that it is the perceived salience of individual maps which is the key factor in transforming global and local individual purposive maps into political behaviour because perceived salience leads to attempts at, and resistance to, influence. We suggest that global schema will be dominant in the long term since they represent dominant values for individuals, whereas local schema represent action tactics associated with those values. *We see politics as an influence process which can be perceived as positive or negative depending on whether one's own 'purposive maps' are being supported or threatened.*

Let us explore further the notions of purposive maps being supported or threatened. In our discussions on organizational politics with managers, there has been a clear split between legitimate and illegitimate influence attempts. In dealing downwards, the successful influence model is essentially a 'comfort process'. Managers attempt to influence downwards through their knowledge of groups and individuals on the basis of what they will be comfortable with. The best implementation of ideas is the product of an influence process based on what individuals understand in terms of their own 'psychological position'. If influence moves by individuals can be re-interpreted and re-phrased to be 'comfortable' to subordinates this approach works to great advantage.

In managing upwards, however, middle managers use a different model. They are so used to leading downwards that they forget that relations upward are also mutual dependence situations. They stereotype the relationship usually in a top-down way and disregard attempts at upward influence, they do not use their highly successful 'comfort model' used for subordinates – they forget that bosses are people! When their stereotypes of bosses behaviour and intentions are threatened or broken, they believe 'politics is being played'. We believe that if insights into the range of dominant schema exhibited by individuals at work can be provided, then the model of 'influence as a comfort' process can be used both upward and downwards. Individuals' psychological positions can be 'massaged' in a positive way.

We describe political processes in terms of global and local purposive maps,

Table 1   Dominant value systems

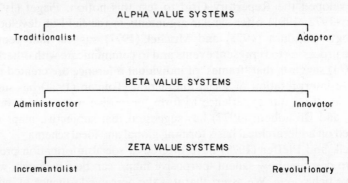

which differ depending on individual cognitive complexity. This complexity involves different perceptions of organization values and role, task, and power dependences in the total organization, subsystems, and small groups.

Our model examines three levels of dominant value systems (dominant schema) and each is represented by a bi-polar range of action strategies (local schema). The three levels are alpha, beta, and zeta (Table 1).

A B Z MODEL

DOMINANT SCHEMA   ALPHA VALUE SYSTEMS (A)

Individuals with alpha value systems match those of the organization. Individuals accept and maintain the power dependences and resource allocation process within the organization. Alpha oriented people emphasize control of group membership. Group values are maintained by paying particular attention to interpersonal interactions.

Alpha people are concerned with maintaining the status quo. People holding alpha values attempt to ensure that resource allocation to their group and to individuals remains constant, as do power dependences. Such effort is geared towards reducing uncertainty and minimizing the anxiety associated with any change.

LOCAL SCHEMA   THE RANGE OF ALPHA ACTION STRATEGIES

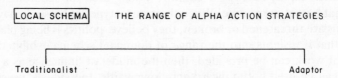

Seeks detailed constancy in resource allocation and power dependences.

Seeks constancy in resource allocation and power dependences, but is

Attempts conservation of detail in internal and external contracts. Conservative, inflexible, and fearful of change.

more flexible and adaptive to the extent that he seeks constancy in the *ratio* of resource allocation and power between departments and groups. He is able to adapt to changes at a detailed level, so long as the ratios are perceived as constant.

Both traditionalist and adaptor will have a high concern about 'system pathology' and perceptions of 'system pathology' will be easily tapped when they are confronted by others holding non-alpha value systems.

DOMINANT SCHEMA   BETA VALUE SYSTEMS (B)

People with predominantly beta value systems are characterized by an acceptance and attempted maintenance of the values of the total organization, but a questioning of the resource allocation and power dependences of particular departments, units, and work situations.

Individuals with beta value systems have developed a cognitive appreciation of how subsystems interact with the organization. They appreciate that their plans cannot progress without involving other parties who may think and feel differently to themselves. Attempts at influence are not necessarily made to be to the advantage of all. Decisions will be arrived at on the basis of what is tolerable to the parties concerned and not necessarily consensual. The acceptance of total organization values could be utilized as justification for redistribution of power and resources.

LOCAL SCHEMA   THE RANGE OF BETA ACTION STRATEGIES

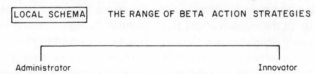

Administrator   Innovator

Has a role orientation to his work and, while questioning power dependences and resource allocation, will do so in such a way that his current role is maintained or, more usually, emphasized and amplified at the expense of others. He will use role amplification incentives to gain support from those not under attack. He will collaborate with others and check before 'making his play'. He needs others on his side before action.

Has a task orientation and is happy to see his role altered on the basis of product or service improvement. He will instigate change in resource allocation and power dependences on the basis of product or service improvement. He will 'test the waters' before 'making his play', but will not be dependent on the support of others before stating his case. Rather, he will use his influencing skills to gain support after stating his case.

The essential difference between the administrator and innovator, besides their role and task orientations, is that the administrator is 'outer directed', i.e. far more influenced by others; the innovator is 'inner directed', i.e. self-directed, more prepared to risk, more assertive, more able to cope with conflict directed towards him and more confident about his own influencing skills.

| DOMINANT SCHEMA | ZETA VALUE SYSTEMS (Z) |

Zeta oriented people question the power dependences, resource allocation, *and* the value system of the total organization. They are characterized not only by a questioning of current dominant values, but also by exhibiting an ability to disengage, or become separate, from the previous values held by the majority in the organization. Zeta oriented people aim towards developing new organizational values and forms. People operating with zeta value systems believe in their visions about long-term trends in the external and internal environment. They have developed what Vickers (1968) described as 'systemic wisdom'. Zeta value system actors operate in relative isolation from other organizational personnel in order to develop new beliefs. Their work philosophies and strategies are dependent on a well identified but personal philosophy concerning the future.

| LOCAL SCHEMA | THE RANGE OF ZETA ACTION STRATEGIES |

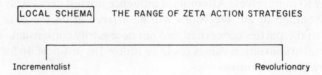

Incrementalist   Revolutionary

Concerned with phased change in the value system of the organization. Replacing existing institutions with new ones. His propensity to risk dramatic change is lower than the revolutionary but higher than those with alpha or beta value systems. He works on principles of 'rolling reorganisation' – phased structural change to produce value changes within the organization. Typically the incrementalist will be part of a complex organization and will have been part of the system for some time. He will have enacted previous values of the organization, and this previous commitment to and appreciation of historical values within

Does not value the process of incremental change, because he has not been committed to previous value systems. He will make great efforts to maintain detachment from previous values and individuals who have been dominant in maintaining those values. Typically a 'new broom', he is able to revolutionize because he manages his own change attempts so as to minimize his commitment to the past and hence perceived dissonance. Despite his non-commitment to the past he will have a good appreciation of how the current system has evolved and how he wants to revolutionize it. Typically he is the entrepreneur or a the organization can produce difficulties in distancing from the past and implementing dramatic change. This is primarily due to perceived dissonance.

'hit man' brought into an 'ailing' organization.

Given these broad definitions, what use are they to individuals and groups who are attempting to influence others? First of all we have found that the model itself is valuable in enabling individuals to understand the previously amorphous area of politics in organizations, through classifying particular values and behaviours. Secondly, it moves people away from thinking of 'politics' as outcomes of unsuccessful influence attempts to the realization that maybe they are already highly skilled as organizational politicians. Once individuals see politics as a process they begin to realize that maybe they can have greater influence on outcomes by using their process skills more effectively.

Table 2   Beta action strategies

Administrator	Innovator
Comfortable with: ● Established procedures and roles ● Lengthy decision-making ● Arguing for policies on committees ● Working within role constraints ● Finding compromises ● Adjusting his behaviour to suit other people ● Manoeuvring for increased personal power ● Maintaining superior/subordinate distance	● Confrontation and conflict ● Working within poorly structured situations ● Thinking and involvement in new ideas and taking the risks ● Using personal influencing skills ● Working with new and different people ● Introducing major changes to improve products or service ● Task orientation in the organization
Uncomfortable with: ● Personal criticism and confrontation ● Sharing with subordinates ● Championing policies or ideas that are considered unpopular or risky ● Putting into practice something new ● Making quick decisions ● Displays of openness, warmth, and empathy by others ● Excessive involvement in group activity	● Working within role constraints and procedures ● Committees and lengthy decision-making processes ● Maintaining group cohesion for its own sake ● Staying in one job for too long ● Increased constraints on initiative and creativity ● Displays of personal warmth and sympathy

With this realization, the next step is to give individuals behavioural benchmarks for the different political schema, differentiating between comfortable and uncomfortable experiences for each profile. Table 2 gives an example for the two beta action strategies. These benchmarks have been devised through observation, discussion, consultancy practice, and from a broad spectrum of trait psychology.

Case Example

A Management Development adviser (beta innovator) had for two years been attempting to influence her boss, the personnel director, to accept a new management development scheme she had devised. The scheme epitomized her own values on how people in organizations should be developed and how task and service operations should be improved. Her boss had consistently refused to accept the scheme. She was interviewed by us and it became clear that such negative outcomes for her were seen as politics. We interviewed her, further about her work situation and asked her to complete the politics questionnaire developed by us. It became clear that her boss was a beta administrator – highly role and status conscious; hence the clash.

With us acting as facilitators, she re-planned her influence moves concerning the new M.D. scheme by suggesting that if introduced, the status of her boss and the strategic aspects of his role would be increased and, as a secondary issue, task and service performance would also increase. Her new scheme was accepted based on what her boss was *comfortable with* – she massaged his meaning of the world.

UNDERSTANDING SUCCESSFUL IMPLEMENTATION THROUGH SCHEME THEORY

As stated above, there exists substantial evidence to suggest that behaviour is driven or motivated by individual cognitive maps. Neisser (1977), for example, has suggested that cognitive maps or schemes are necessary before we can act. We need to anticipate consequences by approximating our experience to the current perception, and then by acting on the basis of those approximations.

A simple scheme might be a tentative plan for the solution of a problem, which is characterized by the start conditions, an outline of the goal to be reached, and some ideas of the route or subgoals that one will go through in order to reach the end goal. The term 'scheme' denotes the regular structure of behaviour in the sense that although repeated activations of a scheme are never absolutely identical, nevertheless there is a regularity in the operations performed and this regularity constitutes the scheme. Scheme theory is an abstract notion used to indicate the fact that there is an organized repeatable series of operations at some level of organization. The level may range from molecular muscle contractions to the vast long-range plans developed for D-Day in Normandy.

Gudrun Ecklad (1980) has suggested that scheme theory can best be described in terms of means–end structures. She argues that: 'Behaviour patterns and hence motivation are best viewed in terms of a lens structure in the sense used by Brunswick' (1952, pp. 25):

> 'In a lens structure, there are two poles or distal points which often function as the start and end phase of a process. Between the two poles there are several paths all starting at the same point and ending in the same point, but following different routes in between – generally, behaviour in a problem-solving situation is *equifinal*, the means vary according to conditions but the final desired state remains the same . . . the lens structure of cognitive motivation resembles a bundle of light rays which pass through a lens. The rays emerge from one point and converge on one point again, but in between they are dispersed by the lens and follow different paths . . . .'

Schemes then have a start or initial state, an end or final state, and a branched middle – the degree of branching dependent upon the current situation, and the degree of 'fit' between the initial scheme and encountered reality.

In applying scheme theory to political behaviour in organizations we suggest that individuals bring a dominant scheme or view of themselves in relation to the organization. This scheme being a product of experience, their values, current perception of their role, power dependences, resource allocation, ambition, and their tolerance ambiguity. In addition, each person will have developed a preferred action strategy in order to successfully implement the dominant values.

Hence, all individuals are capable of enacting alpha, beta, and zeta values, but there will be a preferred dominance of values and of approach in a given environment. Given this, it is possible to represent a means–end structure for an individual schematically as a means–end hierarchy. In the example (Figure 1) a possible political scheme is identified for an alpha traditionalist.

In behavioural terms, the initial state represents a central motivational drive; the final state, the goal; and the mediating paths represent various routes or means to the goal. The structure explains the *orderly* yet *flexible* behaviour of people in organizations. The higher-order schemes (near the outer edges) confers meaning on the subordinate schemes or provides a context for their interpretation. The outermost schemes provide a frame of reference.

Schemes or maps differ in strength or saliency at any one moment in time, dependent on whether the individual concerned is applying a local schema appropriate to the circumstances of the situation. Problems may arise when a person attempts to apply a local schema which is inappropriate to his circumstances. Under circumstances of appropriate schema application to the demands of the situation, we term this process *strength in use*. In situations where an inappropriate schema is deliberately applied, we term this process *circular re-interpretation*.

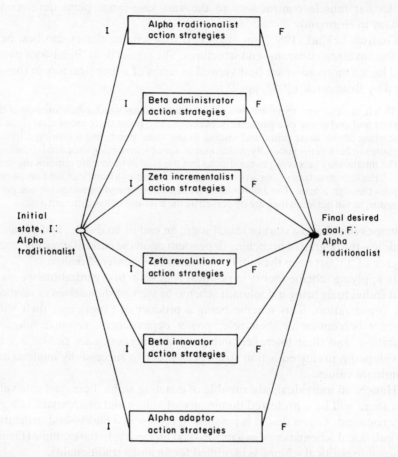

Figure 1. A means–end hierarchy model of political strategy and behaviour. (Initial state, I; Final state, F.)

Strength In Use

When dominant schemes are enacted via the existing strengths in use, the demands of the situation are such that the individual can act out his dominant schema in totality. The implementation skills of the individual and the requirements of the situation, fit. Thus, an individual with a dominant alpha traditionalist strategy is able to act out the behaviours of an alpha traditionalist in practice. There is little ambiguity for him and he is able to take actions consistent with his action strategy. Since his behaviour is consistent, there is little ambiguity for others around him. They can predict his approach and behaviours.

Circular Re-interpretation

When dominant schemes are acted out in a circular way, the environment requires schema and action strategies, other than the individual's dominant schema, to be enacted in practice. The schemes in use are not the scheme in totality – i.e. they do not match the end goal. Their exists ambiguity for the individual. He deliberately engages in action strategies not consistent with his own dominant schema but will do this to achieve his desired final state – through re-interpretation and post-rationalization. Thus, an individual with a dominant beta innovator scheme may find it inappropriate to maintain his strategy in a given environment. He may find himself going round in circles by engaging the same strategy even though it is inappropriate to the situation. The individual has developed such a dominant schema and action strategy that change for him becomes almost impossible.

Secondly, the individual may go round in circles as he engages in behaviour inconsistent with his dominant schema. For example, in order to maintain his beta values, the individual may adopt zeta revolutionary behaviour. In order to achieve his end goal, the individual will engage in other forms of behaviour inconsistent with the dominant schema. Such an approach is effective as long as the individual understands that:

(a) others around him may find his behaviours and motives inconsistent and hence label him as 'acting politically';

(b) he may need skills training to improve his implementation skills in zeta revolutionary behaviour; and

(c) constantly switching from one action strategy to another in order to maintain the dominant schema could be very harmful, as the individual and those around him may lose their sense of direction and purpose and not really understand why they are engaging in certain activities. Under such circumstances, the individual would be labelled devious, political, and untrustworthy.

Thirdly, to go round in circles consistently switching action strategies in order to maintain the dominant schema is indicative of a person whose dominant schema has taken on a compulsive form. The greater the ambiguity the individual faces, the more compulsive the schema, the more inconsistent are his actions, and the more politically devious he is labelled by others. The individual needs to re-examine his dominant schema and consider whether he should withdraw from the situation and maintain his dominant schema, or whether he should enter a phase of fundamental re-examination and re-learning of his beliefs, values, and behaviours.

People who are commonly labelled as being political or devious, i.e. behaviour that has negative connections for those at the receiving end, are people who are going through the process of circular re-interpretation. The term 're-interpretation' is used to indicate that the individual post-rationalizes his behaviour, when he adopts an action strategy inconsistent with his dominant schema in order to gain his preferred final state. The person may say to himself: 'I know what I wanted to achieve was good, but under my particular circumstances, I had to be devious to get there.' More colloquially, this is known as the ends justifying the means. Whether successfully or unsuccessfully applied, ends-justifying-the-means behaviours are generally termed as politics. In this situation, predictions of end goals from means in current use can be totally misleading: they lead to the wrong predictions of outcomes. It is necessary to go beyond means in use, for accurate prediction purposes.

TOWARDS MULTI-RATIONALITY THROUGH TRAINING

Adopting a cognitive approach to the analysis of individual behaviour in organizations assumes that all behaviour in organizations is political. In the majority of circumstances, most individuals find the behaviour of other persons or groups acceptable. Behaviour that is acceptable is behaviour that fits with the schema strategy or map that an individual has both recognized and enacted. Difficult situations develop when an individual or group reject, misunderstand, or respond with inappropriate behaviours to the actions of another individual or group. In other words, the person concerned is unable to mentally recognize the demands and behaviours of the individual or group with whom he is interacting. As stated, the negative consequences of personal and group interaction have largely been interpreted as political behaviour.

A common misconception about organizations or groups is the assumption that there is one single logic or rationality to explain the existence of the organization or group. In fact, all organizations or groups are multi-rational; that is, individuals re-interpret the *raison d'être* in terms of their own dominant schema and strategies for group or organizational existence. The simplest message here being: 'people do things for their reasons not yours!'.

The majority of writers on politics in organizations (French and Raven, 1959; Pettigrew, 1972, 1973, 1975; Schein, 1977; Hersey *et al.*, 1979; Cobb, 1980) adopt the approach of trying to identify those finite behaviours which, if practised, lead to greater personal effectiveness. Such an approach to increasing 'political effectiveness' is inadequate, for two questions remain unanswered:

1. Can the individual concerned recognize what are appropriate political behaviours in the situation?

2. Even when certain behaviours are recognized as political and necessary, could he put them into practice?

The approach we adopt attempts to account for the above two questions by helping participants identify the range of actions and behaviours they have adopted in the past; the range of actions and behaviours others have adopted; and finally identify the behaviours that should be adopted, bearing in mind the demands of each individual's situation. In other words, we help each individual to identify a map of strategic actions – his and others whom he considers relevant to his situation.

Learning Politics

Two social learning theorists, Bandura (1977) and Mischel (1977), emphasize the view that people use symbolic (cognitive) processes to represent events and to communicate with others. Thereby they are capable of choice and self-regulation. In this way, behaviour can be explained in terms of a reciprocal interaction between personal and environmental determinants. People are influenced by environmental forces, but they also make choices as to how they should behave. People are responsive to situations and also influence situations. Through the use of thought and symbols people anticipate future experiences and attempt to prepare the present for the future.

Through the process of *reciprocal determinism* (i.e. the process of valuing certain environmental events, discriminating among situations in terms of their potential, judging one's ability to cope, and deciding which situation to enter and how to behave) and through using feedback to ascertain the results of decisions, the individual is developing a repertoire of *cognitive competences*. This repertoire is the combination of the dominant schema and local action strategies each individual had development in the *A*, *B*, *Z* model.

In terms of training to improve political influence skills, the process involves each participant accepting that he should allow for *behavioural adjustment*, i.e. rejecting certain behaviours and accepting new ones. We consider that behaviour adjustment involves a two-dimensional learning process – *recognition* and *enactment*. In striving for cognitive competency, perceived key behaviours are mentally *recognized* as being relevant. In order to actively utilize these behaviours, they require to be *enacted* into the pattern of the individual's existing behaviours. If the new behaviours do not represent any marked deviation from the existing pattern or map of behaviours, then learning involves increasing cognitive competence within the existing dominant schema and local action strategies. However, those behaviours that have been recognized (seen as relevant) but require substantial changes in the individual's dominant schema and actual behaviours, demand that the individual re-examines the value to himself of his existing schema. Whether increasing personal cognitive competency to change at the local action strategies level or at the dominant schema level, acquiring new cognitive and behavioural competencies involves *modelling* and *guided participation*. Modelling requires demonstrating the desired activities through various models and ensuring that the recipients experience positive consequences, or at least no adverse consequences. Guided participation is the process of breaking-down complete behaviours into subskills and subtasks and assisting the recipients in practising these subskills and subtasks. The ultimate aim is to achieve self-efficacy whereby the individual concerned develops a competence to effectively inter-act in situations he previously found problematic. In effect, we attempt to prevent a person from entering the process of circular re-interpretation by increasing his repertoire of strengths in use. We have developed a five-stage learning process which takes into account the processes of modelling and guided participation. The five-stage learning process is offered as a workshop on developing political skills (see Table 3).

Table 3   Learning process

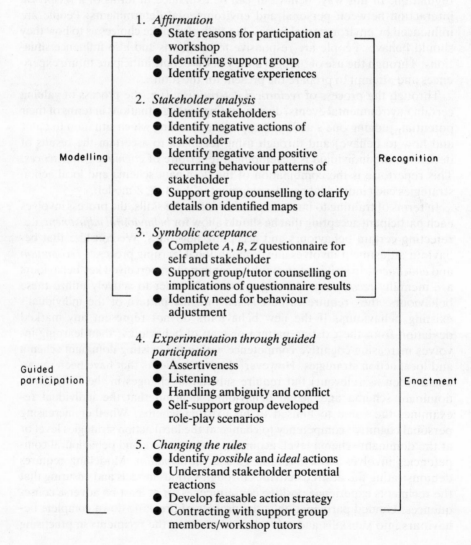

1. *Affirmation*
   ● State reasons for participation at workshop
   ● Identifying support group
   ● Identify negative experiences

2. *Stakeholder analysis*
   ● Identify stakeholders
   ● Identify negative actions of stakeholder
   ● Identify negative and positive recurring behaviour patterns of stakeholder
   ● Support group counselling to clarify details on identified maps

3. *Symbolic acceptance*
   ● Complete *A*, *B*, *Z* questionnaire for self and stakeholder
   ● Support group/tutor counselling on implications of questionnaire results
   ● Identify need for behaviour adjustment

4. *Experimentation through guided participation*
   ● Assertiveness
   ● Listening
   ● Handling ambiguity and conflict
   ● Self-support group developed role-play scenarios

5. *Changing the rules*
   ● Identify *possible* and *ideal* actions
   ● Understand stakeholder potential reactions
   ● Develop feasable action strategy
   ● Contracting with support group members/workshop tutors

Modelling

Recognition

Guided participation

Enactment

Five-stage Learning Process

Affirmation

The participants offer reasons why they are present at the workshop. The trainers note the statements made by the participants. According to the needs and objectives of each individual, people are placed into groups of four – support groups – wherein most modelling and guided participation will occur. A structured workbook is offered to each participant which forms the basis of the workshop activities. The participants are asked to identify any negative experiences they have recently undergone and list these in the workbook. Negative experiences are emphasized at this stage since it was in those situations where the individual remembers that he or she failed to influence adequately or effectively. Each participant has to affirm with the workshop trainer(s) and other participants that he is willing to use these recent negative experiences as data for further exploration in improving individual political influencing skills. The aim of this stage is to obtain the commitment of each participant to examining his influencing skills.

Stakeholder Analysis

The participants in the support group and the trainer(s) help to identify for each participant in turn, the persons who have a 'stakeholding' (a strong interest) in the work, decisions, and behaviour of the participant in question. Particular emphasis is placed on those stakeholders who are considered by each participant to have been influential in stimulating their negative experiences identified at the affirmation stage. A minimum of one and a maximum of two stakeholders are identified. Each participant is asked to isolate the negative and positive recurring behaviour patterns he has witnessed, experienced, or heard others talk about, for each of their stakeholder(s). These behaviours are logged down in the workbook. Each participant then exchanges his workbook with that of another member in his support group for them to read, analyse, question, clarify, and counsel their partner on the statements made so far.

   The stakeholder analysis and didactic counselling are the first stages of the mapping process. Each person has to be clear and succinct about his situation at work and be able to communicate it to someone else. Not only does the stakeholder analysis generate rich data for mapping, but further helps each person realize that simple 'impressions' of the stakeholders are insufficient data on which to plan behaviour adjustment. People need clear and personally meaningful reasons why they should consider changing their pattern of norms, beliefs, values, behaviours, and personal skills. The impression/clarification process is the key to meaningful change attempts.

Symbolic Acceptance

Participants complete the *A*, *B*, *Z* questionnaire for themselves and for the stakeholders. The questionnaire and results feedback sheets are incorporated in the workbook. The results are presented in terms of the distribution of the *A*, *B*, *Z* scores for self and stakeholders, identifying which are the dominant schema and back-up schema for each individual. In addition, the scores at the action strategy level are presented (i.e. traditionalist to revolutionary) indicating a preferred style within each schema.

The participants counsel each other, in their support groups, on the results of the questionnaire, utilizing the workshop tutors as an additional counselling resource. The support groups are advised to pay particular attention (during counselling) to the similarities and differences between the self results and stakeholder results of each person's questionnaire. In particular, five themes are identified for discussion during counselling.

1. To what extent does the self-generated data identified during the affirmation and stakeholder analysis stages match with the questionnaire results?

2. What are the implications if self and stakeholders predominantly enact two different dominant schema?

3. What are the implications if self and stakeholders predominantly utilize different action strategies, for example, if self is identified as having a high beta score with emphasis on innovator, and one of the stakeholders as having a high alpha score with emphasis on traditionalist? What are the likely implications for the individual in his relationship with the stakeholder? Participants are asked to write down what such differences will mean in practice.

4. Do the action strategies in use for the stakeholder present the dominant schema in totality? Has the final goal of the stakeholder been misconceived because a snapshot of behaviour witnessed by the individual has been taken as an appropriate indicator of final goals?

5. How much psychological space does the individual and the stakeholder allow others to occupy? For example, what if the stakeholder and the individual have potential in beta and zeta? It is likely they may have a low need to share values, experiences, and strategies for action with others. The question placed before the support group by the tutors is: Are the individual and the stakeholders trying to push each other into adopting alpha values and behaviours so as to allow their beta and zeta potential to develop unimpeded?

After discussing and counselling each other on the five themes above, the participants have to indicate what the next step should be for them. Some may feel they require counselling as they may need to 'jump' dominant schema. Changing dominant schema is considered a peak learning experience since the individual has to re-examine his values, beliefs, feelings, and thoughts about situations. Counselling may be conducted on a one-to-one basis between trainer and participants or within the support group.

Others may wish to add new behaviours to their existing repertoire and hence limit circular re-interpretation and increase strengths in use. For those that wish to be counselled or to experiment, they naturally continue to stage 4. Some may wish to improve their skills at implementing behaviours already within their existing repertoire. They may stay or leave the workshop. Others may wish to simply leave the workshop. For those that wish to leave, every encouragement is given and 'exit counselling' is recommended.

Experimentation Through Guided Participation

When participants are in their support groups, they are asked to create their own 'role-plays' which, as far as possible, depict their normal work situation. Each participant in turn takes charge of his support group and identifies a scenario and roles for each person in his support group to act out. At the end of each role-play, the support group enters into counselling, examining the learning that took place during the role-play. The workshop tutors are used as an additional resource, whether as counsellors, trainers, or advisers to the role-play exercises. Often it is identified that the participants require training in assertiveness, reflective listening, and handling conflict and ambiguity. The tutors provide whatever additional inputs they consider appropriate or that are requested by the support groups. However, the primary responsibility of identifying and putting into practice behavioural skills through role-play exercises lies with the participants.

Changing the Rules

On the completion of the role-plays in the support groups, the participants are asked to identify in their workbooks what *possible* and *ideal* actions they would like to make in order to improve their position in their workplace. Each participant is then asked to make a list of the possible reactions of the stakeholders to the possible and ideal actions that each participant may put into practice.

Once these two lists (possible and ideal actions, plus stakeholder reactions) have been prepared, each individual is asked to prepare a feasible 'action strategy'. As part of the action strategy, each person has to identify a number of 'influence moves' that he will practise with the stakeholders. The workshop tutors advise that influencing the stakeholders with non-threatening behaviours is likely to produce more positive results for the individual. Furthermore, participants have to indicate for how long they will practise their influence moves (1 hour, 1 day, 1 week, 1 month, 1 year, etc.) and the chronological order in which they will implement the influence moves. In this way each participant has the opportunity to see change as a longer-term strategy. In addition, he has the chance to identify the weakness of his strategy which he can adjust. The individual concerned may realize that to attempt to adopt a new strategy may be too threatening to both himself and the other stakeholders on the 'map', or the simple realization that helping to maintain the status quo can in itself lead to improved performance.

We, the trainers, also emphasize that each person may experience a certain amount of circular re-interpretation. It is almost inevitable that each participant in his workplace may have to adopt an action strategy inconsistent with his dominant schema; he may have to experiment with different action strategies in order to see which fits the situation. This is likely to make others in the situation feel uncomfortable. The participant may in turn be labelled devious and political. Although circular re-interpretation may be inevitable, we stress it should only be entered into for a short period of time in order to achieve maximum effectiveness. Making others feel comfortable rather than uncomfortable is vital for longer-term success.

Finally, the individual contracts with his support group and the trainers that he will attempt to put into practice the influence moves that have been identified. In so doing, each individual is attempting to alter the 'unwritten rules' (norms, beliefs, values in action) of his work situation to, hopefully, his advantage. The contract between the person and the support group or trainers, is that they will contact each other within a specified period indicating how far they have progressed. Some people contact each other over the phone, or meet, but few fail to make any contact.

SUMMARY

Life in organizations is as much about unshared meaning as it is about shared meaning. Living and working with people who do not share one's own values, norms, beliefs in action, and styles of behaviour is as common as having to interact with people who do hold the same norms, beliefs, values, and behavioural characteristics. As Carl Jung (1978, p. 46) has pointed out: 'A sane and normal society is one in which people habitually disagree, because general agreement is relatively rare outside the sphere of instinctive human qualities.'

It is postulated that management education practice has been concerned with generating shared meaning. We state that notions of unshared meaning (i.e. potential negative interactions at work) have been ignored or deliberately rejected in management education.

If management education practice is to have impact on individuals in terms of their implementation skills, then both shared and unshared meaning has to be introduced into the training arena. This means taking into account both the positive and negative interactions that each individual has to face in his workplace. We state that both positive and negative interactions hold political connotations. In order to identify the politics that take place in organizations, it is necessary to map out the differences between people and the reasons for those differences. We achieve this by adopting a cognitive model of human interaction which takes into account personal norms, values, and styles of behaviour. The model had been successfully utilized in a workshop setting, where participants are taken through a five-stage learning process. Our main objective is to increase people's effectiveness at human interaction by taking into account the realities of organizational life.

REFERENCES

Argyris, C. (1964) *Integrating the Individual and the Organisation*, Wiley, New York.
Bandura, A. (1977) *Social Learning Theory*, Prentice-Hall.
Bartlett, Sir F. (1932) *Remembering*, Cambridge University Press.
Broadbent, D. E. (1977) Hidden pre-attentive processes, *American Psychologist*, 32, 109.
Brunner, J. S. (1972) *Process of Education*, Harvard University Press.
Brunner, J. S. (1981) *Beyond the Information Given*, Allen and Unwin.
Burns, T. (1961) Micropolitics: Mechanisms of institutional change, *Administrative Science Quarterly*, 6, 257–281.
Carpenter, H. H. (1971) Formal organisational structural factors and perceived job satisfaction of classroom teachers, *Administrative Science Quarterly*, 16, 460–465.
Cobb, A. T. (1980) Informal influence in the formal organisation: Perceived sources of power among work unit peers, *Academy of Management Journal*, 23, 155–161.
Ecklad, G. (1980) *Scheme Theory: A Conceptual Framework for Cognitive Motivational Process*, Academic Press.
Fiedler, F. (1967) *A Theory of Leadership Effectiveness*, McGraw-Hill, New York.
French, J. R. P. Jr (1956) A formal theory of social power, *Psychological Review*, 63, 187–194.
French, J. R. P. Jr and Raven, B. (1959) The bases of social power, in: *Studies of Social Power*, Edited by D. Cartwright, Institute of Social Research, The University of Michigan, pp. 150–167.
Georgiades, N. J. (1972) A study of organisational climate as a determinant of the difficulties and distastes of secondary school teachers, Unpublished Ph.D. Thesis, Birbeck College, University of London.
Goffman, E. (1974) *Frame Analysis: An Essay on the Organisation of Experience*, Penguin.
Hage, J. and Aiken, M. (1967) The relationship of centralisation to other structural properties, *Administrative Science Quarterly*, 12, 73–92.
Hage, J. and Aiken, M. (1969) Routine technology, social structure and organisational goals, *Administrative Science Quarterly*, 14, 366–375.
Herman, S. M. (1974) The shadow of organisation development, Paper Presented to the N.T.L. Institute Conference on New Technology in O.D., New Orleans.
Hersey, P., Blanchard, K. H., and Nortemeyer, W. E. (1979) *Situational Leadership: Perception and the Impact of Power*, Centre for Leadership Studies, Learning Resources Corporation, pp. 1–5.
Jaques, E. (1976) *A General Theory of Bureaucracy*, Heinemann.
Jung, C. (1978) *Man and His Symbols*, Picador.
Kelly, G. A. (1955) *The Psychology of Personal Construct Theory*, Vols. 1 and 2, Norton, New York.
Litwin, G. and Stringer, R. (1968) *Motivation and Organisational Climate*, Harvard University Press.

March J. G. (1962) The business firm as a political coalition, *Journal of Politics*, **24**, 262–278.

McClelland, D. C. and Burnham, D. H. (1976) Power is the great motivator, *Harvard Business Review*, **March–April 1976**, 100–110.

Mischel, W. (1977) Self Control and the Self, in: *The Self: Psychological and Philosophical Issues*, Edited by T. Mischel, Rowman and Littlefield, New Jersey.

Mumford, E. (1970) Job satisfaction: A new approach derived from an old theory, *Sociological Review*, **18**, 71–101.

Neisser, V. (1977) *Cognition and Reality*, London, John Wiley.

Payne, R. L. and Pheysey, D. C. (1971) G. G. Stern's organisational climate index: A reconceptualisation and application to business organisations, *Organisation Behaviour and Human Performance*, **6**, 77–87.

Pervin, L. A. (1967) A twenty college study of student–college interaction using T.A.P.E., *Journal of Educational Psychology*, **58**, 290–302.

Pettigrew, A. M. (1972) Information control as a power resource, *Sociology*, **6**, 2, 187–204.

Pettigrew, A. M. (1973) *The Politics of Organisational Decision Making*, Tavistock, London.

Pettigrew, A. M. (1975) Towards a political theory of organisational intervention, *Human Relations*, **28**, 3, 191–208.

Pettigrew, A. M. (1977) Strategy formulation as a political process, *International Studies of Management and Organisation*, **7**, 78–87.

Piaget, J. (1978) *Essential Piaget*, Routledge.

Porter, L. W., Allen, R. W., and Angle, H. L. (1981) The politics of upward influence, in: *Research in Organisational Behaviour*, Vol. 3, Edited by B. Staw and L. Cummings, JAI Press.

Pritchard, R. D. and Karasick, B. W. (1973) The effects of organisational climate on managerial job performance and job satisfaction, *Organisational Behaviour and Human Performance*, **9**, 126–146.

Pugh, D. S. (1966) Modern organisation theory: A psychological and sociological study, *Psychological Bulletin*, **66**, 235–251.

Pugh, D. S. and Hickson, D. J. (1976) *Organisational Structure in its Context: The Aston Programme*, Saxon House Studies, Lexington Books.

Pugh, D. S., Hickson, D. J., Hinings, C. R., and Turner, C. (1968) Dimension of organisation structure, *Administrative Science Quarterly*, **13**, 65–105.

Salancik, G. R. and Pfeffer, J. (1978) A social information processing approach to job attitudes and task design, *Administrative Science Quarterly*, **23**, 68–79.

Schein, V. E. (1977) Individual power and political behaviour in organisations: An inadequately explored reality, *Academy of Management Review*, **January 1977**, 64–72.

Slater, P. (1976) *Exploration of Interpersonal Space* Vol. 1, John Wiley, London.

Tolman, E. C. (1924) *Behaviour and Psychological Man*, University of California Press.

Vickers, Sir G. (1968) *Value Systems and Social Processes*, Tavistock, London.

Management Development: Advances in Practice and Theory
Edited by C. Cox and J. Beck
© 1984 John Wiley & Sons Ltd

CHAPTER 3

Developing Organizational Skills

John Beck and Charles Cox

INTRODUCTION

In order to operate effectively within the complex social systems which make up an organization, a manager needs not only to be able to relate successfully to individuals within a group or between groups, but also to develop skills in influencing the wider social processes which run through organizations. This paper describes a training programme and associated conceptual framework for developing such *organizational skills*. This has been recently developed and tested in a number of organizations.

The distinction we are making between organizational and other social skills can be made clearer by reference to the taxonomy of social skills outlined by Cox and Cooper (1976). Briefly this defines five levels of skill in the social domain.

1. *Personal skills* – concerned with personal awareness – the extent to which the person is aware of his own skills, needs, biases, and any gaps in his behaviour repertoire. They include awareness of the effects of the behaviour of others on oneself and clarity about one's own feelings and needs in a situation.

2. *Inter-personal skills* – consisting of the whole range of skills needed to interact effectively with another person or persons. These include such skills as listening, reflecting back, ability to express ideas, ability to express feelings, and giving feedback.

3. *Group skills* – this category comprises the additional skills an individual needs in order to work effectively within a group. They involve an understanding of the effect of the group on behaviour and include an awareness of 'process' issues and interactions within the group and of the effect of work roles and work group norms. They also include decision making and leadership skills.

4. *Intergroup skills* – involve the additional component of the effect of the interaction between two or more groups. Skills in this area include awareness of differences in norms, values, beliefs, and conventions between groups and

41

their effects on behaviour. Other important areas are the effects of intergroup competition, acting as a representative or delegate, and consultancy skills.

5. *Organizational skills* – refer to the skills needed to deal with the extra dimension added by the total organization, e.g. the effect of hierarchies and the function and technology of the organization. These skills include the ability to deal with managers and subordinates in an appropriate style, to manage boundaries, and sense and react to change in the organization's external and internal environment.

It should be noted that the above is more in the form of a taxonomy than a simple classification in that it is hierarchical in nature. That is to say that effective performance at any one level involves skills at all the earlier levels. For example, effective interpersonal skill involves also high-level personal skills. Similarly, to be effective at the organizational skill level involves skills at all other levels – personal, interpersonal, group, and intergroup.

Many programmes and systems exist for developing skills at the first three levels, and some even at level 4. Few, if any, are concerned with organizational skills at level 5. This paper describes one such system.

In concrete terms these organisational skills seem to involve two independent but related activities:

(a) the integration of personal, team, and organizational *goals*, and

(b) the use of appropriate *styles of influence* within the organization to ensure that these goals are accepted and achieved.

GOALS

Based on the views of Cyert and March (1963) a simple taxonomy of goals which are salient to most managers can be identified as follows: *personal goals, team goals,* and *organizational goals.*

Personal goals are associated with the needs and demands placed on a manager as an individual. For the purposes of this model we have chosen to subdivide these personal goals into:

(a) *task goals,*

(b) *development goals,* and

(c) *status goals.*

Personal *task* goals are the objectives which define the nature and scope of responsibilities which the job demands of the individual. They are the task requirements for which the individual has personal responsibility. These objectives may be clear and concrete or relatively unclear and abstract. They may be set after discussion with his immediate superior, or may be imposed unilaterally by the superior, or in other ways by the nature of the technology of production or external influences on the organization. Therefore, depending upon the nature of these influences, the individual may have more or less opportunity to influence the nature of his job, in terms of its objectives.

Personal *development* goals are goals which an individual sets for himself in order to increase the range of depth of his skills and abilities. These goals can be achieved by gaining support from the organization for training, or a new or enlarged organizational role which demands a different set of skills to those which the individual currently employs.

Personal *status* goals are concerned with the individual's standing or formal rank in the organization. These will include not only the promotion to higher levels of authority in the organization, but also the benefits which accrue to the individual with increasing status.

Team goals are concerned with the needs and aims of the work group of which the individual is part. These are goals which have been agreed with other members of the team, and are seen as being of benefit to the team as a whole. We would suggest that team goals are different in kind to the personal goals of the team members, and do not represent a simple coalescence of their personal goals. One crucial difference is that team goals will reveal the extent to which there is interdependence and synergy between the group members and the extent to which it is an effective cohesive unit. A second crucial difference is that there will tend to be a feeling of collective responsibility for the achievement of these goals.

Team *task* goals are the task objectives which recognizable teams or departments are required to achieve. While there may or may not be a feeling of collective responsibility for the achievement of these objectives, in many cases it is the manager or supervisor of the team whose effectiveness is judged by the achievement of team task goals. The way in which these team task goals are set will depend partly on the relationship which the manager has with his members, but also the way in which he interfaces between his team and other teams and more senior management groups. Usually the team task goal requires the successful integration of the individual members' personal task goals. However, in situations in which there is scope for creativity and flexibility in personal task goals, and in which there are effective working relationships between the members, the group output may be different in volume or quality than could be achieved by a simple integration of the personal tasks.

Team *development* goals are goals which the members might agree in order to change some aspect of the team functioning. This might mean changes in the nature of the job, such as changes in production technology or working practices which make the job easier to do. Equally it might mean an extension or change in the quality or range of products which the group is required to output so that the group is doing more interesting work. Alternatively it might mean changes in the way in which the team members relate to one another. So there could be time set aside in which the team members review their interpersonal processes, diagnose any problems, and carry out some activity to change the norms or patterns of relationships within the group.

Organizational goals are seen to be of benefit to the organization and its workers as a whole. These are goals which determine the continued existence and development of the organization as it relates to its environment. These goals are achieved either by increasing the organization's internal efficiency in processing its throughput, or in determining a successful strategy for survival in the changing environment of the organization. To the extent that the organization's goals are clear and agreed, and salient to all employees, then the organization will have a relatively clear identity and an apparent sense of purpose. Again, these goals can be divided into organizational *task* goals and *development* goals.

Organizational *task* goals represent the 'primary task' (Brown, 1960) or mission of the organization. They define the business which the organization is in, and in concrete terms are formally represented by the long-term coporate plan and budget forecasts for any particular financial year. Informally these plans are mediated by the assumptions which the workforce bring to bear about the business which the organization is in, or ought to be in. This sense of corporate purpose will be dependent upon the attitudes which the workers, both blue-collar and management, have about the organization, its products, and its customers.

Organizational *development* goals represent the goals of any programme of change upon which the organization might embark. These might include changes in methods and procedures so that the organization can adapt to developments in its environment, or they might include a fundamental re-think about the organization's mission. Also included would be the goals of any change programme which was designed to affect the climate or culture of the organization as a whole.

For managers who operate at the boundary of a team or organization *inter-departmental* or *interorganization* goals would be included in this taxonomy. This is to suggest that when managers act as representatives of their departments or organization, that they should attempt to set or negotiate goals with the representatives of other departments or organizations which are of mutual benefit to both parties. All too often it seems that negotiations of this nature are conducted in a competitive manner, rather than an atmosphere of co-operation which emphasizes the interdependence of both parties on each other.

Of course, other change and development programmes, such as Management by Objectives (MBO), also emphasize the importance of managing activities against objectives. One difference is that the goals which we ask the participants to identify are broader than the key results of MBO systems.

The model we are offering is therefore prescriptive. We are saying that managers should set, or be aware of, goals at the personal, team, and organizational level, and that they should take responsibility for managing the relationship between these goals. In managing the relationship between these goals the manager will, ideally, be able to find ways of integrating the personal, team and organizational goals which he wishes to pursue. However, if there is unavoidable conflict between these various goals, then he must take responsibility for managing the conflict by compromising or prioritizing the achievement of goals.

Many other writers have emphasized the importance of individuals integrating personal and organizational goals. In particular, the human relations/ resources theorists have suggested that one characteristic of an effective organization is that it allows individuals the freedom to influence the process of setting organizational goals, so that their personal goals can be integrated and incorporated with the organizational goals. In order to enable this integration process to occur these theorists suggest changes should be brought about in the social conditions at work. Thus, by reducing the constraints of close supervision, treating the individual as a mature person, and encouraging a participative managerial style, a climate is created which is conducive to personal responsibility and self-management.

In the developmental programme which is described here we are encouraging participants to accept responsibility for integrating their goals, even when the climate is not conducive. The change target therefore is the individual and not the systems of relationships which surround him. This does not ignore the interdependence between the person and the climate of the organization in which he works, but it does recognize that the skills needed to influence events in organizations which do not encourage participation are different from the skills needed in participative organizations. It is the development of skills which allows the participants to influence organizations in a variety of ways, which is one of the learning goals of this programme. However, as a precursor to that learning one of the crucial determinants of success of the programme is an acceptance, by the participants, of individual responsibility for their destiny in the organization. If that means that some participants have to try to influence organizations which are very resistant to influence, then it means that the skills they require are different from the skills needed to operate and survive in an open participative organization. Nevertheless, the individual must rely on himself to create a situation at work that works for him; he cannot rely on others to create a climate which encourages him to participate.

Participants are asked to identify and set personal status and development goals, which has the effect of legitimizing the achievement of personal non-task goals at work. We ask the participants to consider appropriate goals for their work team, so that agreement on goals is not only between a manager and subordinate, but takes into account the effect on close colleagues as well. Finally, we ask the participant to consider whether, in his opinion and in the particular context of his work, the organization is moving in the right direction, and what changes he would introduce to make the organization more effective. Therefore every individual, and not just senior management, is asked to review and contribute to the organization's survival and developmental strategy.

We may be accused of being naive and idealistic in this approach, particularly by those theorists who have focused attention on the political processes occurring in organizations. They suggest that organizational goals grow out of the personal needs of employees and emerge by virtue of the power which the individual has access to, either because of formal position or because of informal political coalitions with others who are equally motivated by self-interest. Whilst we do not deny that in many organizations this is the way that organizational goals emerge, we do deny that it is the only way that organizational goals can be determined. Equally, we would deny that political behaviour is an inevitable consequence of conflict between an individual's personal goals and the organization's needs. Political behaviour is one way of resolving the conflict in the individual's favour, but it is not the only way or even the best way of resolving that conflict. The approach we suggest is to get individuals thinking organizationally, during which concern with their personal and team needs is suspended whilst they consider what is best for the organization. It is only when a realistic view of what is needed for the organization has been obtained that the relationship between personal, team, and organizational goals can be examined, and ways of reducing or managing conflict between these goals found.

STYLES OF INFLUENCE

These are the means by which an individual influences what happens in his organization in order to get decisions and action which will enable him to achieve the goals he has set. We term these *organizational styles* because they are styles of behaviour which are discrete and internally consistent. Within each style there is a set of skills, beliefs, and values about how to influence events which are characteristic of each particular style. While some people tend to use one style predominantly, we believe that people can be trained to use alternative styles, and part of the training programme is to develop the participants' abilities to use different styles.

The term 'organizational' style is preferred to 'managerial' style, since the latter identifies a way that a manager relates to his subordinates. 'Organizational' style refers to the way in which an individual affects the various decision-making and influence processes across the whole of the organization, and not just within his own department, although it can also apply to relationships within the department. It means influence in lateral relationships, across organizational boundaries, in other departments, divisions, and other organizations, as well as points well removed up and down the hierarchy from where the individual is located. Different styles of influence will be appropriate in different organizations or in different situations in the same organization. We make no value judgements about any particular style, and instead take a pragmatic approach that the 'right' style or mix of styles is that which is most effective in getting the goals achieved. Currently we have identified four different styles which might be used: *formal*, *political*, *open*, and *laissez-faire*.

However, since we are in the process of developing this approach, other or different styles might suggest themselves as we obtain more data from participants.

The *formal* style relies principally on the use of legitimate authority to influence events. This legitimate authority may flow from hierarchical position and the use of formal power to direct and control the behaviour of others – these issues were the principal concern of traditional organisation theorists (Taylor, 1947; Fayol, 1949) and more recently have been the subject of comment by Milgram (1974). The other primary source of legitimate authority flows from the law, rules, regulations, and agreed procedures which make demands upon, and constrain the action of, employees. The power vested in the rules and regulations of a bureaucracy (Weber, 1947; Blau and Scott, 1969) are particularly important since they offer formal power to employees who are low in the hierarchy. By the use, or threatened use, of power vested in legislation (e.g. the Factory Acts) or internal rules, regulations, or established codes, any employee can attempt to influence or resist influence from decision-taking centres in the organization. Skilful use of this style will involve a good working knowledge of the laws, rules, and agreements which apply at work, and a willingness to use formal power or the rules to get what you want. In recent times, with moves towards more participative managerial styles involving attempts to gain consensus in reaching managerial decisions, the use of formal power has been eschewed by many management and organizational development practitioners. But the use of formal power is still a potent means to influence organizational events provided those involved recognize the use of formal power as legitimate. Where they do not, this style runs into problems.

The *political* style relies principally on informal influence to get things done and has two different, but sometimes complementary, strategies. The first of these is the formation of alliances, usually with other organizationally powerful groups or individuals, for mutual self-interest. These alliances will usually be covert, but occasionally strong groups will form an overt axis which they hope will put them in an unchallengeable position. The basis of the relationship within such a cabal is usually the negotiation for the promotion and support of some goal which is of mutual benefit to all parties. If one party ceases to gain benefit, then the alliance might well be broken and the parties will tend to compete against, rather than support, each other's activities.

The second basis of this style of influence relies on the use of information. Information tends to be used in a strategic way. Withholding information partially or completely, timing the release of information, and selecting the appropriate target for the information are calculated to produce the decision that the individual desires. Distortions of information, including impression management, posturing, propaganda, rumour-mongering, and the strategic use of lies, are ways in which the quality of the information is manipulated to have maximum effect on the target.

The picture which is presented by this style is not of a particularly endearing character because of the pejorative connotations which surround the word 'political'. Yet if we spend a few minutes honestly reviewing some of our actions in our own jobs we would become aware that we are not being completely honest and open in all of our relationships within the organization. We do not perhaps reveal all of our intentions or desires at work, we present our activities in their best light, and we gossip with friends about the activities and inadequacies of other colleagues. Therefore in some, if not all, of the transactions which people have at work there is a political dimension, and certainly there are political overtones to many of the decisions made in the organization. If a manager is to be effective in achieving his goals, this political reality has to be recognized, coped with, and skills developed which will enable him to use, rather than be abused by, these political influences.

We wish to emphasize rather than over-emphasize the importance of understanding organizational politics. We do not subscribe to the view proposed by some writers on organizational politics that political behaviour must inevitably follow some conflict of interest within the organization. Pettigrew (1973), Schein (1977), Burns (1961), and Mangham (1979) suggest that organizational politics result from conflicting personal needs within the organization, and represent an attempt to control others' behaviour and not be controlled by them. Kakabadse and Parker (Chapter Two) suggest that a conflict in understanding and values about the organization leads inexorably to political behaviour. While we do not dispute that these theorists often describe very accurately what happens when there is organizational conflict, we doubt whether political behaviour is often the only, or even the most effective, way of resolving this conflict. We see political behaviour as one choice out of a multitude of choices of possible styles which an individual can decide to use to cope with the conflict. This choice of style depends on the strategy which the individual chooses in order to help him achieve his goals. To further distinguish our use of the term 'political' from other theorists, we do not subscribe to the view of Pettigrew (1973) that 'politics is synonymous with strategy'. In our framework the development of an *influence strategy* is an organizational skill which will allow an individual to choose a variety of styles, one of which may or may not be political, in order to achieve his goals. This skill is discussed later in this paper.

The *open* style of influence can generally be seen to be the style which was advocated by Organization Development theorists in the 1960s and 1970s. Essentially it offers an ideal of the *authentic* individual being aware of himself as a whole person with feelings, attitudes, knowledge, skills, and behavioural responses, being prepared to share this awareness of himself with others, and behave in ways which are coherent with what he perceived to be the reality of himself. To foster this development of authenticity it was suggested that organizations needed to create climates of trust and acceptance so that employees could be free to be themselves. This approach has perhaps been over-simplified by some theorists to the 'love and trust' ideology. But by its very nature an open approach also involves being prepared to express feelings of hostility, anger, and confrontation and not just feelings of love and support. The essence of the open approach is therefore to deal with the reality of the situation, where an important part of that reality are the feelings which individuals have about themselves, their colleagues, and the organization as a whole. In dealing with this reality it is hoped that a much more insightful understanding of the problems can be developed, and that solutions to problems will be long-term since they deal with fundamental, as opposed to peripheral, issues.

In a sense the open style can be seen as the opposite of a political style since it values revealing where you stand on issues rather than posturing in order to conceal your position. Because an open style demands the courage to be yourself it is generally seen in the abstract as socially desirable. However, people often fail to realize that the open person is often an uncomfortable guy to have around. He is confronting and will not support the tacit collusions and delusions that help to lubricate much of people's existence in the organization. Again we make no value judgements about this style apart from pointing out that at times confrontation is effective, while at other times it can disrupt an individual's ability to achieve his goals.

The *laissez-faire* style is essentially a style of non-intervention in events when things are going well and according to plan. It is perhaps the most difficult style to get managers to consider because it seems like an abdication of managerial responsibility, but is in fact fairly close to the principle of 'management by exception'. It involves the manager setting the wheels of some project in motion, monitoring how things are going, and only intervening to bring events back on course when things seem to be going wrong, or an unplanned event throws the system out. It involves the manager being able to predict fairly accurately the likely course of events and likely pitfalls, and have a fairly shrewd idea what to do about them.

In general, theorists of managerial style have seen little or no value in a laissez-faire approach. Lewin, Lippitt, and White (1939) demonstrated that a laissez-faire style was associated with poor productivity and low morale in boys' clubs. In organizational settings the term 'Abdicrat' has been applied to managers who leave much of the decision-taking to their subordinates. However, Hersey and Blanchard (1969) have suggested that as a group of subordinates under a manager's control becomes more mature and responsible, then an appropriate style for the manager is to withdraw and allow them to exercise that responsibility.

Again we make no value judgements about the style, and certainly would not see it being adopted in every situation which confronts a manager. It is appropriate where systems, routines, and procedures are fairly clearly established, where the likely problem areas and symptoms of problems are well known, and where the manager has faith in the people who are making the system work. In situations like this, intervention by a manager can have the effect of disrupting a working system, or interrupting a decision-making procedure and thus making it more difficult to achieve his goals.

ORGANIZATIONAL SKILLS

The model of personal effectiveness at work has therefore two broad dimensions: the first is setting realistic personal team and organizational goals, the second is developing the ability to influence others in the organization in appropriate ways to ensure that these goals are achieved. The particular skills which are essential to developing personal effectiveness at work have been developed, based on the work by Miles (1960), who used a similar taxonomy to identify skills developed during sensitivity training laboratories.

Goal management involves setting realistic achievable goals which integrate personal, team, and organizational goals. This will involve the manager identifying needs by himself, and in conjunction with others, which are appropriate goals for each level. It also involves managing the interface between the goals at each level by creatively setting superordinate goals which integrate personal, team, and organizational goals. If this is not possible, it means prioritizing the achievement of the goals, compromising, or satisficing goal achievement; in general terms, managing goal conflict.

A different skill is *sensitivity to organizational dynamics* so that the individual is aware of how things get done in his organization and has a fairly accurate map of the influence processes within the organization. The description of the organizational styles given above can be invaluable in this diagnostic process by identifying the strategies which key figures are using. This sensitivity will also allow the person to identify leverage points within the organization and perhaps give some insight into how to influence these points.

A related skill is the development of an *influence strategy* in which an individual plans who and how he proposes to influence in order to achieve his objectives. It involves the individual identifying the influence style or styles which are most likely to be effective in influencing a person or decision-taking body, and also thinking through the likely conequences of adopting any particular strategy on his credibility and relationships in the long term.

Finally, the individual requires the appropriate *behavioural skills and flexibility* in order to be able to implement his influence strategy. This involves being able to adopt any particular style which is thought to be appropriate in a given situation. The ability to act out a particular style will involve behavioural skills developed in interpersonal or group interaction, so that the individual is aware of the impact that his behaviour is having and is capable of modifying that behaviour if it does not seem to be effective in achieving the goals.

DEVELOPING ORGANIZATIONAL SKILLS

The authors have now run a number of workshops and seminars with the objective of developing the skills defined above. In the usual design these involve three distinct phases.

Stage 1 – Awareness and Diagnosis

In the usual five-day programme this phase lasts one day, and can be seen as the *unfreezing* stage in Lewin's (1947) *unfreeze, change, refreeze* model. It starts with a brief introduction, aimed at clarifying expectations, based on the learning cycle proposed by Kolb *et al.* (1971). It is explained that since this is an experiential programme, a series of exercises (or experiences) will be presented. If they are going to learn from these, participants must be open to that experience, be prepared to reflect on it, and develop insights about what is happening. These insights should lead them to experimenting with new behaviours. This, in turn, will lead to new experience, and thus start the cycle again. Short lectures and written inputs are also used to help conceptualization.

The first exercise is a group decision task, where groups of six to nine participants are given about one hour to reach a group decision. In the review which follows a number of aspects of the group process are examined. These include such issues as who has influenced the group and in what way. This begins to develop the concept of influence styles. The clarity of, and agreement on, objectives is also reviewed, together with the assumptions about how such objectives could be achieved. This is related to a modified version of Thompson and Tuden's (1964) model for organizational decision-making. The purpose of this is to introduce the notion of clarity of objectives (or goals) and its importance for organizational performance, and relate this to the need to clarify how goals are to be achieved.

Phase 1 concludes with a second cycle of the above process. Participants are given another decision task, this time one which also requires implementation. This tests the group's commitment and clarity about its decision. The main purpose of this exercise is, however, to provide an opportunity to test insights developed in the first exercise, i.e. another circuit of the learning cycle. It sometimes emerges at this stage that participants are not effective enough in the interpersonal and group skills. If this is the case it is possible to modify the programme to spend more time developing skills at those levels of the taxonomy.

Stage 2 – Elaboration of Concepts and Skill Development

This stage starts the process of change and utilizes two main approaches. First, the elaboration of concepts concerning organizational influence, and, using these concepts, the development of greater self-insight into the individual's traditional approach to getting things done in organizations. Secondly, to provide opportunities for participants to develop and practise the new skills needed if their approach is to change. There are four main elements to this phase, although not all will, necessarily, be used in any particular programme.

(i) *Cognitive input*. This consists of a short lecture and discussion of the organizational goals and influence styles model outlined above. In conjunction with this participants complete and score a questionnaire which gives feedback on their own preferred styles of influence. This is used as a starting point for self-review and discussion and is not presented as infallible feedback. Where possible, parallel feedback is also obtained, prior to the programme (via questionnaires), from bosses, subordinates, and colleagues. All these data are reviewed at this stage so that the individual can start to identify strengths and weaknesses, and decide which styles he needs to develop.

Another device sometimes used at this stage is *critical incident*. Participants are asked to identify a critical incident, such as the last time they were in conflict with someone in the organization. Then think through how they handled that situation, decide what style they used, and whether this is typical of their behaviour.

(ii) *Simulation exercises*. A number of exercises involving organizational simulations are used. In these, participants are required to define their goals and the influence style they intend to use to achieve them. Their effectiveness is then reviewed after the exercise. A procedure found to be useful here is the organization of *learning pairs*. Each person teams up with another, and before each exercise explains to the other what his learning goals for the exercise are, and how he intends to achieve them. After the exercise each pair review their learning. This process serves to facilitate learning by encouraging each participant to move more explicitly through each phase of the learning cycle by requiring him to think about what happened in the last exercise and its implications for the next. Usually people stay in the same learning pairs throughout the workshop.

(iii) *Plan a group activity*. This is an exercise in which individuals have to define and agree goals at all three levels – individual, team, and organizational – and then have the opportunity to practise skills at achieving these goals. The task is to plan an activity which the whole community (i.e. all workshop participants) will actually carry out together, usually (but not necessarily) during one evening of the course. In general the only constraints are that everyone must take part in the same activity and that it must be active not passive (i.e. spending the evening in the pub or watching television would not meet the constraints). Other constraints can be added if it is wished to emphasize particular learning goals. Time is given for individuals to define their own goals and hence the activity they would favour, and also to think about team (i.e. group) and organizational (i.e. community) goals. They are also encouraged to plan how they will attempt to influence the community towards their goal. The groups are then given time to work on term goals before interaction is allowed between all groups to reach a final decision on the activity.

The main value of this exercise is that it confronts participants with the need to set and negotiate goals so that there is compatibility between all three levels, and also provides practise at influence styles. It has a 'real-life' element in that participants are actually going to spend the evening doing the activity planned; hence, motivation is high and real feelings are involved, an ingredient often missing in simulation exercises. The exercise, therefore, has the virtue (and the dangers) of being 'real-life' but is also short cycle so that learning can be easily reviewed.

(iv) *Action replays*. In this activity participants are asked to define and describe real-life incidents which they perhaps feel they had not handled very well. With a small group of colleagues they then think through and define alternative strategies. To test these they then brief colleagues on the other roles involved and try out the strategy in a role-play re-run of the incident. This type of exercise comes appropriately towards the end of Stage 2 since it provides a bridge to Stage 3, which is concerned with *re-entry* and *re-freezing*.

Stage 3 – Application

This stage is usually not more than one day – often, in fact, the final half-day. The purpose is to facilitate transfer of learning from the course back to the work situation. The usual method is simply to give time for each individual to think through and define his future goals at all three levels, both short- and long-term, and to plan his influence strategies. The next stage is to work in small consultation groups of three or four people, where each person outlines his plans and talks through possible difficulties. The function of the others is to act as consultants helping to define unclear areas and solve problems. This process helps both to clarify the plans and develop commitment. Participants are then encouraged to write precise action plans with goals and time scales clearly stated. Much of this is, of course, quite conventional practice on any social skills course.

Another device which can be helpful (if time and geographical constraints allow) is the formation of support groups back in the organization. These are ideally based on the consultation groups of Stage 3, and consist of people who have been through the programme together and who meet periodically to review progress with the plans made at the end of the course, and who provide support and encouragement for each other when organizational pressures threaten to overwhelm attempts at change.

CONCLUSION

The key feature of this programme is the development of *organizational* skills, by which we mean the ability to influence events across organizational boundaries. We are concerned to enable participants to become better *operators* in their organization. An effective operator is aware of his own goals, and can integrate those goals with the goals of others and the demands placed upon him by the organization. He has available a wide and flexible range of behaviours to influence organizational processes. He is pro-active rather than re-active and is a potent force for change and development in the organization, rather than simply responding to events as they occur.

There are a number of features of the programme which aid the development of these skills.

1. It highlights the area of goals. By encouraging participants to clarify and set personal goals it legitimizes the achievement of personal needs within an organizational setting, an important factor in motivation. Emphasis is also put on the need to find compatibility between personal, team, and organizational goals.

2. Insight into organizational dynamics is developed. Participants become more aware of what happens in the organization and develop a greater understanding of how events are influenced and by whom.

3. Participants are encouraged to think strategically. That is, to appraise their goals in the context of the organization and, bearing in mind the realities of that organization, to develop a pro-active strategy to achieve their goals.

4. A high value is placed on developing behavioural flexibility in implementing the influence strategy.

In essence the message is to be clear what you are trying to achieve and how that relates to what others are trying to do, and to be flexible in how you set out to achieve it. While this, obviously, has much in common with other philosophies and training programmes, we feel that the system described here integrates a wider diversity of factors within one conceptual framework than most other theories can offer. The associated training, therefore, offers a more comprehensive approach to developing skill at working in organizations.

REFERENCES

Blau, P. M. and Scott, W. R. (1969) *Formal organizations: A comparative approach*, Routledge and Kegan Paul.
Brown, W. (1960) *Exploration in Management*, Heineman, London.
Burns, T. (1961) Micropolitics: Mechanisms of Institutional Change, *Administrative Science Quarterly*, 6, 257–281.
Cox, C. J. and Cooper, C. L. (1976) Developing OD skills in Japan and the UK: An experiential approach, *Journal of European Training*. 5(1), 4–12.
Cyert, R. M. and March, J. G. (1963) *A Behavioural Theory of the Fir h*, Prentice-Hall, Englewood Cliffs, N.J.

Fayol, H. (1949) *General Industrial Management*, Pitman, London.
Hersey, P. and Blanchard, K. H. (1969) *Management of Organizational Behaviour: Utilizing Human Resources*, Prentice-Hall, Englewood Cliffs, N.J.
Kolb, D. A., Rubin, I. M., and McIntyre, J. M. (1971) *Organizational Psychology, An Experiential Approach*, Prentice-Hall, New Jersey.
Lewin, K. (1947) Group decision and social change in: *Readings in Social Psychology*, Edited by T. Newcomb and E. Hartley, Holt, Rinehart and Winston, New York.
Lewin, K., Lippitt, R., and White, R. K. (1939) Patterns of aggressive behaviour in experimentally created social climates, *Journal of Social Pscyhology*.
Mangham, I. M. L. (1979) *The Politics of Organisational Change*, Associated Business Press, London.
Milgram, S. (1974) *Obedience to Authority: An Experimental View*, Tavistock, London.
Miles, M. (1960). Human relations training, processes and outcomes, *Journal of Counselling Psychology*, 7.
Pettigrew, A. M. (1973) *The Politics of Organisational Decision Making*, Tavistock, London.
Schein, V. E. (1977) Individual power and political behaviour in organisations: An inadequately explored reality, *Academy of Management Review*. 2(1), 64–72.
Taylor, F. W. (1947) *Scientific Management*, Harper, New York.
Thompson, J. D. and Tuden, A. (1964) Strategies, structures and processes of organisational decision, in: *Readings in Managerial Psychology*, Edited by H. J. Leavitt and L. R. Pondy, Chicago, University of Chicago.
Weber, M. (1947) *The Theory of Social and Economic Organization*, The Free Press, Clencoe, Illinois.

Management Development: Advances in Practice and Theory
Edited by C. Cox and J. Beck
© 1984 John Wiley & Sons Ltd

CHAPTER 4

The Use of Assessment Centre Simulations to Evaluate Decision-making Skills in Selection

Joe Kelly and A. Bakr Ibrahim

The recent spread of the assessment centre method, ever since the pioneering studies by Dr Douglas Bray in 1964 at AT&T, has been phenomenal.

WHAT IS AN ASSESSMENT CENTRE?

An assessment centre is a standardized selection method that uses a variety of different techniques, includings tests, interviews, and case studies to evaluate and select potential managers. Using this variety of techniques, a company can observe and objectively evaluate a promising candidate in terms of his managerial potential. The hallmark of this approach is its emphasis on behaviour rather than on delineation of traits.

FROM ESPIONAGE TO THE AT&T STUDIES

Perhaps a brief historical frame of reference of the assessment centre approach is in order. The use of a formal assessment centre can be traceable to the German and Japanese military and later, during the Second World War, to the British War Office Selection Boards (WOSB). The idea then moved from the WOSB to the U.S. military – The American Office of Strategic Service (OSS). The history of the OSS assessment centre was published in 1946 in an article in *Fortune* magazine entitled 'A Good Man is Hard to Find', and later in *The Assessment of Men*, a book published by the OSS (1948). The main objective of the OSS assessment centre was to select and train spies during the Second World War. While the Germans used observation techniques to identify the skills and potentials under pressure situations, the real contribution and breakthrough in the assessment techniques was the development of the 'real-life' situation type of exercise by the OSS staff led by Dr Henry Murray (of Harvard).

However, the credit for introducing the assessment centre approach to industry goes to the American Telephone and Telegram (AT&T) and the pioneering work of Dr Douglas Bray in 1956 known as the Management Progress Study, a longitudinal study of the career development of young managers at AT&T. No doubt this early study has played an important role in establishing the validity of the assessment centre approach, the reported results of the management progress studies confirmed the high predictive power of the assessment techniques to subsequent performance.

The success of the AT&T longitudinal study encouraged others to follow the bandwagon. Standard Oil of Ohio was the second to apply the assessment centre approach, followed by IBM, Sears, General Electric, and Caterpillar Tractor. In 1981, more than 2,500 organizations were applying the method to select potential managers. In Canada, this includes Steinbergs, Bell Canada, Bank of Montreal, CN, the Federal Government (CAP programme), and others.

Although emphasis has been on the selection of candidates for first level managerial jobs, use of the assessment technique to select high-level management's potential is growing. The assessment centre approach has also been used to select salesmen, schools' superintendents, engineers, junior accountants, and others.

THE ASSESSMENT CENTRE PROCESS

The assessment centre process can be outlined in five sequential steps.
1. Identification of job dimensions.
2. Selection and design of the instruments of measurement.
3. Observation and reporting.
4. Evaluation.
5. Feedback.

Within each of these steps more discrete stages can be identified, as shown in Figure 1. Each of these sequential steps can now be discussed in order to give an idea of how an assessment centre actually works.

Identification of Job Dimensions

The first step requires the translation of job requirements into measurable dimensions relevant to success in the management job. For example, we grouped the different behavioural variables that are necessary in a typical management job in 15 dimensions, as shown in Figure 2.

It would be worthwhile at this point to elaborate on the way these dimensions or managerial skills have been selected. Previous assessment efforts (Wollowich and McNamara, 1969; De Costanzo and Andretta, 1970; Thompson, 1970; Moses, 1973; Bray *et al.*, 1974) reported several dimensions necessary for

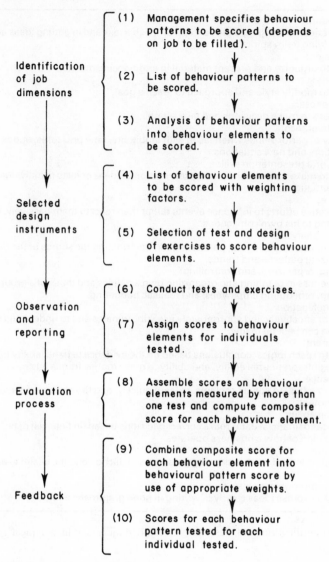

Figure 1. The assessment centre process

success in managerial positions, based on their evaluations of six different assessment programmes. Bray *et al.* (1974) reported seven factors to be responsible for the 25 dimensions stated in their assessment programme at AT&T. Thompson (1969) identified five factors in his managerial assessment programme. However, in general, two main factors seem to be the common dominator in most of the studies: oral communication and influence construct.

1. Leadership:
   Effectiveness in bringing a group to accomplish a task and in getting ideas accepted, and building team spirit.
2. Persuasion:
   Ability to organize and present material in a convincing manner.
3. Flexibility:
   Ability to modify style and approach to reach a goal.
4. Decisiveness:
   Readiness to make decisions and take action.
5. Stress tolerance:
   Stability of performance when faced with ambiguity, time pressures, opposition, frustration, and new situations.
6. Formal oral presentation skills:
   Ability to make a persuasive, clear presentation of ideas or facts in individual or group situations.
7. Initiative:
   Exerts active efforts to influence events rather than react to them passively. Acts according to his own convictions.
8. Problem analysis:
   Effectiveness in seeking out pertinent data; determining the source of the problem; recognizing patterns and trends.
9. Planning, organizing, and controlling:
   Effectiveness in planning and organizing own activities and those of a group, ordering, scheduling employees, and realistic budgeting.
10. Use of delegation:
    Ability to effectively and appropriately use subordinates and to understand where a decision can best be made.
11. Judgement:
    Ability to reach logical conclusions based on the evidence to hand, ability to evaluate people, entrepreneurial ability, and ability to make money from a business.
12. Intelligence:
    Ability to adapt, to solve problems, to learn quickly, and to sensibly understand an environment.
13. Financial ability:
    Understand financial data; make correct decisions based on financial data; appreciation of how a business operates.
14. Motivation:
    The importance of work in deriving personal satisfaction and the desire to achieve at work.
15. Written communication skills:
    Ability to express ideas clearly in writing in good grammatical form.

Figure 2. Identification and description of job dimensions in a typical managerial position

Based on the above studies and our factor analysis of different assessment programmes, we were able to identify the 15 dimensions shown in Figure 2.

Selection and Design of Instruments of Measurement

This step requires the selection of the various psychological instruments, such as the interview, the case study, the irate customer role-play, and the in-basket exercise. The key objective in this step is to decide which instrument is to measure which behavioural dimensions. We will discuss briefly some of these instruments commonly used in industry.

The Background Interview

This exercise is designed to gather information about the candidate (assessee). It could last from 5 minutes to 2 hours and is conducted by one or two of the assessors, and is usually structured to some extent. The main purpose of the background interview is to measure behavioural variables such as personal philosophy towards management process, personal impact, energy, and oral communication skills. The assessee is usually asked to complete a background questionnaire prior to the interview. This questionnaire is used by the assessor or interviewer as a general guideline during the interview. In addition, the assessor may ask several questions related to the behavioural dimension the exercise is designed to measure.

Leaderless Group

This exercise is commonly used in assessment centres. The exercise involves role-playing, i.e. a group of assessees are assigned to particular roles and are given a discussion question by the assessment staff. Then they are asked to come to a group consensus in order to arrive at an answer. This exercise is designed to measure dimensions such as problem analysis, decisiveness, oral communication skills, judgement, initiative, convictions, impact, stress tolerance, leadership, planning and organizing energy, or motivation. Group discussion may be developed on specific issues involving promotional, disciplinary, or operational problems. The 'who to promote' exercise is commonly used in leaderless group discussion, this group exercise lasts between 15 and 30 minutes.

Pressure or Stress Interview

In light of the fact that hiring and appraisal interviews often occupy substantial time for the manager or supervisor, many organizations include mock interviews as a measure of testing major skills. This exercise usually involves role-playing where the assessee is placed in a particular role. For example, the candidate might face a committee about unethical practice. The main object of the pressure interview exercise is to measure behavioural variables such as stress tolerance, self-confidence, flexibility, personal impact, and convictions.

Role-playing

This type of exercise is quite relevant to some managerial jobs where the manager or supervisor has to spend a great deal of time interacting with customers or clients. In the role-playing exercise the candidate is placed in the target role, where he has to act. For example, he may be asked to deal with an irate customer. The main objective of such role playing exercise is to measure behavioural variables such as persuasion, customer relation sensitivity, problem analysis, flexibility, conviction, oral communication skills, stress tolerance, and judgement.

Lecturette

An individual presentation lasting 5–10 minutes is quite common at assessment centres. An opportunity is thus provided to evaluate assessees on behavioural variables such as oral communication skills, flexibility, conviction, personal impact, energy, stress tolerance, planning and organization, and ingenuity and creativity.

Other Methods

Written exercises, paper and pencil tests can also be used to measure other behavioural variables.

Observation and Reporting

Candidates go through an assessment centre in small groups (usually between six and twelve) and assessors observe and evaluate their performance. A typical assessment centre activity lasts two to three days. Assessors are often in a ratio of one assessor to every two candidates and can either be professional psychologists, line managers, or a combination of both. During the assessment time candidates may play a business game, complete an in-basket exercise, participate in group discussions, and be interviewed. The assessment staff observe the candidates and evaluate them on a specially prepared form.

Evaluation

At the end of the assessment activities assessors get together to evaluate all the data they have gathered and assess each candidate and come to a group consensus. A general rating or score for each assessee is arrived at for each dimension originally selected and an overall rating, usually in terms of his potential success on the job, is agreed upon. The assessors spend two to three days comparing observations and making a full evaluation report of each candidate.

Feedback

A final condensed report on each candidate is then developed including items such as overall prediction of success, strengths, weaknesses, potential, and development need. This information is important in career planning decisions. A feedback meeting is usually conducted with each participant where the evaluation report is relayed to him by the assessment staff or his responsible line manager.

ASSESSMENT CENTRE AND HUMAN RESOURCE POLICY

To conclude this part, we have attempted to provide a brief overview of the assessment centre approach. However, before we move to the second part of this paper we wish to point out that the assessment centre method is just one issue in what we consider a total human resource policy. Perhaps an elaboration is in order at this point.

The assessment centre is only a method of appraisal and selection, and unless it is supported by an effective human resource policy, we may not be able to reap the expected benefits. The components of an effective Human Resource Policy (HRP) can be summarized as follows.

1. The human resource policy is part of the comprehensive organizational goals. The organizational goals are based on a consistent evaluation of the internal and external factors (i.e. environment, market, values, structure, strengths and weaknesses of the organization, etc.).

2. The human resource policy is based on a thorough analysis of current and future human resource situations internally and externally (i.e. at the organizational level and industry wide). Analysis of current human resources is based mainly on the ability of the organization to maintain an up-to-date skills inventory of its organizational members and of the industry and total community. Future human resource analysis, on the other hand, is based mainly on the ability to forecast accurately organizational needs of human resources. This in part depends on how accurate the first step was (organizational goals) and how effective the current skills inventory.

3. The policy implementation phase. The first two steps, or what we call policy formulation, would be useless unless put into action through an effective implementation process (this includes hiring to firing).

4. Finally, we think an effective human resource policy has to have a feedback mechanism to enable the policy-maker to adjust his plan whenever he feels the need to do so.

THE ASSESSMENT CENTRE –
A CLINICAL PREDICTION APPROACH

Perhaps we should say a final word before we move to the second part concerning the type of prediction the assessment centre employs.

Meehl (1956) identified two approaches in prediction: actuarial and clinical prediction. The main distinction here is how the data are employed in making the prediction. The actuarial approach employs the data rationally. The clinical approach depends mainly on the judgement of the clinician or personnel officer. On the other hand, the actuarial approach depends on a systematic procedure (i.e. any individual or machine could carry out the procedures and the end-result would be the same).

It is obvious that the assessment approach to personnel selection is what Meehle (1956) termed the 'clinical type of prediction'. The rater, or assessor's, observational skills and experience are the final judge in predicting the success or failure of the candidate. In this case the decision-making process is influenced by many factors (i.e. the assessor's skills, the order of information given by certain candidates, and the perceptual defence mechanisms).

With this in mind, let us now turn to the second part of this chapter.

THE USE OF ASSESSMENT CENTRE SIMULATIONS TO EVALUATE DECISION-MAKING SKILLS IN SELECTION

We have developed a complete set of exercises which capture assessment information exclusively through video tape recording (VTR). The main objective is to evaluate the decision-making aspect (skills) in selection. We anticipate that with the easy availability of VTR, our simulation programme could have a marked effect on assessment centre techniques and on developing observation skills for the assessment staff (the assessors).

WHY VTR

We have found VTR to be very useful in manipulating variables in our experiment, i.e. information order, recency and primacy effect, perceptual defence such as stereotyping, halo effect, and projection. While it may be true that a video recording of an interview does not have the same impact as the true interview situation, a number of studies suggest that video tape viewing of a person and face-to-face viewing produce substantially the same ratings (Moore and Lee, 1974; Lewin, Dubno, and Akula, 1975).

In order to understand the decision-making process, a recent study by Tullar, Mullins, and Caldwell (1979) has identified two measures of decision time that could be possible by the VTR approach:

> if an overt behaviour (such as checking a sheet when the decision is made) is required, then the experiment can covertly time the interval between the start of the tape and the behaviour. Or alternatively subjects can be required to give a stream of consciousness report of their impressions indicating the critical point at which the decision was made (talk-through time).

METHOD

Using the five sequential steps described above, subjects (assessors) receive an evaluation booklet (AEB).

The Assessor Evaluation Booklet (AEB)

The booklet contains three parts, and is designed to evaluate the decision-making skills in selection.

Contents and Descriptions

Part I: Background information about the assessor. This part is mainly designed to correlate the assessor's background with the decision-making, i.e. male/female, black/white, Anglophone/Francophone, etc.

Part II: Job description. This part is designed to give the assessor background information about the job and the behavioural variables relevant to success in such a job.

Part III: Evaluation forms. In this part different forms are designed together with the behavioural dimensions relevant to the instrument (exercise) used and the job skill analysis.

Procedures

Assessors are instructed to watch each exercise on the VTR and evaluate the different actors (assessees) based on the behavioural dimensions relevant to the exercise.

Assessors are asked to make two types of decisions.

1. Talk-through time decision (TTTD). This type of decision is made at the end of each exercise for each candidate. Talk-through time decision is designed to measure the decision skills based on the nature and order of information input (i.e. information favourableness, type, ambiguity, location in the information flow, and contrast), recency/primacy effect, and perceptual defence such as stereotyping, halo, and projection.

2. Complete information decision (CID). This second type is a comprehensive decision, and is designed to measure the decision skills based on complete information about the candidate after observing the different behavioural variables relevant to success on the job. This type of decision is made after observing the different sets of exercises and business games for each candidate.

PROSPECTIVE

Beside the main objective of evaluating the decision-making skills in personnel selection, we see a tremendous potential in the use of the VTR assessment programme, specifically:

1. As a training device for assessors and personnel officers to improve their observational skills.

2. The ability to manipulate the information input (i.e. the order of information input, the favourableness of information, the applicant's characteristics, and the characteristics of the previous applicant). This, we believe, can play a vital part in the progress and development of clinical prediction in personnel selection.

3. The collective experience shared by the different assessors who watch the VTR assessment programme could have a great effect on the behavioural change process of the organization.

REFERENCES

Bray, D. W., Campbell, R. J., and Grant, D. L. (1974) *Formative Years in Business: A Long-term AT&T Study of Managerial Lives*, Wiley–Interscience, New York.

De Costanzo, F. and Andretta, J. (1970) Implementation of an assessment center in a federal agency, *ASTD Journal*, **September 1970**.

Lewin, A. Y., Dubno, P.; and Akula, W. G. (1975) Face-to-face interaction in the peer nomination process, *Journal of Applied Psychology*, **60**, 495–497.

Meehl, (1956) *Clinical vs Actuarial Prediction, In Proceedings of the 1955 invitational conference on testing problems*, Educational Testing Service, Princeton, 136–141.

Moore, L. F. and Lee, J. (1974) Comparability of interviewer, group and individual ratings, *Journal of Applied Psychology*, **59**, 163–

Moses, J. L. (1973) The development of an assessment center for the early identification of supervisory potential, *Personnel Psychology*, **26**, 569–580.

Office of Strategic Services (OSS) (1948) *Assessment of Men*, Rinehart, New York.

Thompson, H. A. (1969) *Internal and External Validation of an Industrial Assessment Center Program*, Case Western Reserve University.

Tullar, W. L., Mullins, T. W., and Caldwell, S. A. (1979) Effects of interview length and applicant quality on interviewer decision time, *Journal of Applied Psychology*, **64**, 669–674.

Wollowich, H. B. and McNamara, W. J. (1969) Relationships of the components of an assessment center to management success, *Journal of Applied Psychology*, **53**, 348–352.

Management Development: Advances in Practice and Theory
Edited by C. Cox and J. Beck
© 1984 John Wiley & Sons Ltd

CHAPTER 5

The Task for the '80s: Training Women Managers

Mike Smith and Sandra Langrish

IS THE TRAINING OF WOMEN MANAGERS THE TASK FOR THE '80S?

Crystal ball gazing is a hazardous affair. It is doubly hazardous when it aims to predict what future management educators will nominate as the major development of the present decade. With the infinite advantage of hindsight, they will be able to identify which of the many contenders was the main development of the decade. Without this hindsight it is difficult for us to distinguish between the training flavour of the month and the real task of the decade. Criteria will be needed to aid our contemporary distinction. Four criteria spring immediately to mind.

First, the task of the decade will address a problem which is manifestly obvious to a large proportion of the population. A second, related criterion is that the size of the task will be large. Third, the task will have its origins in socio-cultural trends which have been in existence for some time. Finally, the task of the decade will need to promise a substantial benefit to the community. The training of women managers meets all the criteria and it must be considered as a serious nominee as *the* management educators' task of the '80s.

Importance of Training Women Managers

The problem concerning women in management is that there are too few. The British workforce contains about 42% of women, yet only a tiny percentage of managers above supervisory level (less than 10%) are women (Cleverdon, 1980). A part of the difference can be readily explained by the fact that not all women want to be managers. But, it is equally true that a proportion – possibly a smaller proportion – of men are also reluctant to become managers. Even when a possible differential between willingness of the sexes to become managers is taken into account, there remains a large discrepancy between the proportion of women in the workforce and the proportion of women managers.

Furthermore, the imbalance is not restricted to Britain. As Table 1 shows, the imbalance is present in both developed and undeveloped countries.

The problem seems particularly acute at middle and senior management levels. It seems *relatively* easy for women to reach junior management positions; the immediate supervisor in the sewing machine room, or in the general office is almost certain to be a woman. Above this level there is the equivalent of an 8-foot wall topped with barbed wire and supported in depth by tank traps, machine gun towers, and seismic detectors.

The Size of the Training Problem

The scale of the problem is enormous. Supposing it would be acceptable to adopt the objective where the ratio of women managers to women workers is about half the male ratio (e.g. 21% women managers compared to 42% women workers), a ten-year program to achieve this objective will need the education of thousands of female managerial recruits. The more extreme members of the women's movement would regard such half parity as a 'wet' sell out. Yet, even a wet sell out of this kind would require management training facilities which far exceed the present capacity.

The Socio-cultural Forces

Many of today's training issues are relatively short-term. The training of women managers does not fall into this category since it stands at the confluence of two long-term trends in society. The *first* of these trends is the *increasing professionalism* of management and the increasing emphasis upon formal management education. It will take years before past cohorts of 'mechanic managers' reach retirement. The days when the accepted route into management ran from apprenticeship to head mechanic to factory manager and finally to general manager are slowly drawing to a close. A survey by Guerrier and Philpot (1978) shows that younger managers tends to have better educational qualifications than previous generations. The trend towards specific education for managers has continued since the establishment of the Business Schools in the United States in the early part of the century. Similar developments in the United Kingdom occurred rather later, but by the mid-1930s management education was being pioneered in the United Kingdom by both the London School of Economics and the University of Manchester Institute of Science and Technology.

Formal management education has shown continued expansion since the 1930s. Indeed, plans indicate that this will continue, even against a background of cuts in other areas of university teaching. Although UMIST is the market leader and is probably the biggest management department in Europe, its experience is not atypical of other U.K. management departments.

Table 1 Cross national comparisons of womens' share of higher-level occupations

Census year	Country	Percent of women among:			Census year	Country	Percent of women among:		
		All professionals	Managers administrators	Total labour force			All professionals	Managers administrators	Total labour force
Western Europe					*Latin America (Cont'd)*				
1970	Denmark	55	17	37	1971	Panama	51	12	26
1975	Norway	48	13	38	1970	Chile	50	17	23
1975	Sweden	48	11	42	1975	Venezuela	50	7	28
1971	Italy	46	6	27	1973	Costa Rica	47	11	19
1975	Finland	45	18	46	1975	Mexico	38	19	22
1968	France	43	12	35	1972	Peru	33	5	21
1971	Great Britain	38	8	37					
1971	Austria	37	20	39	*Middle East and Africa*				
1970	Germany (FD)	34	14	36	1970	Lebanon	38	2	17
1970	Spain	33	4	20	1971	Bahrain	35	7	5
					1975	Kuwait	34	2	12
Eastern Europe					1966	Iran	26	3	13
1970	Poland	50	27	46	1966	Egypt	24	4	7
1970	Hungary	47	15	41	1970	Syria	23	2	11
1971	Yugoslavia	46	9	36	1966	Algeria	21	6	4
1970	Czechoslovakia	42	14	45					
					Asia				
North America					1970	Philippines	57	29	32
1976	Canada	48	20	37	1973	Thailand	49	9	45
1975	USA	42	20	39	1971	Hong Kong	44	8	34
					1971	Sri Lanka	41	6	26
Latin America					1975	Japan	38	5	37
1970	Brazil	59	11	21	1975	Singapore	30	7	30
1972	Paraguay	55	15	21	1971	India	18	2	17
1970	Argentina	55	7	25					

Source: C. Hakim, *Occupational Segregation*, Department of Employment, London, 1979.

The second societal trend has an even longer history. The movement towards equality between the sexes goes back at least as far as the married
women's property act of 1870 and was subsequently reflected in such events as
the adoption of equal franchise in 1928 and the establishment of the Equal
Opportunities Commission in 1975.

Benefits to the Community

A sustained training effort must hold the promise of benefits to the community.
An increase in the proportion of women managers may well improve the level
of managerial talent. The rationale has an almost mathematical simplicity.

Suppose that the least talented 20% of male managers could be replaced by
the most talented females, then the national pool of managerial talent would be
improved by several percentage points. However, this argument needs to be
approached with care – it makes very defensible assumption that men and
women have equal managerial ability. It also makes a less defensible assumption that the incompetent men would be replaced by competent women: in
practice, competence often plays a minor role in selection and placement
decisions. Often, selection is based upon assertiveness or verbal spontenaity:
the incompetent men could instead be displaced by assertive, but equally
incompetent women.

STRATEGIC ISSUES

Once the challenge of increasing the propotion of women managers has been
accepted, a number of strategic issues must be faced. All aspects of the problem
cannot be tackled simultaneously and a ground plan is needed to identify
priority areas. Probably the most important distinction is between the training
needed to *increase* a higher proportion of women managers and the training
needed to *maintain* a higher proportion. The two types of training needs should
be approached in different ways.

Training to Increase the Proportion of Women Managers

The training required to increase the proportion of women managers has the
ethos of an uphill, pioneering struggle. It takes place against the conventional
background where, in the initial stages, women managers will be the exception
and will need to operate in an environment which is largely attuned to male
needs and attitudes. Often, this type of training will be concerned with those
who are already in the labour force and will involve 'older' women. Their
maturity and experience are both a boon and disadvantage. Training methods
appropriate for older workers, such as discovery learning, will need to be
chosen in preference to other techniques and time and effort may need to be

devoted to unlearning certain attitudes. On the other hand, the previous experience and knowledge of the trainees should help them assimilate information and place it in its proper context. Furthermore, the pre-existence of experience should mean that after training, promotion can take place quite rapidly.

Training designed to increase the proportion of women managers will be distinguished by two further characteristics: the calibre of the trainees and the organization of the training. It could be contended that in the initial stages at least, the women trainees will be of a higher calibre since they have survived a rigorous process of elimination. While this argument may be true in the majority of circumstances, its validity is not necessarily universal. Good connections also help. Women whose husbands are already successful and who can provide resources, information, and contacts, are not necessarily subjected to such a rigorous elimination procedure as their husbands. The total iconoclast will add a further note that, if organizations are under pressure to demonstrate their commitment to equal opportunities, they may be tempted to abandon their normal standards of competence.

The organization of training to increase the proportion of women managers involves the issue whether the training should take place in a 'women only' environment. The arguments against 'women only' training are strong: most women managers will work in an environment where the majority of colleagues will be men. Consequently, it would seem sensible to maximize the transfer of training by including men in the training programme.

However, there are even stronger arguments in favour of 'women only' training. A large part of a training program for potential women managers is not relevant to potential male managers. For example, few men need to obtain skills to enable them to work in an environment which is dominated by the opposite sex. Similarly, few men need advice on how to manage the 'career gap' which child-rearing entails. A second argument in favour of 'women only' training is that the presence of male participants influences the social interactions and the training 'atmosphere'. The presence of male participants carries the danger that traditional patterns of interaction will be preserved and reinforced: there is the danger that men will adopt the active leadership roles while the women will take the line of least resistance and adopt a subordinate role. In 'women only training', at least some women will need to adopt the leadership roles. The social atmosphere is particularly important in training designed to encourage women to experiment with new patterns of behaviour. Such training needs to be conducted in a trusting non-threatening atmosphere. Whilst the precise effect will depend upon the particular men or the particular women involved, it is possible that a group containing both sexes is less conducive to the development of this atmosphere of social support.

In practice, the decision whether to use 'women only' training is not the difficult dilemma suggested by the previous argument. Indeed, the optimum strategy may call for both mixed and 'women only training'. The best results might be achieved by organizing a programme so that the early part of the training is conducted on a 'women only' basis while later parts involve both men and women.

Training to Maintain a Higher Proportion of Women Managers

Even if the initial objectives are achieved and an equitable proportion of managers are women, management educators will still need to devote resources to the training of women managers. But, the problem will take on a different hue. The need to train women to overcome career barriers and cope with being the only female manager with whom her male colleagues interact, will, optimistically, disappear. The generation of women entering managment will, hopefully, have received opportunities which are comparable to their male colleagues. Consequently, much of their training will be identical to the training given to male managers.

One separate training need will remain. For as far ahead as can be seen, women managers will be much more likely than men to break their careers. Unless the career break is properly managed, it could constitute a continuous drain upon the pool of women in management positions. Unless positive action is taken, it could, within the space of a decade, return the proportion of women managers to present levels.

Career break counselling and 'returnee training' will be important elements in answering the problem. However, they must not be viewed in isolation since restructuring of career patterns and changing traditional attitudes will also play an important role.

Levels of Action

Whether the training is designed to increase or to maintain the proportion of women managers, action can be taken at five different levels.

First, there are the *women themselves*. Self-development is one of the most potent methods in management education and it has been the method used by the majority of today's women managers. Individual women must continue to take a large share of the responsibility for their own management education. They need a willingness to widen their horizons, challenge traditional stereotypes, and enrol for relevant courses.

The second level of action concerns *companies* as employers. Companies acting on their own, or as a part of a trade federation or training group, are uniquely placed to provide compensatory training for the women themselves and, perhaps, the training of male managers in an attempt to remove traditional attitudes which may prejudice the advancement of women with managerial potential.

The third level of action concerns the *trade unions*. Here the possibilities for action include acting as a pressure group to encourage the provision of facilities. Unions should also provide relevant training for their own staff and they should enable women to take up positions of responsibility within the unions. Finally, unions are in a unique position to make their members more aware of the issues involved.

At the fourth level, there is the *state*. A government which makes a policy decision in favour of equal opportunities will need to support the decision in ways that are both directly and indirectly relevant to training. The actions directly relevant to training include pump-priming activities, such as taking a far-sighted view and commissioning relevant training programmes. Government can also award grants to encourage companies to offer special training. In addition, the problem of training management trainers and educators can only be effectively tackled by the state or one of its agencies.

The fifth and final level concerns *supranational organizations* such as the EEC or the United Nations. They can undertake some of the functions of national governments such as increasing levels of awareness or providing sources of funds over and above those provided at national level. The distinctive contribution of supranational organizations stems, however, from their unique perspective. They have a wider view of sociological changes and they are able to collate information from a wide variety of sources. Supranational organizations are in an ideal position to stimulate new action by bringing together training experts, policy-makers, and managers. They can also compare the effectiveness of different programmes and disseminate the experiences gained from different approaches to the problem.

Synthesis and Progress Report

The identification of levels of action and the distinction between the two types of training need can be brought together to provide a useful 'ground plan'. The ground plan can then be used to guide further action. Each cell of Table 2 lists *some* of the possible training activities and the state of the art in each area can be assessed.

For example, there has been considerable research on sex role stereotyping and means of widening the career horizons of female school leavers. Equal opportunities legislation has also been enacted in most European and North American nations. In many countries commissions have been established to enforce the legislation and increase awareness of the problems of sex discrimination. Other areas where progress has been made include the provision of compensatory training together with the provision of grants and other pump-priming activities. At a supranational level, a good start has been made in providing some funding and facilitating the exchange of experience.

On the debit side, very little activity has taken place to help our understand-

Table 2 A classification of some of the training concerning women in management

	Individuals	Companies	Unions	Government	International agencies
Training to *maintain* a higher proportion of women managers	breaking down stereotypes	same job training as men	provision of training for own staff	developing equality within educational system	increase awareness
	widening horizons beyond traditional sex roles	managing career break		enactment of equal opportunity legislation	unification of training infrastructure
Training to *increase* the proportion of women managers	confidence building	compensatory training	pressure for training courses for women	pump-priming grants	increasing awareness
	encouragement to enrol	establishing attitudes of male managers	raising levels of awareness	training of trainers	provision of additional funding for comparative research
					exchange of experiences

ing of the attitudes of male managers, the techniques needed to manage the career break, and the reasons why many women do not enrol for courses of compensatory training. The role of the educational system in promoting equal opportunities has long been recognized but the task of bringing about change is gargantuan and progress seems painfully slow.

NEEDS ANALYSIS FOR COMPENSATORY TRAINING

Compensatory training is an area of direct concern to management educators and trainers. Whilst the concept of compensatory training is evident from its name, the *content* needs to be based on an analysis of training needs. A review of various sources (e.g. Cotton and Allied Textile Industry Training Board, 1977; Langrish and Smith, 1979, 1981; Ashridge Management College, 1980) suggests that four broad training needs exist: women's issues; career planning; interpersonal skills; and management knowledge.

Women's Issues

The most obvious training needs is to prepare women for the issues they will face as *women managers*. Here, the women need to be familiar with, and come to terms with, the *attitudes and stereotypes held by senior male managers*. For example, they need to be aware of research work which suggests that male managers tend to attribute the causes of women's promotion to factors other than the women themselves and that a majority of males in personnel posts believe that a woman applicant is likely to be inferior to a man in respect of all the qualities considered important (Hunt, 1975; Deaux, 1976). The tendency for men to dislike 'liberated' women while assigning them a higher status and men's tendency to like and give high status to 'equalitarian' women (Dufresne, 1971) are other examples of relevant research findings in this area (see Langrish, 1981, pp. 19–31 for a detailed exposition). It should also be noted that *women's* attitudes towards *women* managers may be equally important. At anecdotal level there is some evidence to suggest that the task of women managers may be made more difficult by the negative attitudes of other women – especially older women.

A second important 'women's issue' is the *styles of operation* which women managers can adopt. These range from the 'Queen Bee' to the 'Old Dragon' to the situation where the woman manager adopts a style which exhibits more machismo than Tarzan. The advantages and disadvantages of each of these styles can be compared and more realistic role models provided.

A third major women's issue involves the guidance on how to operate in an environment which is dominated by the opposite sex. Two particular issues under this heading concern *networking* and *visibility*. One of the facets of managerial work, illuminated by Mintzberg (1973), is that managers need a network of formal and informal contacts to provide a readily accessible source of up-to-date information. Such a network may also provide a source of emotional support which can be used in times of stress. These networks evolve over a long period of time and are often based upon informal contacts made in single-sex settings such as the men's sauna, the football club, or even the public school. Male networks can be used to exclude female managers and put them at a disadvantage. Women potential managers need to be aware of this possibility and be prepared to consciously establish networks of their own (see Welch, 1980).

Previous work (e.g. Humphreys and Shrode, 1978; Langrish and Smith, 1979) suggest that women concentrate upon completing the *task* at hand efficiently and without fuss. Because problems do not arise from their work they are not noticed and are taken for granted. Thus, they may well be overlooked in promotion decisions. A part of the training for women potential managers should draw the problem to their attention and equip them with some skills for achieving higher visibility. A final 'women's issue' concerns the possibility that a 'male backlash' may be provoked by arrogant, expedient, and unduly assertive behaviour of female managers.

Career Planning

Career planning is not normally included in training for male potential managers and this omission may be justifiable. Veiga (1977) suggests that men themselves stress the need for planning not only career goals but also the methods of attaining them: many men felt the need to give opportunity a hand.

The omission would not be justified in a training programme for women potential managers. Veiga points out that in contrast, to work hard and await the rewards of virtue is the strategy which *women* consider to be the most effective. Veiga describes this as a self-perpetuating cycle of passive acceptance in career strategy.

It can be argued that the task of planning a career is more difficult for women. Occupational sex role stereotypes have customarily reduced the range of jobs available to women. The range of jobs available to women may also be restricted by the fact that fewer women have any educational qualifications in science and technology. Furthermore, there is the added complication of the break in career which child-bearing usually entails. On the basis of the evidence cited in this section, there is a clear need for a substantial component on career planning to be included in a programme for women potential managers. There is also evidence (O'Neil *et al.*, 1978, 1979) that such career planning can be successful in encouraging women to think of a wider range of careers.

Personal and Interpersonal Skills

A number of writers (e.g. Vaught, 1965; Maccoby and Jacklin, 1974; Schwartz and Waetjen, 1976; Larwood and Wood, 1977; and Place, 1979) have produced results that indicate women are less confident than their male colleagues. *Lack of confidence* may also be related to a difference between men's and women's motivation. The level of achievement motivation (McClelland *et al.*, 1953) in women has been closely investigated following Horner's (1970, 1972) suggestion that women have lower motivation to achieve because they fear success. Horner claimed that success is feared because, for her subjects, success is associated with loss of femininity and social rejection. Reviews of the research literature on fear of success have been undertaken by Ward (1978) and by de Charms and Muir (1978).

Thus, it seems that there is a training need to increase confidence and increase the levels of achievement motivation. Although it is possible to devise specific training to increase achievement motivation (Alschuler *et al.*, 1970; McClelland, 1972) by teaching participants to think, talk, act, and set goals like an individual with high achievement motivation, these objectives can be achieved by the appropriate organization of training. For example, most participative exercises can be handled in a way which encourages the setting of objectives with moderate risks (a characteristic of individuals with high achievement motivation). Success in achieving these objectives can then be handled in a way which builds confidence and does not threaten the participant's feminine self-image.

An analysis by Langrish and Smith (1979) and research by Humphreys and Shrode (1978) indicate that, contrary to the popular image, women potential managers think largely in terms of the task at hand, while their male colleagues will think in terms of personnel and leadership. Vinacke and Gullickson (1964) found that in competitive activities, women tend to form coalitions in an accommodative manner, while men are more exploitive and use coalitions to gain advantage. The work of Kotter (1977) and McClelland and Burnham (1976) indicate that the social skill of acquiring power may be an important managerial characteristic, and Schein (1978) points out that women may have fewer opportunities to acquire this skill. Furthermore, at an anecdotal level, it has been claimed that women have a lower level of skill at working in groups because their socialization has included fewer group activities such as team sports. The evidence is far from conclusive. But, it may be that training in group skills and interpersonal skills is more important for female potential managers than for their male counterparts.

Management Knowledge

Examination of occupational statistics reveals that women, including women managers, are concentrated in a relatively narrow range of industries. They also tend to be concentrated into particular management functions such as personnel or other jobs which are outside the mainstream career path of line management.

Many women's experience of industry is reduced still further by the fact that there is a break in their careers during child-rearing. Thus, women potential managers may know less about the management function than their male counterparts. This relative lack of knowledge interacts with their lower self-confidence and may result in a reluctance to enrol for training or to seize development opportunities because they fear humiliation at not being able to understand management jargon. Training in management theory might prevent a downward self-fulfilling prophesy whereby a lack of management knowledge leads to a reluctance to enrol for training which then leads to lack of promotion which in turn prevents the improvement of knowledge about management.

The exact training need must be analysed with care. A management course such as those given to male management trainees is not required at this stage (but hopefully it will be required at a subsequent stage). The training needed has strictly limited objectives. It should aim to overcome the fact that the woman's experience of management is often restricted to certain specialist functions. Consequently, it should aim to broaden women's view of the management process so that they can see their own experiences in context. The second objective is to demystify the management process. The third objective should be to teach a limited range of vocabulary so that the content of subsequent courses can be assimilated quickly.

ETHICAL ISSUES

The ethical issues involved in training women managers are often ignored but they are of great importance.

First, there are ethical issues concerning the trainees themselves. At the time they commit themselves to a training course, participants may have little insight into the implications of the training upon their lives. The danger varies according to the precise content of the training. Instruction to improve knowledge of management techniques is relatively safe. Training concerned with assertiveness, transactional analysis, or sensitivity training, carry greater dangers since in essence they aim to alter the behaviour of the individual. Transactional analysis, assertiveness, and group training are useful counter-measures against manipulation by others. But, unless training in these techniques is handled with integrity, they can lead to the extreme egocentricity of the Texan and Californian 'I am' culture which is anathema to many European values. Some of these types of training can cause the individual psychological damage. Indeed, it can be argued that the most vulnerable individuals are attracted to this type of course. Much can be done to mitigate these dangers: participants can be carefully selected and given information that enables them to exercise their own choice. In most practical situations, however, the trainer unilaterally makes a decision that to change participants in a particular way is a good thing.

Training for women potential managers can cause harm in other ways. Inevitably, the level of the woman's ambitions are raised. Yet, the means of fulfilling these ambitions often lie outside the control of both the woman herself and the management educator. The net result of such training could be frustration, resentment, and anger. The outcome could parallel the denouement of Shaw's *Pygmalian*: Eliza can neither return to her previous life nor easily take her place as a duchess in society. Meanwhile, her educators, blinded by the technical success of her education, remain oblivious to both her predicament and the eddies of her emotions.

The ethical issues arising from the training of women managers go beyond those involving the woman herself. The training can have an indirect impact upon marriage and the woman's spouse. It can also affect the way that children are reared and, in due course, this could alter the society in which we live. Some of these changes will be for the better of all. Some will be for the worse. In many situations it is the trainer who plays God and decides whether the advantages outweigh the risks. It is an awesome responsibility. It is a responsibility which must be faced and discharged with care and integrity as management educators set about their task for the 1980s.

REFERENCES

Alschuler, A. S., Tabor, D., and McIntyre (1970) *Teaching Achievement Motivation, Middletown*, Educational Ventures Inc., Conn.

Ashridge Management College (1980) *Employee Potential: Issues in the Development of Women*, London Institute of Personnel Management.

de Charms, R. and Muir, M. S. (1978) Motivation: Social approaches, *Annual Review of Psychology*, **29**, 95.

Cleverdon, J. (1980) *Women in Management*, The Industrial Society, London.

Cotton and Allied Textiles ITB (1977) *Women in Management in the Textile Industry*, CATITB, Manchester.

Deaux, K. (1976) Sex: A perspective on the attribution process, in: *New Directions in Attribution Research*, Vol. 2, Edited by J. H. Harvey *et al.*, Erlbaum, Hillsdale, N.J.

Dufresne, M. M. (1971) Differential reaction of males to three different female sex roles, Ph.D Thesis, University of Connecticut.

Guerrier, Y. and Philpot, N. (1978) *The British Manager: Careers and Mobility*, Management Survey Report No. 39, British Institute of Management, London.

Horner, M. S. (1970) Femininity and successful achievement: a basic inconsistency, in: *Feminine Personality and Conflict*, Edited by J. Bardwick *et al.*, Brooks, Cole, Belmont, California.

Horner, M. S. (1972) Towards an understanding of achievement related conflicts in women, *Journal of Social Issues*, **28**, 157–75.

Humphreys, L. W. and Shrode, W. A. (1978) Decision-making profiles of female and male managers, *MSU Business Topics*, **Autumn 1978**.

Hunt, A. (1975) *Management Attitudes and Practice Towards Women at Work*, HMSO Office of Population Censuses and Surveys, London.

Kotter, J. P. (1977) Power, dependance and effective management, *Harvard Business Review*, **55**, 125–136.

Langrish, S. V. (1981) Women in Management: Comparative Studies using Repertory Grids, Ph.D Thesis, University of Manchester Institute of Science and Technology.

Langrish, S. V. and Smith, J. M. (1979) *Women in Management: Their Views and Training Needs*, Training Services Division of the Manpower Services Commission, Sheffield.

Langrish, S. V. and Smith, J. M. (1981) *Report on a Programme to Develop Women for Management Practices in the Textile Industry*, Training Services Division of the Manpower Services Commission, Sheffield.

Larwood, L. and Wood, M. M. (1977) *Women in Management*, D. C. Heath, Lexington.

Maccoby, E. E. and Jacklin, C. V. (1974) *The Psychology of Sex Differences*, Stanford University Press.

McClelland, D. C. (1972) What is the effect of achievement motivation training in schools, *Teachers' College Records*, **74**, 129–145.

McClelland, D. C. and Burnham, D. H. (1976) Power is the great motivator, *Harvard Business Review*, **54**, 100, 110.

McClelland, D. C., Atkinson, J. W., Clark, R. A., and Lowell, E. L. (1953) *The Achievement Motive*, Appleton Century Crofts, New York.

Mintzberg, H. (1973) *The Nature of Managerial Work*, Harper Row, New York.

O'Neil, J. M. *et al.* (1978) *A Developmental Preventative and Consultative Model to Reduce Sexism in the Career Planning of Women*, J.S.A.S. Catalogue of Selected Documents in Psychology, 8: 1689.

O'Neil, J. M. *et al.* (1979) Research on a career workshop to reduce sexism with women, Paper presented to 87th Annual Meeting of the American Psychological Association, New York.

Place, H. (1979) A biographical profile of women in management, *Journal of Occupational Psychology*, **52**, 267–276.

Schein, V. E. (1978) Sex role stereotyping, ability and performance: Prior research and new directions, *Personal Psychology*, **31**, 259–268.

Schwartz, E. B. and Waetjen (1976) Improving the self concept of women managers, *Business Quarterly*, **44**, 4, 20–27.

Vaught, G. M. (1965) The relationship of role identification and ego strength to sex difference in the rod and frame test, *Journal of Personality*, **33**, 271–283.

Veiga, J. F. (1977) Women in management: An endangered species, *MSU Business Topics*, **25**, 3, 31–35.

Vinacke, E. and Gullickson, G. R. (1964) Age and sex differences in the formation of coalitions, *Child Development*, **35**, 1217–1231.

Ward, C. (1978) Is there a motive to avoid success in women? *Human Relations*, **31**, 12, 1055–1067.

Welch, M. S. (1980) *Networking: The Great New Way for Women to Get Ahead*, USA.

Management Development: Advances in Practice and Theory
Edited by C. Cox and J. Beck
© 1984 John Wiley & Sons Ltd

CHAPTER 6

Coping with Change and Managerial Obsolescence

Andrew N. Jones

INTRODUCTION

It is often said that one of the most prevalent and obvious characteristics of modern life is change. It occurs in dramatic and often violent ways but also in more subtle and unobtrusive ways. We are all influenced by it. It has consequences for all aspects of life from the food we eat, the clothes we wear, the way we rear our families to the jobs we do. How well we cope with change is a reflection of our psychological well-being and ability to adjust to new situations. Managers in particular have a great need to be able to cope with change from a technological, occupational, and organizational standpoint, in addition to being flexible in their managerial practices. The success of today's industry depends greatly on the updatedness of its managerial staff. Those who are out of date in terms of knowledge and skills for their jobs are said to be obsolescent.

THE MANAGER AND CHANGE

There are four main types of change which make demands on managers' knowledge and skills (see Figure 1). The first of these is *technological change*. This is highly visible in the form of new products being created by new methods of production. Automation alone has revolutionized organizational processes, ranging from purchasing to production scheduling and control. The introduction of the 'silicon chip' has taken automation a further leap forward in terms of manufacturing practices and information retrieval.

The second major change is *occupational change*. This is clearly evidenced by the fact that workers in white-collar occupations with higher skill requirements now outnumber those in blue-collar jobs, many of who have been eliminated as a result of technical progress.

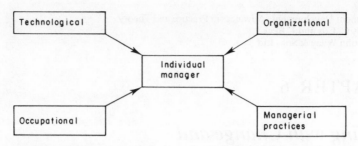

Figure 1. Model of changes affecting managers. *Source*: A. N. Jones and C. L. Cooper, *Combating Managerial Obsolescence*, Philip Allen Publishers, Oxford

Organizational change is the third major form of change which affects ever-increasing numbers of companies each year. These occur through mergers, acquisitions, development of new products, expansion of markets, especially those overseas, and the introduction of computers. Major structural changes can also be brought about by external forces such as political alliances, for example the European Economic Community (EEC), the oil crises of 1973 and 1979, and the introduction of the European Monetary System (EMS).

Finally, there are changes in *managerial practices*. These are reflected in the widespread use of operations research and systems analysis techniques, which emphasize quantitative and computer methodology to facilitate and improve management information, decision-making, and forecasting. Management techniques also increasingly utilize behavioural science findings to improve motivation and productivity, as well as provide a more comfortable working environment for all. The effects of these changes on the practising manager are enormous. For, besides having to cope with 'knowledge changes' in his own discipline, he must also cope with those of others if he hopes to maintain his effectiveness.

WHAT IS MANAGERIAL OBSOLESCENCE?

A problem faced by all researchers and writers in the field of obsolescence is one of definition. Burack and Pati (1970). Mahler (1965), Horgan and Floyd (1971), Shumaker (1963), and Siefert (1963) have all defined obsolescence in terms of a reduction in skills or performance over time. Burack and Pati (1970) found that managers and professionals generally experienced obsolescence when their knowledge or skills were not adequate to meet their job demands. Mahler (1965) described obsolescence as the failure of a manager to do his job with the same degree of competence as once expected. Horgan and Floyd (1971) use two terms to describe obsolescence: *Professional obsolescence* 'refers to those whose technical "know how" does not include the furthest reaches of knowledge and technique which exist within their discipline'; and

Job obsolescence which refers 'to a situation in which the individual's knowledge is insufficient when compared to the body of knowledge that is pertinent to the specific technical tasks that he is required to perform in his current job'. Shumaker (1963) defines obsolescence as a reduction in technical skills resulting from a manager's inability or unwillingness to keep up to date with new technological and other developments since leaving formal education. According to Siefert (1963): 'obsolescence is the measurement at some point in time of the difference between the knowledge and skills possessed by the practicing professional who may have completed his formal education a number of years previously, and those possessed by a recent graduate of a modern curriculum'. Mali (1970) developed what he called the obsolescence index (OI) in order to define the concept of obsolescence:

$$OI = \frac{\text{current knowledge understood by managers}}{\text{current knowledge in the field}}.$$

The equation is based on the rate of change versus time. High rates of technical obsolescence are related to high rates of growth.

There are a variety of reasons why a manager or professional might be considered to suffer obsolescence. First, it may be that he/she, on completing training, moved into a routine and unchallenging job that required little use of his/her knowledge or skill. Secondly, it may be that the individual over-specialized during professional training and so severely curtailed his/her knowledge or skill. Thirdly, he/she may have entered a field of research or work which, through changing technology or economic factors, became obsolete, e.g. manned space technology. Fourthly, the manager may have entered his/her job with the requisite knowledge and skills but failed to maintain or build on them through management education and training, and finally, he/she might have moved from a technical position to one of administration or management which no longer required a high technical competence and, at the same time, did not provide the fundamentals of management knowledge and skills required to do the job.

Therefore, the common elements of most definitions suggest that a manager or professional is suffering from obsolescence if he has inadequate knowledge or skill to meet the current demands of his work. Whether this is due to failure to keep up to date or movement to a new discipline without adequate training, or recent promotion, the resultant effects are the same in that the job will not be done as efficiently or effectively as might be expected of one who was up to date.

IDENTIFYING OBSOLESCENCE

As an illustration of how to recognize symptoms of obsolescence Malmross (1963) has identified five characteristics which are prevalent among engineers:

(1) they become less and less inclined to apply rigorous mathematical techniques to obtain solutions to problems;

(2) they encounter increasing difficulty in reading new technical papers and feel frustrated at their inability to follow the mathematics;

(3) new technical concepts are confusing to them;

(4) new tasks and assignments look too difficult to be practical; and

(5) contemporaries no longer seek their advice.

The Stanford Research Institute study (1968) found that mature industries with recent advances in technology or with innovation through large research and development activity were highly susceptible to obsolescence. Small industries with a high reliance on technical engineering and science managers for man management and administrative jobs are likewise susceptible. Obsolescence-inducing trends are identified as new forms of organization, new management methods, new technologies, new markets and marketing techniques, new services, new inputs from basic and applied sciences, and new social, political, cultural, and regulatory developments. A further finding reported by this study was the fact that twice as many companies with low management obsolescence had high rates of growth as had low rates of growth. Companies with high management obsolescence tended to have low rates of growth.

What are the real danger signals for a manager or professional? Or is it best to assume we are all susceptible and so commit ourselves to lifelong learning, formally and informally. How realistic is this and who pays for it? These are as yet unanswered questions for most of us.

SIGNIFICANT VARIABLES IN RELATION TO MANAGERIAL OBSOLESCENCE

The variables listed in Table 1 have been found to be significantly related to managerial obsolescence. They are exemplified here as they relate to the characteristics of high and low obsolescent managers as found in recent studies (Jones, 1979; O'Reilly, Jones, and Coldrick, 1980).

These results indicate that there are many variables which seem to influence managerial obsolescence, so that any attempt to explain this phenomenon must take account of all of them. However, the most important variables seem to be managers' perception of their learning ability and the extent to which they enjoy new work-related learning. An examination of the significant variables in the studies suggest that the most important group were the personal variables, dealing with managers' learning ability, their perception of the importance of updating, and their motivation to keep up to date. The career variables appear to be next in importance, particularly those relating to decision-making, job challenge, and the extent to which managers' jobs utilize their professional skills and abilities. The third group in terms of explaining managerial obsolescence were the organizational variables, especially those relating to encour-

Table 1 Profile of high and low obsolescent managers

Category of variable	High obsolescent	Low obsolescent
Demographic	Younger	Older
	Low level of educational attainment	High level of educational attainment
	Negative perception of their learning ability	Positive perception of their learning ability
	Decline in learning ability in recent years	Improved learning ability in recent years
	Do not enjoy learning activities	Enjoy learning experiences
Personal	Do not think it is important to keep up to date, either for career development or maintaining job	Think it is important to keep up to date both for maintaining job effectiveness and career development
	Not motivated to keep up to date	Motivated to keep up to date
	Experience difficulty keeping up with professional literature	Can keep up with professional literature
	Not members of professional associations	Members of professional associations
Career	Likely to work in Production or R&D	Likely to work in Finance or Personnel
	Work at junior/middle management level	Work at senior/board level
	Will have many years' management experience	Will have less management experience
	Will not have held management posts in other companies	Will have held management posts in other companies
	Would not be willing to work outside the country in the future	Willing to work outside the country in the future
	Will not be contributing much to decision-making	Will be contributing a great deal to decision-making
	Will not find their jobs challenging	Will find their jobs challenging
	Their skills and abilities will be underutilized	Their skills and abilities will be well-utilized
Organizational	Likely to work in Food, Drink, or Tobacco or Printing and Paper companies	Likely to work in Engineering companies
	Likely to work for a large company (500+)	Likely to work for a medium or small company
	Their organizations do not have a policy for career planning	Their organizations do have a policy for career planning
	Their organizations do not reward high management performance	Their organizations do reward high management performance
	Their organizations do not encourage innovation	Their organizations do encourage innovation
	Their organizations are poor at responding to change	Their organizations are good at responding to change
	Their superiors will not be interested in their careers	Their superiors will be interested in their careers
Personality	More affected by feelings	More emotionally stable
	More intelligent	Less intelligent
	More suspicious	More trusting
	More humble	More assertive
	More reserved	More outgoing
	More group dependent	More self-sufficient
	More imaginative	More practical
	More forthright	More shrewd
	Have low motivation to achieve	Have high motivation to achieve

agement of innovation, organizations' ability to respond to change, and bosses' interest in subordinates' professional growth and development. The least important group of variables were the demographic ones. Figure 2 illustrates these findings in diagrammatic form.

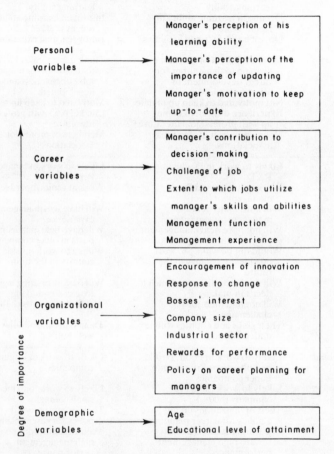

Figure 2. Variables influencing managerial obsolescence

THE PERSONALITY OF THE OBSOLESCENT MANAGER

The main traits of the obsolescent manager's personality are illustrated in Figure 3. The major differences between high and low obsolescent managers were on entrepreneurial traits, adjustment, level of motivation to achieve, and creativity. The remaining two characteristics differed little between the two groups of managers.

Low on entrepreneurial traits

Less well adjusted

Low level of motivation

High on creativity

Above-average ability to learn
and grow in a new job

Slightly below average mental
health

Figure 3. Personality of the obsolescent manager

These results suggest that the obsolescent manager does not appear to possess the traits traditionally associated with the successful manager. The importance of this finding is the fact that managerial personality may be used as a way of identifying the obsolescent manager from his more up-to-date colleague. The following variables were not found to be significantly related to managerial obsolescence.

1. A manager's professional/technical qualifications.
2. Number of years in present post or company.
3. Number of management posts held in present company.
4. Previous employment outside the country.
5. Availability of, or participation in updating activities.
6. Particular areas requiring updating.
7. Whether the employing organization had a policy for staff updating or not.
8. Influence of organizational policy on staff updating and manager's decision to undertake further education.

DISCUSSION

This discussion is concerned with the main elements of each of the foregoing sets of variables. It is presented here in concise form in order to illustrate the interaction of each set on the other.

The main conclusions arising from the examination of personal characteristics of managers are that age alone is not a very significant variable in relation to managerial obsolescence. However, it is important in terms of learning ability. Yet, if managers have a positive perception of their learning ability irrespective of their educational/technical qualifications, they can and will keep up to date. If, on the other hand, they have a poor perception of their learning ability, this is usually associated with a negative attitude to updating and hence a ready recipe for obsolescence. Managers' work experience was found to be very important in keeping them up to date. It is necessary for managers at all levels to have challenging and worthwhile work which provides them with plenty of stimulation and job satisfaction. The absence of this can lead to mobility which is not necessarily a solution and, in fact, can often be used as an escape rather than for professional growth and development. Membership of professional associations is important for managers because of the benefits derived from attending seminars, meetings, etc. and the opportunity they provide for colleagues to discuss common problems and experiences.

The most important and helpful updating activities that managers engaged in were educational courses taken in their own time and on-the-job problem-solving. The most commonly engaged in activities are, however, reading work-related books and journals, on-the-job problem-solving, and attending seminars and conferences.

In terms of personality variables, the results show that a positive self-concept is an important trait of managers who are up to date.

Those with a high self-esteem are more likely to ward off obsolescence because they are independent, confident, and willing to take risks in order to further their careers. Managers who were capable of coping with change were found to be less vulnerable to obsolescence because they were open to new ideas, flexible, risk-takers, and interested in keeping up to date. Intelligence appears to be a factor influencing susceptibility to obsolescence. Those with a high intellectual ability tend to pursue updating activities more readily than those with lower ability.

Achievement motivation has been found to be a major factor influencing vulnerability to obsolescence. Managers with high achievement needs tend to set more demanding goals for themselves, expend larger amounts of energy trying to achieve them, and use their initiative more than those with lower achievement needs. Finally, it has been found that 'cosmopolitan' managers are less likely to become out of date than 'local' managers because they are more determined to keep abreast of change and developments in their particular profession.

In terms of the Jones (1979) study of managers, the high obsolescence group of managers were similar to the low obsolescence group in terms of mental health, but slightly higher in terms of ability to learn, capacity to grow in a new job, and creativity. They were less entrepreneurial, less well adjusted, and had a lower level of motivation to achieve than the low obsolescence group of managers.

In relation to career characteristics, a number of points are worth noting. The first of these is that different functions appear to be more or less susceptible to obsolescence, with Finance and Personnel being less than Production and Research and Development (R&D). The reason for this seems to be related to the length of time managers engage in study during their careers. The former two groups appear to study longer into their careers than the latter groups who may be better qualified academically, but are likely to have completed their formal studies prior to embarking on their careers.

The hierarchical level of managers seems to influence their level of obsolescence, but not in any clearcut fashion. Many junior/middle managers become obsolescent because of unchallenging work or frustration caused by lack of promotion. They may also experience misutilization or underutilization of their knowledge and skills. Senior managers, on the other hand, may be kept up to date because of the stimulating nature of their work and their willingness to take risks, which of course may relate to why they are senior managers in the first place.

Managers' decision-making responsibilities and job challenge appear to be related. Those who are actively engaged in functional and company decision-making, in other words those who are listened to, seem to be the most likely to be kept up to date. Managers with challenging jobs which utilize their professional skills and abilities tend to find it easier to keep up to date than others. These findings emphasize the importance of challenging job assignments, whatever the function or level in the hierarchy in maintaining updatedness.

In relation to supervisory behaviour, the conclusions are that although supervisors should encourage their subordinates to engage in updating activities and help to provide the necessary resources to do so, it is still very much up to the individual manager to take responsibility for his own updating. It has been found that no matter what a supervisor may or may not do, if an individual manager is determined to keep up to date he will do so, for ultimately he alone has to participate in, and derive benefit from, updating activities. If he neglects this, he will undoubtedly become a victim of managerial obsolescence.

From an organizational viewpoint, it was found that different industrial sectors seem to experience managerial obsolescence to varying degrees. This is related to the type of technology present in the industry and the rate of change within that technology. Managers in smaller companies appear to be less prone to obsolescence than their counterparts in larger (500+) companies. This is related to the fact that they have to deal with all aspects of their function, while the others generally tend to specialize in narrow aspects of their functions and hence do not keep up to date quite so readily from a functional viewpoint.

The presence or absence of a company policy on updating or career planning does not seem seriously to affect managerial obsolescence, for it is the manager himself who must take responsibility for his own updating. However, this is not to say that organizations can ignore the question, for it is still beneficial if they encourage their managers to keep abreast of change and provide the facilities to do so. Career planning is important in order to ensure that managers will have challenging job assignments throughout their careers and that their knowledge and skills will not go into decline through lack of use. Rewards for high management performance can provide effective incentives for managers to keep up to date, but it is important that these rewards be recognized by managers and be related to the jobs they do.

Encouragement of innovation can help to ensure that managers utilize their creative potential to cope with the ever-changing demands of their jobs. This in turn can have a beneficial effect on everyday problem-solving which facilitates managers' professional growth and development.

Organizational response to change has been found to affect managerial obsolescence, for if a company is good at responding to change, this influences the willingness or attitude of managers towards engaging in updating activities. It also affects and influences the degree of job challenge available for managers which, as pointed out above, is related to how up to date their knowledge is.

COMBATING OBSOLESCENCE

In terms of coping with or preventing the onset of managerial obsolescence, the following are of note. From the individual's viewpoint it is essential that a manager engages in continuous learning activities whether formal or informal. This involves learning to learn so that he/she derives benefit from new job experiences. It also involves taking responsibility for one's own learning and not waiting for others to make suggestions or provide opportunities. The up to date manager is one who takes the initiative, whatever the situation, and strives to keep abreast of new knowledge and skills as related to his discipline.

From an organizational standpoint many approaches can be used to help cope with or prevent the onset of managerial obsolescence. These include promotion, demotion, job rotation, special assignments, on-the-job training, job enrichment, career planning, industrial encouragement of innovation, rewards for high performance, and incentives to engage in updating activities. Management development generally, and those engaged in the provision of development in particular, need to examine closely both the content and methodologies employed in their programmes. Many managers express a need for further input on such topics as Finance and Personnel, but these are not necessarily related to the traditional inputs provided under these broad headings. Many non-financial managers need a greater understanding of Finance, but this of necessity must be non-technical, for otherwise it will not be understood. In the area of Personnel, the greatest need appears to be in the field of interpersonal communications, man-management, and motivation, rather than the technical aspects of the discipline. Managers indicate that their greatest learning often comes from on-the-job problem-solving which, by its very nature, is experiential and informal. This suggests that greater use could be made of this form of learning than exposing managers to numerous lectures and highly structured learning experiences. Professional associations also have a role to play in providing a service to their members which will help them to keep up to date with changes in their disciplines.

Finally, the effects of managerial obsolescence can be felt at many levels, first by the individual manager who may no longer be capable of carrying out his duties as efficiently or effectively as before. Secondly, by his department or section which may suffer as a result of this individual's incompetency which in turn will affect the overall company. Then, collectively, companies who are having difficulties due to managerial obsolescence will affect the economy of a country. This may sound somewhat alarmist, but if one examines the logic of it, it is understandable.

Because of this it is necessary to tackle managerial obsolescence at a variety of levels, from government to organizational to individual. However, it is my conclusion that it is the individual manager who is the key to the successful handling of the problem for he must ultimately take the major responsibility for his own updating.

REFERENCES

Burack and Pati, G. C. (1970) Technology and managerial obsolescence, *M.S.U. Business Topics*, **Spring 1970**, 49–56.

Horgan, N. J., and Floyd, R. P., Jr. (1971) An MBO approach to prevent technical obsolescence, *Personnel Journal*, **50**, 687–693.

Jones, A. N. (1979) Managerial obsolescence and its associated factors, Doctoral Dissertation, U.M.I.S.T., Manchester.

Jones, A. N., and Cooper, C. L. (1980) *Combating Managerial Obsolescence*, Philip Allen, Oxford.

Mahler, W. R. (1965) Every company's problem – Managerial obsolescence, *Personnel*, **42**, 8–10.

Mali, P. (1970) Measurement of obsolescence in engineering practitioners, *Continuing Education*, **3**, 1–5.

Malmross, A. (1963) Obsolescence of engineering and scientific personnel in industry, Paper presented at Mid West Conference on Reducing Obsolescence of Engineering Skills, Illinois Institute of Technology, Chicago.

O'Reilly, A. P., Jones, A. N., and Coldrick, A. J. (1980) Keeping up-to-date as a manager: A study of occupational obsolescence among managers in Ireland, AnCO, Dublin.

Shumaker, C. H. (1963) Presenting the case for engineering and professional societies, Paper presented at the Mid West Conference on Reducing Obsolescence of Engineering Skills, Illinois Institute of Technology, Chicago.

Siefert, W. W. (1963) The prevention and care of obsolescence in scientific and technical personnel, *Research Management*, **13**, 2, 143–154.

Standford Research Institute (1968) *Managerial Obsolescence*, European Long Range Planning Service, U.S. and Switzerland.

Management Development: Advances in Practice and Theory
Edited by C. Cox and J. Beck
© 1984 John Wiley & Sons Ltd

CHAPTER 7

Developing Creativity

R. J. Talbot and T. Rickards

INTRODUCTION

Education for managers in a formal sense can be traced back to the evolution of business departments or schools from older established university faculties – primarily from departments of economics. Historically there has been a strong tradition of respect for the notion of scientific management following the pioneering efforts of Taylor (1912), Fayol (1949), Follett (1941), and others.

More recently there have been challenges to the concepts of scientific management and a growing interest in humanistic approaches following Maslow (1954), McGregor (1960), and the field theory school of Lewin (1948). A recent conference of business school educationalists from Europe and America (1980) concluded that business education was going to have to develop new approaches to difficult but important issues collectively categorized as 'non-cognitive skills'.

The changes have in part been brought about by awareness of the changing business environment. A widely accepted view by management scientists is that we are experiencing an increasingly complex, uncertain, 'turbulent' environment – powerfully expressed by Ansoff (1979) at a theoretical level, and Toffler (1970) at a more popular level.

One response to the perceived uncertainty in the environment is to move towards problem-centred training. In the absence of guidelines as to the nature of problems to be faced, the manager needs skills of flexibility, imagination, vision. This is the position of those trainers engaged in courses aimed at stimulating creativity, and the one we will be presenting in the rest of this paper. Our practical experiences are shared by members of a network of associates in the United Kingdom, Holland, Belgium, and elsewhere in Europe with whom we have worked in a range of different types of management training courses.

The major influences on creativity network participants include the earlier American educators of the creative problem-solving school, and in particular

Osborn and Parnes at Buffalo; Paul Torrance at Minnesota; Prince and Gordon at Cambridge; as well as more indirect influences such as Jung, Barron and Taylor, Lewin, Kolb, Koestler, MacKinnon, and Guilford. In particular we single out one theoretical influence that has increasingly enriched our thinking and led to integration of theory and practice. We refer to the works of George Kelly (1955), the philosophy of constructive alternativism, his theory of personal constructs, and methodology of eliciting and interpreting individual construct systems (repertory grids).

With the benefits of hindsight it is clear why Kelly has had such an impact on our work. The general implicit assumption of creative problem-solving courses is that each individual has unique needs that respond to individualized learning (Rickards and Freedman, 1979), and that creativity is often blocked by internal and external factors which can be weakened or removed 'with a little bit of help'. Creative insight is part of a process of individual change and reinterpretation so that 'the familiar becomes strange and the strange familiar' (Gordon, 1961). This approach fits well with Kelly's theory which proposes for each individual a personal construction of the world on which is based (and from which is derived) anticipation and the prediction of future events.

In this paper we briefly review the creative problem-solving paradigm with attention to its impact on European attitudes and practices of creativity training. Kelly's work is examined as it relates to our understanding of creativity and as it has led to changes in our training courses.

THE CREATIVE PROBLEM-SOLVING PARADIGM

We owe the notion of a paradigm in the field of pure science to Thomas Kuhn. He used the word in various ways in his analysis of scientific change. Here we refer to a paradigm as an accepted framework within which gradual developments are made. According to Kuhn (1967), the gradual or normal development that occurs inside a scientific paradigm is based on a settled consensus view 'acquired from scientific education and reinforced by subsequent life in the profession'. Kuhn, in the same article from which the above quote is taken, suggests that in applied research there may be no fully relevant paradigm. We have therefore chosen to view the practitioners and researchers concerned with creativity as engaged within a rather loose paradigm. For it is certainly possible to identify implicit beliefs widely if not universally shared by the community of published writers on creativity: the existence of something called 'creativity', for example, although no universally agreed formal definition exists; the belief that creativity (whatever it is) is a good thing, often severely suppressed by personal and environmental factors; the acceptance that creativity can be fostered, or at least that the blocks to creativity can be weakened progressively following certain types of training experience.

It has been suggested that creativity as a subject for research and training owes much to a critical incident in the history of space exploration, namely the launch of the first Russian satellite – the sputnik. This in turn produced a receptive climate in America to appeals for research funds, not only into space exploration but into understanding the nature of creative talent, and how it might be channelled into successful innovation. The decade following sputnik proved to be the most productive for research into the creative process. Guilford (1967) (who as president of the American Psychological Association made the famous and successful post-sputnik plea for funds for research into creativity) led a long-term study into the structure of intellect using factor analytic techniques to demonstrate relationships between convergent, divergent, and problem-solving skills, and the creative abilities of his subjects. Other dominant theoretical influences were MacKinnon (1978) who investigated personality factors which correlated to creative performance, and Torrance (1962) who has devoted the greater part of an illustrious academic career to understanding and stimulating creative talent in school-age children.

In retrospect the substantial work of a few major researchers, such as those mentioned above, contrasts with much misdirected research of the 'number of angels on a pin' variety. (For instance, in the 1960s there was the large number of papers on the rate of production of ideas in brainstorming sessions under various conditions – a misdirection of energy that has now thankfully gone out of fashion.) The theoretical state of the subject was highlighted in a series of important conferences at the University of Utah in the late 1960s. What emerged was recognition of the extreme difficulty in pinning down the 'ultimate criteria' for creativity. Perhaps this contributed to a decline in interest in creativity as a research area. Guilford, MacKinnon, and Torrance continued their long-term research projects, but in general the subject was no longer seen as an academically 'hot' one.

A major contribution of a more practical nature came from Alex Osborn with his invention and development of brainstorming. His best selling book *Applied Imagination* (1957) produced a wave of enthusiasm for group creativity sessions in industrial, educational and social contexts (see, for example, Parnes, 1977). After Osborn's death his work was extended at the Creative Problem-Solving Institute at State University of New York, Buffalo, directed by Professor Sydney Parnes. Buffalo can be viewed as the centre of the creative problem-solving paradigm. Its journal is one of the longest established in the field; its annual conference now attracts over 600 participants to study creativity either at an introductory level or at an advanced level. Workshops are held on related topics: techniques, research methods, meditation, self-awareness, biofeedback, industrial problem-solving, human information processing, and systems analysis are all to be found represented.

One related system for stimulating creativity also deserves special mention for its influence among our network of European colleagues: synectics. This system was developed by Gordon (1961) and Prince (1970) as a means both of 'operationalizing' principles that favour creativity and of introducing a framework for healthy interrelationships in shared or small-group problem-solving.

THE CREATIVITY NETWORK: A EUROPEAN INITIATIVE

In time synectics and brainstorming stimulated interest and spun-off a range of other American systems for stimulating creativity (Rickards, 1980). In Europe the development of enthusiasm for creativity techniques was rather less spectacular. (To put that statement in context it might be added that even in America the paradigm has struggled to make an impact on mainstream educational and industrial training. But at least it could number many universities and colleges engaged in research and teaching.) As was pointed out in an earlier article (Rickards and Freedman, 1979), on this side of the Atlantic management trainers tended to include the subject 'creativity' as a half-day or one-day specialist topic within longer general management courses. No research school had established itself, either through publications or through training programmes. Diffusion of American ideas was slow, and impetus to the introduction of the subject of creativity was to come 'second hand' or from writings of the two European authors, Koestler (1964) and de Bono (1971), whose works had gained some popular recognition.

Geographically isolated from the established training centres of the American workers, and lacking any academic focal point for training or research, an informal network of trainers and consultants developed. A 'creativity club' was founded in Manchester by representatives of major regional organizations and universities. The club was to become the focus for the informal network, and in 1973 led to the establishment of a quarterly newsletter (*Creativity Network*, published from the Manchester Business School). In time the network grew from its original membership of thirty to several hundred subscribers. Its members include trainers, consultants, technical professionals, and representatives of other professions concerned with practical or theoretical aspects of the creative process.

Since its inception training initiatives by creativity network members have occurred in nearly a dozen European centres including France, Sweden, Germany, Italy, Holland, Belgium, Ireland, and the United Kingdom. One project in particular illustrates the changes that have taken place in our teaching procedures through international collaboration. We will trace the development of an annual one-week course into today's design which incorporates features strongly influenced by Kelly's personal construct theory.

'Creativity Step by Step'

In 1975 a group of creativity network members from Holland and the United

Kingdom agreed to collaborate in designing and executing a one-week course on creative problem-solving. The original team was five tutors, all actively engaged independently in occupations involving stimulating creative behaviour. We wanted to advertise the possible benefits in the long term of creativity training – for individuals and organizations.

The course was called 'Creativity Step by Step' and its declared purpose was

> to permit participants to make another step in their efforts at operating creatively in their jobs and their personal lives . . . the step must be self motivated . . . [the tutors] can offer information . . . only you can relate these facts to your personal circumstances and needs . . . Our teaching goals are to demonstrate that as well as a process for producing imaginative new products, creativity can be displayed in diagnosing the causes of problems; in accepting the needs for multiple viewpoints and actively seeking them; in treating all ideas as starting points to improved ideas; and in seeking to integrate your needs with those of others involved in order to bring about a desired change.

Implicit in the approach is the linking of creative problem-solving very closely with personal problem-solving (Rickards and Freedman, 1979). During the course problems are treated as 'owned', preferably by an individual who is present and who has a need to achieve some goal without knowing how to do it. Creative/personal problem-solving is the process of discovery for that individual. The creative problem-solving techniques (CPSTs) are presented as mechanisms through which the individual, often assisted by others in a team, becomes aware of more possibilities and then perceives a possible way forward (the start of a possible solution to the problem). The way forward is sometimes recognition of a new formulation of the problem more likely to be resolved than the initial formulation. It is therefore important that the course operates with 'real, owned' problems.

The mechanisms of creative problem-solving techniques were introduced as aids to providing a richer set of possibilities and therefore a higher chance of a new perspective. The critical mechanism for convergence or closure is acceptance by the problem-owner of a reformulation of his problem or of a possible solution to it. The design of the course was itself a step-by-step one. The steps of a generalized process of creative problem-solving were represented (for teaching purposes only) as: recognition (of a problem); definition; exploration (idea generation); development (of an improved idea); and implementation (with emphasis on personal action planning and commitment). The techniques of brainstorming, synectics, morphological analysis, and lateral thinking were introduced as mechanisms that could be freely adapted and interchanged to assist in one or more of the five stages of the problem-solving process. (See Rickards, 1980, 1974, for more details of these techniques.)

By way of illustration, we give an example of a session using a (definition stage) technique: a problem-owner may explain that his problem is about a colleague who 'is giving me all sorts of troubles'. This typically vague statement is taken as a starting point (or 'problem-as-given'). Assisted by a syndicate group of about six participants the problem-owner might spend some time towards the beginning of the course looking for a fresh approach practising 'goal orientation' (Rickards, 1974). Perhaps a dozen or so 'how to' statements are generated:

How to deal with Fred.

How to help Fred.

How to get Fred to help himself.

How to be fair to all my workers.

How to find Fred work he wants to do.

How to measure and feedback progress to Fred.

How to 'level' with Fred.

How to run a tight ship.

Sometimes the problem-owner can become 'unstuck' as a result of the goal orientation approach. We believe this is the clue to a process of escaping from assumptions about the nature of the problem. Gordon (1961) talks about the problem-as-given being converted through a creative leap to the problem-as-understood. At this stage, it is interesting to note, creativity occurs not at the idea-generation stage but at the problem-defining stage.

Only then do we begin idea generation and development of ideas into possible solutions. At each of these stages technique elements can illustrate the principles of creative problem-solving. For idea generation our preference is brainstorming ('. . . in what ways might we'), with or without a 'morphological' matrix for systematically exploring the idea space. As for problem-finding, progress is made by the problem-owner indicating the ideas he finds new and interesting from the large numbers generated. The group provides a rich set of options, but the problem-owner decides which he prefers to examine.

Once a few promising ideas have been identified, each is approached in a positive manner. The problem-owner explains, as best he can, 'what's good about it'. The idea-development stage does not ignore the concerns the problem-owner might have about the idea, however. After its merits have been considered, the group helps the client work on his concerns. These can be expressed as 'residual objectives' or problem statements. It will be appreciated that progress is being made if the residual objectives are, or appear to be, easier to obtain than the problem-as-given. If they are, in contrast, just as difficult, or even more difficult to tackle then the original problem, the process has been unhelpful. It has then entered a rather vicious spiral leading to failure to make any impact on the problem.

In our experience the process 'works' and the residual objectives become easier to reach, as the problem-owner moves towards a problem-as-understood which recognizes his personal involvement in the solution. For example, an initial position of 'How to get Fred to change' might become 'How can I deal better with Fred'. Subsequent action planning emphasizes the need for creativity and personal responsibility at the implementation stage of problem-solving. The criteria suggested for an idea are novelty, relevance, and implementability.

In our early courses we worked from a textbook which listed these techniques (Rickards, 1974). Later we stopped using it as being too constraining. Instead, we used a brief set of notes covering the various exercises which were supplied 'step by step' for a looseleaf folder. This was augmented by a few key back-up references on theoretical and practical aspects of the creative problem-solving paradigm, also supplied at appropriate times for inclusion in the folder. The additional material referred to *en passant* during the week was available for inspection, and copies could be provided for any participant who wanted them. (With the exception of one or two more academically oriented participants, no one showed any strong desire to acquire the complete set of forty articles.)

As experience was gained we began to see possible improvements to the design. We realized that the dominant but unintentional message left in participants' minds was that creativity was about using techniques like brainstorming. What we wanted to imply was that creativity was more likely to occur under conditions of postponed judgement *such as occur* in well-run brainstorming sessions. But instead of the technique reinforcing the message, it swamped it. Secondly, the sequential day-by-day approach left people waiting until Friday to experience tackling problems to the stage of commitment to action (implementation) by real problem-owners. Finally, we had no powerful bridges with a theoretical framework.

The Current Design (1981)

In seeking to improve the course we gradually revised the design, drawing on experiences of creativity network members. Buijs (1979) had found it important in creativity training to pay attention to the implementation phase of problem-solving, particularly when dealing with industrial innovation projects. Our own participants on the annual course had also indicated difficulties in making progress after the course, and more recent designs have addressed themselves to this issue. The title of the annual course was changed to 'Ideas into Action' to emphasize the importance of carrying ideas through. We also invited members of the creativity network to come along to talk about practical experiences at work which illustrated the importance of creativity and determination in implementing ideas.

The one-week event is now presented as Stage 1 of a continuing learning experience. At the end of Stage 1 each participant begins to implement an action plan. Some three to six months later the group reassembles to share experiences and examine possible reasons for difficulties encountered.

The overall structure of the course has also changed. In particular, day 1 has 'awareness' as its theme. During the day participants discover through paper and pencil exercises and relatively simple puzzle-type problems the underlying principles that are the rationale for a creative approach to problem-solving. Specifically it is shown that individuals process information differently, a phenomenon that can lead to creativity or conflict in group work. The differences between open and closed problems are also explored (Rickards, 1974), and the impact of climate on performance studied. The aids to a creative climate are introduced: establishing a positive, opportunity-sensitive attitude or mind set (Brown, 1979); supportiveness in communications; and how to erode cultural blocks to openness and imagination. By the end of day 1 the participants will have received all the background information needed to develop more flexible behaviours. The rest of the week is application, reinforcement, and assimilation of the key principles introduced in day 1.

In day 2 a few of the better-known creative problem-solving techniques are presented in order to reinforce the principles already mentioned. The point is made that often you are best operating the techniques at an intuitive level. For example, brainstorming is what actually happens in a creative climate if a group (or even an individual) is exploring solution possibilities without evaluation. Lateral thinking is what actually happens when someone escapes from one confining viewpoint and perceives another.

Days 3 and 4 have become a kind of problem workshop – a course within a course. Emphasis switches from exercises and puzzles set by the tutors to illustrate various teaching points, to the tackling of real problems submitted by participants (it will be noticed that in earlier versions we introduced 'owned' problems earlier in the week). This method seems to help in the re-focusing from learning from the tutors to learning about oneself and one's personal approaches. Day 5 remains the necessary interface between the training and continued work experiences. Implementation and action planning are important themes of the final day of the week. Efforts are made to emphasize that learning will have to continue if any permanent gain is to arise from the week.

Overall this design has proved itself robust; that is to say, it can be adapted with appropriate modifications to a range of circumstances – numbers and backgrounds of participants, workshop topics, and tutorial resources. Typically it can be run with two full-time tutors assisted by one or more guests for the occasional session. By drawing on different tutors from the pool of five who initiated the course we are all able to maintain a level of competence by regular involvement and continue to learn from one another.

To illustrate the flexibility of the design we can compare a version run for R&D specialists in one organization with a course for middle line management in another. In the first instance the course was located in the training rooms on the site of a large research complex. During the workshop periods participants were encouraged to use all the available facilities of the site. One project team moved to the engineering test laboratory. Other members of the course went to the library which was also on site. At the workshop review on day 5 a 'product in a bottle' or prototype was displayed with an action plan for initiating a research project to commercialize the product. (It seems that the achievement is customarily blocked during training because it is assumed to be impossible. If the course tutors believe it possible, and *expect* a tangible result from the two-day workshop, the feasible is attained to great learning gain.)

In contrast, the other version of the design which we now describe concerns a company wishing to equip its managers for the greater flexibility required from them in the next decade. The creativity in the first instance was to manifest itself in day-to-day behaviour, especially in decision-making. The objectives of the course were summed up as follows in the course manual:

> The course concerns itself with two conflicting processes in human behaviour – the process of discovery and the process of routinisation. We make most decisions 'intuitively' ('without thinking'). It is possible to discover new and imaginative options in many tasks. That is what we mean by creative decision-making. During the week you will be experimenting with real and hypothetical problems requiring decisions. It is our hope that you will get an increased awareness of the potential for creative decision-making in your job, and a few guidelines for developing flexible and creative decision-making behaviour.

The basic framework described above has been retained. In the awareness exercises of day 1 more emphasis is placed on automatic or habitual behaviour as contrasted with developing additional responses (imaginative or creative behaviour). One particular consequence of dealing with 'open-ended' problems is highlighted, namely that the more open-ended, personal, 'owned', and unusual a problem is, the less appropriate become the so-called rational decision-making processes. The creative problem-solving techniques of day 2 come particularly into their own if creative decision-making is appropriate.

This theme of responsibility for ownership and creative decision-making carries over to the workshops of days 3 and 4. Participants discover the possibility that in the past perhaps there have been times when they have been blocked from constructive action by over-reliance on the power of quantification in decision-making. And that 'analysis to paralysis' accompanies a disengaged and uncommitted approach to problems. These messages can be particularly powerful to managers with a technical education, who have never really thought through the nature of the evaluation process when it applies to intangibles such as ideas. As we put it: an idea is as good as you choose to make it.

Day 5 remains a period of considering re-entry issues and implementation. As with day 1 the reflective exercises here owe much to Kelly in their design and are described in that context below.

The impact of the course on participants is more in terms of personal awareness than of extrinsic products invented. This is reflected in course reviews. At one course the typical benefits were considered as: '. . . allowed us to see the wood for the trees . . . no definite answers to our problems, perhaps

Day 1: Problem-finding (exercises in defining and redefining problems)

Day 2: Idea-finding (exercises in idea generation)

Day 3: Idea-development (exercises in developing ideas into feasible solutions)

Day 4: Implementation (exercises in anticipating and dealing with blocks to acceptance of a new idea)

Day 5: Integration (tackling problems using all the techniques introduced in days 1–4)

Figure 1. A typical technique-centred course on creative problem-solving. (See Parnes, Noller, and Biondi, 1977, for examples of variations of this type of sequential design of creativity training.)

definite maybes (!) . . . you can have fun while you are working hard . . . maybe I am too concerned with avoiding all risks . . .'. Interestingly few mentions of techniques. The timetables of the two courses are shown in Figures 1 and 2.

Creating an Appropriate Climate for the Courses

From comments of participants who had attended other courses on topics related to creative problem-solving it seems likely that the impact of the course cannot be assessed by the contents on a timetable. The involvement of the tutors is of critical importance. It has been a repeated challenge to tutors from the creativity network group to commit themselves to the courses in a highly involving way. It seems to us that if we believe in the benefits to be gained from a creative and positive approach to one's job, we have to convey that attitude in our practise of our trade, in training courses.

For example, we avoid using the same exercises and puzzles too frequently, or we try to find new and deeper significance in the puzzles for which we

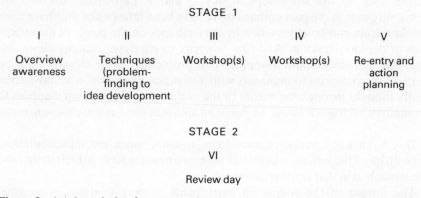

STAGE 1

I	II	III	IV	V
Overview awareness	Techniques (problem-finding to idea development	Workshop(s)	Workshop(s)	Re-entry and action planning

STAGE 2

VI

Review day

Figure 2. A robust design for a two-stage course on topics relating to creative problem-solving. (Developed by members of the European Creativity Network, for managerial and professional participants, to enhance reinforcement of learning in an interim phase between Stages 1 and 2.)

develop a particular affinity. In one exercise we signal our own willingness to do what we ask others to do by taking part in the first two acts of a three-act play written by one of the tutors – and then asking the other participants to write and act out a creative resolution to the play during the course (Rawlings, 1981). This helps us from falling into a trap of trying to show how creative we are at coming up with 'answers' to owned problems of the participants, as such behaviour conflicts with important messages in the course and is counter-productive.

An important metaphor for the learning process is often used during the week. We talk about learning through a new experience as adding a new element to a kaleidoscope (Parnes earlier used the metaphor to illustrate idea generation; in Osborn, 1957). Each new element of learning has an influence on all the other elements. There is a unity – a holism – about learning that is often overlooked in the need to teach things 'step by step'. One exercise actually called 'kaleidoscope' is a tape-slide package of slide photographs of participants and tutors obtained on the first day, favourite slides and music on cassette brought by the participants on request, and captions including key messages of the course plus comments heard and overheard from tutors and participants. This collage is the action plan of the tutors, completed while the participants are engaged on their own action plans during the workshop days.

The recapitulation also has a kaleidoscope nature. A combined team of all participants and tutors compile a brainstormed list of remembered (and there-fore memorable) items with a brief exposition on each item. The argument is that if some item has been overlooked it will have made no impact or linkage with any other item in any of our personal kaleidoscopic recollections. It is best left unremembered.

These are some of the ways we have found of setting a climate in the course that expresses the open and creative climate we refer to in our more formal presentation sessions. The climate is of particular importance for experiential learning. However, we have also considered how to bring about more reflective learning. For that we draw heavily on our increasing understanding of Kelly. The impact of Kelly in our designs, execution of the course, and theoretical thinking is the main subject of the rest of the paper.

Impact of the Courses

Over a period of years we have tried to assess the impact of our courses on participants. Perhaps the assessment can be broadened to examine the impact on tutors as well.

A modest level of organizational change can be claimed. We can identify cases of individuals returning to their workplaces and redirecting their efforts, drawing on ideas or skills acquired in the course. In other instances attendance is followed by requests for assistance in running workshops on organizational problems. One R&D laboratory, for example, ran a programme on identifying new product opportunities. A public sector administration department has followed through with workshops to improve the effectiveness of a reorganization (objectives: better team-work and joint problem-solving skills).

PERSONAL CONSTRUCT THEORY AND CREATIVITY

Kelly's (1955) work is appropriate to creativity in three important ways. The philosophy on which Personal Construct Theory (PCT) is based is particularly appropriate to attitudes implicit in the creative problem-solving paradigm. The theory itself provides copious opportunities for interpreting and understanding creative processes, and the technology arising from PCT – repertory grid methodology – has been adapted and used in our creativity training courses.

Philosophy

PCT is based on the philosophy of Constructive Alternativism, which can be summarised in three statements.
1. Events are subject to a great variety of alternative constructions.
2. All our constructions are open to question.
3. We can only make assumptions about what reality is and then proceed to test these assumptions.

This philosophy is particularly appropriate to creativity training in that it encourages the participant to search for alternative ways of looking at a situation, to question habitual ideas and ways of behaving, and to identify and check assumptions he might be making about a given situation. In particular, it implies that a person can deal with a problematic situation by finding a way of re-construing that makes more sense than the current (problem-causing) construction.

Adoption of this philosophy implies a movement away from the position commonly held by decision-makers and problem-solvers, namely that there is only one right way of interpreting and dealing with a given situation. A central feature of our creativity teaching is that there are many available ways of tackling a problem and, further, that their might be better ways if we care to try and create them.

One of the most common inhibitors of successful creative problem-solving is the adoption, often unconsciously, of self-imposed constraints or assumptions by the problem-tackler. He makes assumptions about the type of problem he is faced with (see the section below on 'Practice' for an elaboration of this point) and he makes assumptions about what the important features of a problem are. We believe that the identification of such assumptions and at least a temporary, experimental relaxation of them can lead to more, and possibly better, solutions.

Some writers (e.g. Ackoff and Vergara, 1981) place great emphasis on the role which assumptions play in causing a person to have problems. Ackoff defines creativity in problem-solving and planning as 'the ability of a subject in a choice situation *to modify self-imposed constraints* so as to enable him to select courses of action or produce outcomes that he would not otherwise select or produce, and are more efficient for or valuable to him than any he would otherwise have chosen' (our emphasis). (Elsewhere Ackoff equates 'self-imposed constraints' with 'assumptions'.) The literature is liberally strewn with puzzles and problems illustrating the ways in which habitual assumptions can prevent the solution of problems. The nine-dot problem is one of the more well-known examples:

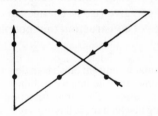

Join the dots with four straight lines without lifting the pen from the paper and going through each dot once only.

Those that have difficulty with this puzzle do so usually because they assume that the lines must be drawn within the boundaries of the dots – an assumption which makes a solution impossible. By identifying and relaxing this assumption (or self-imposed constraint) one can solve the problem:

Interestingly, if one identifies and relaxes other assumptions, solutions using three straight lines and indeed one straight line can be discovered (invented?) without folding the paper.

The philosophies underlying both PCT and creativity training appear to have much in common. In essence one is asked to treat one's model of events as a personal theory which one *lives with* – discarding aspects that do not work, developing those that do – rather than as a dogma which one *lives by*. (A distinction expressed most succinctly by Bannister and Fransella, 1971, in their introduction to personal construct theory, *Inquiring Man*.) This attitude is particularly important at those times when one is confronted with a problematic situation. It may just be that the cause of the problem lies in one's reluctance to relinquish cherished ideas.

Theory

Kelly presented his theory in a somewhat formal and extensive manner in a two-volume work published in 1955. It is not possible in this paper to give anything other than the briefest description. A good introduction to PCT can be found in the previously mentioned book by Bannister and Fransella. A brief summary can be found in Talbot (1981). At the centre of the theory is an (explicit) assumption that a person acts as a scientist, in that he is in business to make sense of himself and the world he inhabits. The theory describes the ways in which a person constructs, evaluates, and changes his current model in the light of his experiences. Kelly offers explanations of the ways in which a person's model (his 'construct system') may become inappropriate for coping with events with which he is confronted, and suggests the conditions necessary for and ways in which a person may change his model, with and without the help of another. (In Kelly's case this meant the use of the theory by a psychotherapist to help a client change his construction of himself and his relationship with other people.) PCT is sometimes thought of as a cognitive theory, largely, we think, because Kelly has managed to represent in explicit and sometimes complex ways his understanding of people. Perhaps one needs to be somewhat cognitively complex oneself in order to understand the theory. However, Kelly does attempt to describe the relationship between cognition and affection – between thinking and feeling. Unlike some theorists, he does not see these as opposites. Emotions are associated with *changes* in a persons's construing. Among Kelly's set of what he calls 'transition constructs' are two cycles of construing that can give rise to changes in construing. Kelly refers to them as typical sequences of construction that people employ in order to cope with everyday situations.

> Two of these invite particular attention: one has to do with action decisions and the other with a person's originality. The first we call the C–P–C cycle and the second the Creativity Cycle. The C–P–C cycle (Circumspection–Preemption–Control) has to do with decision making in which the self is involved. The Creativity Cycle has to do with the way in which a person develops new ideas (Kelly, 1955, pp. 514 and 515).

One of us (Talbot, 1981) has described a model of creative problem-solving which is based on a combination of these two cycles of construing. An adapted version of this description is provided below.

The C–P–C cycle is a sequence of construction involving, in succession, circumspection, pre-emption, and control, and leading to a choice which precipitates the person into a particular situation.

Circumspection is the process of looking at a situation in a multi-dimensional manner, of perceiving it from a number of different perspectives, of placing a variety of constructions upon the situation. 'This situation is X. Now what else can we say about it.' Generating redefinitions of a problem is one way of circumspecting, as is the use of analogies. Circumspection provides material for answering the question: 'What sort of situation is it?'

Pre-emption involves the selection of what the individual regards as the best way of looking at the situation, and he temporarily – or permanently – disregards the relevancy of all the other issues that may be involved. 'Thus by preemption, he sets up a choice point, a cross-roads of decision. He may say, like Hamlet, "To be, or not to be: that is the question . . ." ' (Kelly, 1955, p. 516).

Control involves choice, choosing which way to go, whether 'to be or not'; which pole of the construct provides the best base for action.

Problem Identification (Jacques and Talbot, 1977; Talbot and Jacques, 1977a, 1977b) can be seen in Kellian terms as an attempt to elaborate the Circumspection phase of the C–P–C cycle, the purpose of problem identification being to 'find an enabling basis for action'. Involvement in the problem identification process reduces what Kelly calls 'impulsivity – a characteristic foreshortening of the C–P–C cycle'. (Of course, there are dangers inherent in an overemphasis on circumspection. The person who delays pre-emption for too long can be described as 'indecisive'. 'Indecisiveness' is our version of the contrasting pole to 'impulsivity'.)

The end result of the C–P–C cycle is a decision to take action. Based on the person's reading of the situation he says to himself: 'If I do this then that will be the result.' Also implied in this sort of statement is a prediction of what will not happen. This 'differential prediction', as Kelly terms it, is based on the bi-polar nature of a construct. To construe a person as intelligent is to predict that in a given situation he will do some things and not others; in particular he will not do the things a stupid person would do. What taking action does is to provide information on the basis of which the person can check out his prediction. Logically, there are three possible outcomes of an action. The predicted consequences occur; or the outcome is one which was predicted as not occurring; or, thirdly, an outcome occurs that was neither expected nor ruled out.

In the first case the person's construction of events is confirmed – he pre-empted appropriately and made the correct choice. The other two cases lead to disconfirmation of the person's construing. In the second case he pre-empted appropriately but made the wrong choice, and in the third case he pre-empted inappropriately – he chose a wrong way of looking at the situation. It is this third case which is particularly relevant to problem-solving. Faced with this sort of outcome the person has three choices: either he can look for another way of construing the situation, or he can finish with the situation, or he can temporarily leave it unresolved.

Let us look at the first option. What the person does can be construed as entering into another C–P–C cycle, and looking for a different way of construing (maybe taking his construing of the outcomes of his first action into account). This time he may pre-empt appropriately. If he does, he will have achieved control of the situation and maybe also will have achieved some useful learning that might come in handy for dealing with future situations – particularly if he can figure out why he initially misconstrued the situation.

If he again pre-empts inappropriately, he is once more faced with deciding whether or not to continue looking for another way of construing the situation. What considerations could affect this decision? The C–P–C cycle starts when a person decides he has to take an action relevant to a situation. (He may decide for himself, believing that a situation requiring action is imminent, or he may be asked by someone else to do something.) Importantly, however, the person believes or assumes that there is something efficacious that he can do (otherwise he would not consider the situation). A succession of disconfirmations of his anticipations may, however, suggest that he revise his construction of himself as capable of handling the situation satisfactorily. This is one place where Kelly's transition constructs (see Figure 5 below) are relevant. 'Negative emotions follow unsuccessful construing' (McCoy, 1979), and a person's responses to these feelings have a significant effect on the course of the problem-solving process. If 'anxiety' is too great, for example, the person may seek to disengage from the problem situation – to finish with it without finding a solution. He decides (not necessarily consciously) that revision of his construction system (of himself in relation to the problem situation) is likely to be more painful than disengaging.

Sometimes a person cannot leave things like that; he believes he can still sort things out, somehow. Having tried all he can currently think of he may break off his engagement with the problem, with the intention of returning to it at some later date. It is our guess that this 'shelving' of a problem (as opposed to finishing with it unresolved) is what creative people do. What follows is the incubation period, where the person actually continues working on the problem at what Kubie (1958) calls the 'preconscious' level. Circumspection continues while the person's attention is on something else. The moment of illumination (Eureka!) is a pre-emption that feels appropriate. It is a way of construing the situation that appears to make sense of it.

The *Creativity cycle*, according to Kelly, 'starts with loosened construction and terminates with tightened and validated construction'. We interpret this as follows. A tight construct is one that leads to unvarying predictions. For example, if a drawing is construed as a triangle, then it follows that the internal angles total 180 degrees. A loose construct, on the other hand, leads to varying predictions, but without losing its meaning. Thus, if one were to speculate about a triangle whose internal angles did not add up to 180 degrees, one might perhaps invent a new geometry, as Riemann did. (You can draw a triangle on the curved surface of a sphere whose internal angles total 270 degrees.) Loosening construing appears then to involve asking the question: 'What if?' Many of the available structured aids to creative problem-solving (or creativity techniques) appear to be directed at facilitating this loosening of construing.

The central rule of brainstorming, for example, is 'postpone judgement'. This is essentially an invitation to *not* think through the implications of one's ideas, at least not for the time being, and in particular to avoid anticipating the less desirable implications. Again, the use of metaphor can be construed as a means of facilitating loosening. Instead of working directly on one's construction of the problem situation, one works on an analogous situation and identifies courses of actions applicable to it. Then one tries out these ideas on the original situation. Sometimes, this can suggest actions which concentrating only on the problem would not have done.

It could be argued that one has a problem because none of one's anticipations concerning its development, brought about by courses of action one can conceive, is acceptable. It may be, however, that there are potential actions which one would not normally see as applicable. The use of the analogy makes these available for consideration. Metaphorical thinking loosens construing; the discovery of a course of action that looks as though it might solve the problem permits re-tightening; and the implementation and evaluation of the solution involves validation.

In our courses we sometimes ask participants to use ideas for recycling glass bottles, as stimuli for suggesting solutions to the problems of redundancy. An analogous situation has some similarities with a given problem situation – that is what makes it analogous. But it also has differences, and it is these differences which can be the source of new ideas for tackling the problem situation. They enable the problem-solver to pose to himself the question: 'What if I treated the problem situations like the analogous situation?'

As Kelly suggests, the C–P–C cycle and the Creativity cycle are in some respects related 'since a new act often involves a new construct and one finds himself on the verge of new constructs as a result of his venturesome acts' (Kelly, 1955). Thus, although action might lead to disconfirmation, it might at the same time suggest new ways of looking at the situation. Also, continual disconfirmation can lead to loosening which can in turn lead to a different organization of constructs (or to new constructs) which is then checked out in a further C–P–C cycle. The loosening phase may be 'unaided', as in incubation, or helped by using one or other of the structured aids to problem-solving. Validation of the new construct system is achieved through taking action and seeing if the expected outcomes occur.

Figure 3 is a representation of the whole process. It might be better to represent the process as a spiral rather than a cycle, since each successive cycle is informed by previous experiences, and there might well be a gradual 'homing in' on the solution (or on the fact that the person does not have the appropriate construction of events). The feeling that one is getting closer to a solution is an important influence on the decision to continue searching. (This is another place in which transition constructs are relevant, but this time we are concerned with positive rather than negative emotions). Two further comments concern-

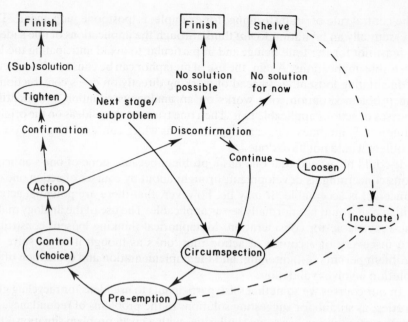

Figure 3. A model of creative problem-solving based on Kelly's C–P–C and creativity cycles

ing the model are worth making. First, various events are represented in somewhat black and white terms. For example, it has been implied that a person's predictions are wholly disconfirmed. In reality they will only be partly disconfirmed. So a person may decide to finish with the situation even though he has not achieved a perfect solution but one that is good enough (the 'satisficing' solution). Secondly, it will be necessary in a future version of the model to distinguish between what might be called 'real' actions and 'hypothetical' actions. A 'real' action is one which affects the situation being considered and might change it, and how it might develop. A 'hypothetical' action is one that is taken on a model of the situation: the model might, for example, be a drawing or a person's 'mental picture' of the situation. Hypothetical actions enable the person to experiment or rehearse prior to taking real action. As such they do not change the actual situation but they may alter the person's construing of the situation.

Indeed, it seems reasonable to assume that any process of problem-solving involves several C–P–C cycles. Recycling does not only have to follow disconfirmation. For example, if a problem-solver is following the 'recognize–define–explore–develop–implement' procedure outlined above, he might, in his own opinion, successfully 'recognize', 'define', 'explore', 'develop' (each stage involving one or more cycles of construing with *confirmation leading to the next stage*). Since no action has yet been taken on the actual situation, these stages can be regarded as hypothetical. The test comes when implementation occurs, when real action is taken.

Practise

Although the use of the theory to understand creative behaviour is still in its early stages of development, we have found it possible to use some central features of PCT as aids to designing several exercises for use on our creativity courses.

Each exercise involves the participants in construing some aspects of their experience and presents them with the opportunity of using the results of that construing for purposes of taking some action. 'Construing' is interpreted basically as identifying significant similarities and differences between events.

For example, in an exercise called PROBLEMS (usually introduced in day 1) we ask participants to tackle three problems. Then we hold a discussion, aimed at identifying and clarifying similarities and differences between the three experiences. It is possible to choose three problems that illustrate what we believe are important ways in which problems can be construed. Some problems have an elegant solution – one right answer – which anyone with the appropriate knowledge and skills will achieve. On the other hand, some problems have many answers which differ only in how good or bad they are. There is no perfect solution, only solutions which have a variety of strengths and weaknesses. Different people will produce different solutions, according to their experience, interests, and preferences. Again some problems are 'closed' in the sense that solving them has no further implications for the solver, whereas others are such that implementing solutions may well give rise to further problems. Another important distinction is that between 'owned' and 'unowned' (or 'not owned by me') problems. Other people's problems often appear easier to tackle than one's own; one does not have to live with the consequences of tackling non-owned problems to quite the same extent as with owned problems.

One possible implication of identifying different sorts of problems is that maybe they should be approached in different ways. In particular we teach that 'closed-ended' (Rickards, 1974), 'tame' (Rittel and Webber, 1974) and 'well-defined' (Hayes, 1978) problems are susceptible to attack using well-tried logical and analytical approaches. On the other hand, 'open-ended', 'wicked', or 'ill-defined' problems involve and require a more imaginative approach both in defining the problems and producing and developing ideas for solving them. One version of the PROBLEMS exercise has this contrast in approach built into it.

We present the following puzzle (see Figure 4) to two groups of people from the course. Usually both groups quickly construe the diagram as representing

Management Development

two co-planar right-angled triangles with a common hypotenuse with lengths of sides as shown. If this is so, then application of Pythagoras's theorem will yield the length of *AB*. Either of the triangles can be used to calculate *AB*. Both should yield the same result. However, the action of calculating *AB* from the two triangles yields *different* results. (A disconfirmation of anticipations.)

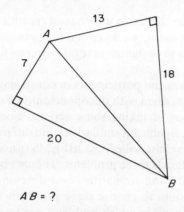

$$AB = ?$$

Figure 4. A puzzle used for illustrating some principles of problem-solving

From this point onwards the two groups are treated differently by their trainers. In one group, questions from members are, as far as possible, answered with a 'Yes' or a 'No'. For example, someone usually asks the trainer if the two triangles are actually in different planes, e.g. one tilted upwards. The trainer responds with a 'No'. Again, if someone asks whether the units of measurement differ from one triangle to another, the answer is again 'No'. What people seem to be doing is identifying assumptions they might have made concerning various features of the figure and checking them out with the trainer. (Each question can be viewed as an action resulting from a circuit around the C–P–C cycle. The confirmation or disconfirmation is provided by the trainer.) By behaving in this way the trainer is reinforcing the assumption that this is a puzzle with one unique solution, which can be reached through a systematic process of identifying and relaxing assumptions. If the group does question the trainer in such a way as to show that they have identified *the* blocking assumption, he answers 'Yes'. We refer to this group as the YES/NO group. On most occasions, someone in the YES/NO group comes up with the solution. The blocking assumption *is* difficult to identify, partly because it is so habitual, and partly because it involves for most people a construct with what Kelly calls an implicit pole: 'The *implicit* pole of a construct is that one which embraces contrasting context. If contrasts with the *emergent* pole. Frequently the person has no available symbol or name for it; it is symbolised only implicitly by the emergent term' (Kelly, 1955). (There should be enough clues in the above for readers to find the elegant solution for themselves.)

The second group is treated somewhat differently by its trainer. If he is questioned, for example about whether the right angle symbols really represent right angles as measured (rather than as they appear from the point of view of the perceiver), he answers: '*Yes*, there is a solution if those are right angles, *and* there may well be solutions if you care to interpret them differently.' (We refer to this group as the 'YES AND' group.) He usually adds that other groups have generated whole ranges of different solution ideas, some leading to particularly interesting solutions. Usually, the group tries initially to identify and question aspects of the figure. This process generates a variety of solutions. At some stage in the process someone (possibly the trainer) suggests reconstruing the whole figure. One person suggested that the figure was a map showing three routes between work (A) and home (B) of the trainer, and that the numbers represented addresses of mistresses on the two roundabout routes. The trainer's unwillingness to divulge the address of his mistress on the direct route prevented a solution from being achieved, however.

Another suggestion was that the figure represented a Critical Path diagram giving a solution for AB of $13 + 18 = 31$.

One group, perhaps feeling a little frustrated, produced the answer '42' (this being the answer to 'the question of the meaning of Life, the Universe and all that').

What usually comes out of the review of the problem-solving activity are the following points.

1. A problem can be treated *either* as having only one best, elegant solution *or* as having many possible solutions. By implication it follows that some problems *do* have one solution and that others have many possibilities. Perhaps, more often than not, problems facing managers are of this second type.

2. For problems of the first type a systematic, logical (YES/NO) approach will produce the solution given that the problem-solver (or problem-solving group) has the appropriate knowledge and abilities.

3. For problems of the second type an initially divergent, adventurous, imaginative (YES AND) approach will produce a large number of solution ideas which will vary in quality.

4. It is also implied that a YES/NO approach to a problem of the second kind will not lead to any solution, or at least it will take much longer to generate a satisficing solution than will the 'YES AND' approach.

5. Finally, the solution eventually settled upon will be very much a function of the people tackling the problem and will also be shaped by the influences other interested parties (sponsor, manufacturer, customer, etc.) may bring to bear.

Another awareness-raising exercise, THE CREATIVE PERSON, requires participants, individually and/or collectively, to identify constructs pertaining to a creative person they know, an uncreative person, perhaps a famous creative individual, themselves as they are (Actual Self), and themselves as they would like to be (Ideal Self). As well as provoking discussion on the nature of creative people, the exercise can be used to help participants to identify individual change goals to be worked on during and after a course. These goals can be derived from actionable differences between Actual and Ideal Self characterization.

Another exercise, HERE AND THERE, is an end-of-course exercise designed to help course participants make a bridge between their experiences on a course ('HERE') and those back at work ('THERE'). Opportunities arise to identify similarities and differences between the sorts of problems tackled, the ways of tackling problems, group/organizational climate, permissible ways of behaving, and so on. This sort of information can be used as a basis for deciding how to make use of the course experiences back at work (and also for deciding what not to do).

A related exercise, PAST, PRESENT, and FUTURE, provides participants with the opportunity to identify problems, opportunities, and goals relating to their personal development, themselves in their job, their company, and its environment. They are asked to identify what for them are significant features in some or all of these areas and to describe how these have changed and how they might and should change in the future. In this way possible trends can be identified and explored. For example, a manager may see his company's business environment becoming increasingly volatile and complex, and yet not see his own capabilities as developing sufficiently to cope. This could be seen as a problem he can do nothing about, or as a source of developmental goals.

This exercise is highly flexible in that participants can choose what area they wish to work on. They may, for example, wish to concentrate on their career prospects, or on future challenges facing their organization. On the other hand, they may choose to use it as an opportunity to reflect on their current position in the company. We normally introduce PAST, PRESENT, AND FUTURE towards the end of a course, as an alternative to HERE and THERE; allowing participants to choose their own areas for work enables them to identify and begin to work on issues of current importance to them.

The emphasis we place on the participant's construing of events reflects another important commonality between our approach to teaching creativity and Kelly's philosophy.

In answering the question: 'Why is it that two people in exactly the same situation behave in different ways?', Bannister and Fransella (1971) suggest:

> the answer is of course that they are not in the 'same' situation. Each of us sees our situation through the 'goggles' of our personal construct system. We differ from others in how we perceive and interpret a situation, what we consider important about it, what we consider its implications, the degree to which it is clear or obscure, threatening or promising, sought after or forced upon us.

A course participant is, we believe, more likely to benefit if he is enabled to make sense of course experiences in his own terms with relevance to his own circumstances.

Discussion

It should first be emphasized that the amount of space we have devoted to Personal Construct Theory in this paper does not reflect its overt contribution to our courses. It is quite likely that someone unfamiliar with Kelly's ideas could go through one of our Ideas into Action, or Creative Decision-Making weeks without realizing that PCT has played any part in influencing events. This is partly because we think it unnecessary to expound the theory to participants and partly because we have only begun the process of relating PCT to creativity training.

Other influences are much more visible to course participants, e.g. Kolb (1974) (learning and problem-solving styles), Prince and Gordon (synectics), and Osborn (brainstorming). We chose to emphasize PCT in this paper because it is new in the creativity training context and because its use holds out promise for a rich diversity of future developments.

There are a number of interesting challenges facing creativity trainers which might benefit from the adoption of a Kellian perspective. The theory offers explanations of certain events and might be used to suggest ways of dealing with them. For example, one of the main purposes of our courses is to invite participants to experiment with what to them might be new ways of tackling problems. We do not, incidentally, ask them to reject conventional and logical, analytic approaches to problem-solving. Rather, we suggest that they try to integrate with these procedures more imaginative approaches. For example, we suggest that the initial formulation of a problem is not the only possible formulation, and may not be the best. We invite them to postpone rejection of ideas until they have generated a large number rather than deal with one idea at a time. We suggest that a weakness in an idea can be looked upon as an opportunity to improve it rather than as a reason for rejecting it.

We have to work hard to get the message across, even with interested participants acting in a supportive climate. This is not so much because the suggestions are difficult to understand, but because they are difficult to implement in many organizations. If, for example, it is customary to accept without question a superior's formulation of a problem; if the method of dealing with is by debate with a strong reliance on expert opinion; and if fantasy and fun are seen as inappropriate to problem-solving meetings, then a course participant, however convinced he might be of the value of a more creative approach, will face a considerable challenge in introducing and using the new attitudes and techniques. He may well be violating organizational norms. Furthermore, the changes in him might be difficult for his colleagues to handle. He has changed and therefore become less predictable, giving rise to feelings of anxiety in his colleagues. (Kelly's definition of 'anxiety' is shown in Figure 5 below.) If their preparedness to try to look at things through his eyes (in Beck's, 1980, terms, if their *acceptance* of him) is low then he might well become labelled as odd and discounted as a serious influence on their activities. If, on the other hand, acceptance is high, they may, as Beck (1980) suggests 'experience confrontation of their current constructs, particularly if the accepted person is seeing the world in a very different way'. Such confrontation may not be welcomed. Clearly, attempting to change the construing of one's colleagues is a complex process. Perhaps a Kellian approach to understanding the personal and interpersonal facets of re-entry might suggest ways of handling the situation.

Another possible reason for re-entry difficulties might stem from the way we run our courses. Much of the work done by participants on our courses is done in groups. We recently became aware of one way this might be causing difficulties for participants on arrival back at work. Some, not unnaturally, have assumed that to introduce creative problem-solving into the work situation required setting up, training, and running groups of colleagues. If they lack the authority to get a group together, or if they lack the skills to train groups, then the chances of successful introduction of new approaches are small. We are therefore currently developing a course design which places less emphasis on group work and more on individual work. Particularly exciting is the idea of collaborative work with, say, one other person. A better strategy for introducing change might involve a progression from individual through collaboration to group work. Perhaps we can find ways of helping our course participants identify work colleagues with whom collaboration is possible, using, for example, a modified form of a repertory grid.

Feelings and Problem-solving

We suggested above that tackling a problem involves changes in construing, and that changes in construing are associated with feelings or emotions. Thus, problem-solving would not appear to be a purely cognitive process, although as a topic for study it is confined largely to the cognitive psychology literature. Personal experience and informal observation of others tackling problems suggest that feelings *are* involved in problem-solving. Dissatisfaction with a situation, frustration associated with the failure of current solution attempts, elation at discovering a promising solution, disappointment when it does not work out, satisfaction when it does, are easily observed feelings involved in problem-solving.

Our current understanding of the role of feelings in problem-solving is somewhat rudimentary. We do not know, for example, whether feelings direct the course of problem-solving or whether they are merely a by-product of cognitive processes. We do not know if feelings can be identified and used by a problem-tackler to help him in his endeavour. Our current hope is that a person who is aware of his feelings and of the reasons for experiencing them will be more effective at solving problems than otherwise.

Beck (1980) presents a description of changes in construing which incorporates the influence of transition states, and suggests that the successful elaboration of the system will depend in part on the way in which the participant copes with the confirmation or disconfirmation of his current model and the emotions generated by the experience. However, inspection of Kelly's set of transition constructs (see Figure 5) suggests that the feelings associated with reconstruing have as yet been neither systematically nor exhaustively identified. Three ways of construing these constructs suggest ways of elaborating the set.

Threat:	Threat is the awareness of an imminent comprehensive change in one's core structures.
Fear:	Fear is the awareness of an imminent incidental change in one's core structures.
Anxiety:	Anxiety is the awareness that the events with which one is confronted lie mostly outside the range of convenience of one's construct system.
Guilt:	Guilt is the awareness of dislodgement of the self from one's core role structure.
Aggressiveness:	Aggressiveness is the active elaboration of one's perceptual field.
Hostility:	Hostility is the continued effort to extort validational evidence in favour of a type of social prediction which has already been recognized as a failure.
CPC cycle:	The CPC cycle is a sequence of construction involving in succession, circumspection, pre-emption, and control, leading to a choice precipitating the person into a particular situation.
Creativity cycle:	The creativity cycle is one which starts with loosened construction and terminates with tightened and validated construction.
Impulsivity:	Impulsivity is a characteristic foreshortening of the CPC cycle.

Figure 5. Kelly's constructs relating to transition

First, Kelly deals mainly with core construing (construing the self and one's relations with others). Problem-solving does not always involve self-reconstruing. McCoy (1979) suggests some additions which deal with peripheral or non-core structure. For example, she defines the non-core equivalent of 'threat' as 'Bewilderment: awareness of imminent comprehensive change in non-core structure'.

Secondly, some of Kelly's transition constructs appear to deal with change that is about to happen ('imminent change'), with change that is currently happening (see 'anxiety' for example), and change that has just happened (see 'guilt' for example). For our purposes elaboration of the set of transition constructs relating to feelings before, during, and after tackling a problem would be useful. It seems not unreasonable to assume that feelings play a part in *generating* problem-tackling activities, that feelings occur *during* such activity and play a part in *directing* it, and that feelings *follow* problem-tackling and contribute to the *interpretation of its outcomes*.

The third aspect of the transition constructs worth examining relates to their names. Several of Kelly's set refer to bad feelings, or 'negative emotions' as McCoy (1979) calls them, e.g. 'anxiety', 'threat', 'fear', 'guilt', and 'hostility'. First of all it is fairly obvious that there are good feelings associated with reconstruing, particularly in respect of problem-tackling. McCoy's expanded set of construct theory emotions contains some of these good feelings – satisfaction, happiness, contentment, and so on. However, her positive emotions are associated with the validation of construing, and her negative emotions with unsuccessful construing. For example, she defines 'contentment' as 'awareness that the events with which one is confronted lie *within* the range of convenience of the construct system' (our emphasis); contentment is thus seen as a contrast to 'anxiety' (where events lie *outside* the range of convenience). While this set of formulations makes a lot of sense, we think it would be interesting also to distinguish between the structural change referred to in the definition of transition constructs and the reception of that change by the person. To clarify this, consider someone tackling a problem who becomes aware that the events with which he is confronted lie outside the range of convenience of his construct system, i.e. he realizes he does not understand what is going on. It is conceivable that this may be a welcome realization rather than an unwelcome one.

We remember hearing an astronomer saying that the aspect of astronomy he liked most was that every solution to a current problem led to further challenges. His work was for him a never-ending series of challenges; it provided him with a lifetime of opportunities for elaborating his construct system. His response to the awareness of his ignorance was positive. It seems a little odd to us to label this feeling with the term 'anxiety'. The best way we can think of describing his feelings is that he was *excited* by the challenge. It might be interesting therefore to distinguish between the nature of the construct system change and the person's response to awareness of that change. Thus, we would use the term 'anxiety' to define a negative response to a person's awareness of his lack of understanding, and (perhaps) 'excitement' to define a positive response. What we have done is to produce a construct 'anxiety' vs. 'excitement' to describe the range of possible responses to awareness of non-understanding. And this suggests that somewhere in between these two poles might lie something like 'indifference'. We are well aware of our non-understanding of a great many events with which we might be confronted, but which neither bother us nor excite us. We believe we can deal similarly with others of Kelly's transition constructs.

An interesting implication of this particular way of construing transition is that the person can choose to respond to changes (imminent, in progress, or occurred) in his construing in either a negative or positive way, or indeed somewhere in between (with 'modified rapture'?). As mentioned above, we suggest to course participants that the initial formulation of a problem might not be the best one, we invite them to try different ways of generating ideas and to consider weaknesses of ideas as opportunities for improvement. We are inviting them to construe themselves, problems, and problem-tackling processes in new and, initially at least, somewhat incomprehensible ways. If accepted, these invitations could lead to experiences that produce negative feelings (anxiety, threat, fear, etc. in the original Kellian sense). However, we further invite participants to respond positively to disconfirmation.

We suggest they have a choice when faced with a problem they cannot currently solve. They can feel bad about it or about themselves and find a face-saving (construct-system preserving) way of disengaging from the problem, or they can treat the current failure as an opportunity to extend their construct system. There is always another way of formulating a problem; there are always new ideas, and any idea can be improved.

McCoy (1979) suggests that 'since man seeks to be able to make his world predictable and for this purpose develop a construct system, *positive emotions are those which follow validation of construing. Negative emotions follow unsuccessful construing*'. We believe this to be true only when a person is seeking to preserve (i.e. further define) his construct system. (Of course, this does happen in problem-solving, particularly when a person is attempting to verify a good-looking solution.)

If, on the other hand, he is seeking to *extend* his construct system (incidentally we prefer to describe man as seeking to make *more and more* of his world predictable), positive emotions can follow disconfirmation of his construct system. In effect, such a person might say to himself: 'Things are not as I expected; Good. This is an opportunity to learn something.' For us this sort of response is the epitome of creativity. A creative person not only expects the unanticipated to occur, he actively seeks it and uses it as an opportunity to develop.

REFERENCES

Ackoff, R. L. and Vergara, E. (1981) Creativity in problem-solving and planning: A review, *European Journal of Operational Research*, 7, 1–13.

Ansoff, H. I. (1979) *Strategic Management*, Macmillan, London.

Bannister, D. and Fransella, F. (1971) *Inquiring Man*. Penguin, Harmondsworth.

Barron, F. and Taylor, C. W. (Eds) (1963) *Scientific Creativity: Its Recognition and Development*, Wiley, New York.

Beck, J. (1980) Changing a manager's construction of reality, in: *Advances in Management Education*, Edited by J. E. Beck and C. J. Cox, Wiley, pp. 215–230.

de Bono, E. (1971) *Lateral Thinking for Management*, McGraw-Hill, U.K.; AMA, U.S.A.

Brown, M. (1979) Management's set solutions, *Management Today*, **April 1979**.

Buijs, J. (1979) Strategic planning and product innovation: Some systematic approaches, Long Range Planning, **12**, 23–34.

Fayol, H. (1949) General principles of management, Chapter 4 in: *General Industrial Management*, Pitman.

Follet, M. P. (1941) The giving of orders, pp. 50–70 in: *Dynamic Administration*, Edited by H. C. Metcalf and L. Urwick, Harper, pp. 50–70.

Gordon, W. J. J. (1961) *Synectics*, Harper and Row, New York.

Guilford, J. P. (1967) Intellectual factors in productive thinking, in: *Explorations in Creativity*, Edited by R. L. Mooney and T. A. Razik, Harper and Row, New York.

Hayes, J. R. (1978) *Cognitive Psychology: Thinking and Creating*, Dorsey Press, Homewood, Illinois.

Jacques, R. and Talbot, R. (1977) Problem identification for design, *Studies in Design Education and Craft*, Keele University.

Kelly, G. A. (1955) *The Psychology of Personal Constructs*, Norton, New York.

Koestler, A. (1964) *The Act of Creation*, Hutchinson, London.

Kolb, D. (1974) *Organisational Psychology, An Experiential Approach*, Prentice-Hall, New Jersey.

Kubie, L. (1958) *Neurotic Distortion of the Creative Process*, University of Kansas Press.

Kuhn, T. S. (1967) *The Structure of Scientific Revolutions*, University of Chicago Press, Chicago.

Lewin, K. (1948) *Resolving Social Conflicts*, Harper.

McCoy, M. M. (1979) Positive and negative emotion. A personal construct theory interpretation, Paper presented to the Third International Congress on Personal Construct Psychology, Breukehen, Netherlands.

MacKinnon, D. W. (1978) *In Search of Human Effectiveness*, The Creative Education Foundation, Buffalo, New York.

McGregor, D. V. (1960) *The Human Side of Enterprise*, McGraw-Hill, New York.

Maslow, A. H. (1954) *Motivation and Personality*, Harper and Row, New York.

Osborn, A. (1957) *Applied Imagination*, Scribner, New York.

Parnes, S. J. (1977) CPSI: The general system, *Journal of Creative Behaviour*, **11**, 1.

Parnes, S. J. (1981) *The Magic of your Mind*, Creative Education Foundation, in association with Bearly Ltd, Buffalo, New York.

Parnes, S. J., Noller, R.B., and Biondi, A. M. (1977), *Guide to Creative Action*, Scribner, New York.

Prince, G. (1970) *The Practice of Creativity*, Harper and Row, New York.

Rawlings, B. (1981) By your acts shall ye be known, *Creativity Network*, **7**, 2.

Rickards, T. (1974) *Problem-Solving through Creative Analysis*, Gower Press.

Rickards, T. (1980) Designing for creativity: A state of the art review, *Design Studies*, **1**, 5.

Rickards, T. and Freedman, B. (1979) A re-appraisal of creativity techniques, *JEIT*, **3**, 1.

Rittel, H. W. J. and Webber, M. M. (1974) Dilemmas in a general theory of planning, *DMG/DRS Journal*, **8**, 1.

Talbot, R. J. (1981) Construing problems, *Design: Science Method*, Edited by R. Jacques and J. A. Powell, IPC, Guildford.

Talbot, R. J. and Jacques, R. (1977a) Open University problem identification game I, *SAGSET Journal*, **7**, 2.

Talbot, R. J. and Jacques, R. (1977b) Open University problem identification game II, *SAGSET Journal*, **7**, 3.

Taylor, F. (1912) Testimony to the House of Representatives Committee; see Taylor (1947), *Scientific Management*, Harper and Row, New York, pp. 39–73.

Toffler, A. (1970) *Future Shock*, Pan Books, U.S.A. and U.K.
Torrance, E. P. (1962) *Guiding Creative Talent*, Prentice-Hall, New Jersey.

Management Development: Advances in Practice and Theory
Edited by C. Cox and J. Beck
© 1984 John Wiley & Sons Ltd

CHAPTER 8

Living with the Future – The Adaptive Manager

John Bessant and George Lester

INTRODUCTION

'A slow sort of country!', said the Queen. 'Now *here*, you see, it takes all the running you can do to keep in the same place. If you want to get somewhere else, you must run at least twice as fast as that!' (Lewis Carroll, *Through the Looking-glass*).

The predicament in which Alice found herself is not dissimilar from that facing managers nowadays. Without restating too much what is already an over-described area, it will be useful to review the kinds of changes which are taking place in today's complex environment: Tables 1 and 2 give some examples.

Essentially, the changes in the quality of the environment can be summarized as:

● an increase in the *number* of relevant and influential elements which have a bearing on the firm;
● an increase in the *variety* (the number of different elements);
● an increase in the level of interconnectedness;
● an increase in the rate at which they are changing.

The consequence of this is that the firm has to deal with an increasingly dynamic, complex, and varied environment which exerts a growing influence. Additionally, the likelihood must be that as the potency of these environmental influences increases, so each company environment will become unique. Further complications to the problem arise because firms are not homogeneous, but are themselves made up of varied, complex, and interrelated elements – all of which factors influence the speed, type, and effectiveness of responses to environmental changes. Environmental proliferation will mean that forecasting by any one group (e.g. corporate planning) or based on one group's expert knowledge (e.g. R&D, Marketing) will be less likely to reflect the variety of the environment. This has important implications for the responses open to the firm.

Table 1   The complexity of the industrial environment and the boundaries of that environment

Aspect	Industrial (1900–1950)	Post-industrial (1950–19??)
Type of activity	Commercial	Socio-political
Turbulence level	Stable	Changing
Boundary of company environment	Well-defined	Vague
Susceptibility of environment to change	Non-permeable	Permeable
Boundary of industry blurred	Industrial sectors	Industrial lines blurred
Interest groups	Few actors	Many actors
Influence courses in environment	Mainly direct	Direct and indirect
Power sources	Firm as centre of power	Political/diffuse power locations
Knowledge source	Common shared knowledge	Many types of specialized and privileged knowledge

Source: Ansoff (1979).

COPING STRATEGIES

As has already been indicated, such problems are well known and well described in the literature. From this discussion, it is possible to find some answers to the general question: What coping strategies can be used?

One of the most basic methods is undoubtedly structural differentiation; that is, an attempt on behalf of the organization to match the variety (Ashby, 1956) of the external environment by creating new agencies (Child, 1977) – setting up particular specialist departments and so on. Such decentralization of functional responsibility can also be linked to delegation of decision-making authority down to units in the organization nearer to the environment and able to react more quickly to environmental changes (Galbraith, 1977a). Both of these options are common coping strategies, but whilst successful to some extent in dealing with the environment, can create new internal problems of integration and control (Lawrence and Lorsch, 1967).

Another option is to improve the organization's capability for information-processing; that is, to improve the quality and handling of information about the world outside so as to improve decision-making effectiveness (Beer, 1974). With the recent changes in the availability of computer systems, such approaches have gained in popularity; however, their success is limited by the quality and speed of information input to the system and by the design of the system itself, especially in respect of its organizational acceptance (Argyris, 1971).

Table 2   Some views on important environmental influences (This list is compiled from various sources; the many apparently contradictory views held by different commentators are included to illustrate the difficulty of forecasting environmental changes)

Decline of big business corporations
Emergence of state capitalism and expanded private sector
Decay of bureaucracy
Labour alienation and decline in mobility
Rise in meritocracy
Technological convergence
Decline of traditional sectors/deindustrialization
Increasing structural unemployment
Increased emphasis on the leisure society!
Discontinuous rates of change
Centralization of knowledge
Information society
Growing North–South polarization
Emergence of newly industrializing countries
Continuing decline of less developed countries
Increasing protection policy
Growing political/military intervention
Decline in 'bigness is best' philosophy
Failure of the free market economy
Decline of growth ethic
Decentralization of organizations
Growing stratification in society
Increasing unemployment
Alienation of economics and technology from social values
Population growth
Shortages of materials, energy, food, etc.
Growth in pollution and adverse technological developments
Growing political instability
Lack of policy-making
Lack of control

Sources: Drucker (1970); Toffler (1970); Bell (1972); Schumacher (1973); Cole *et al.* (1974); Child (1975); Macrae (1975); Sheane (1976); Galbraith (1977b); Barron and Curnow (1979); Bessant *et al.* (1980).

Another option is to use various types of forecasting in an attempt to anticipate the ways in which the environment might be expected to change in the future (Holroyd, 1979; Rivett, 1979). Here the problem appears to be that changes in environmental quality towards increasing complexity, variety, and turbulence make it very difficult to forecast with sufficient certainty on which to base decisions. Ansoff's description of the problem is useful here: using a military analogy, he says 'that the range of the radars for early recognition of potential attackers is shrinking and the speed with which the attackers fly is increasing . . .'. (To this might be added that there are also more attackers involved.)

Other strategies can be identified in the literature. These include both increasing formalization of procedures within the organization and decreasing it in favour of high internal flexibility. Another is to increase environmental control through external contacts and influences – joint ventures, political coalitions, diversification, and integration policies (Chandler, 1962; Stopford and Wells, 1972). Child (1977) calls this type of response 'environmental management'. The essential features of these solutions are that, alone or in combination, they are not sufficient answers to the problem of managing in a complex environment. In many cases they may exchange one set of external problems for a new set of internal ones – as with the differentiation/integration issue. Clearly, what is needed to make such options work, and to continuously adapt and improve on them in the face of new external and internal changes, will be highly flexible skills on the part of managers. Whatever approach is adopted, organizational flexibility and learning can be considerably enhanced by these adaptive capabilities. Yet, in the context of response strategies, the skills enhancement of managers has received relatively little attention.

THE ROLE OF PEOPLE AS ADAPTIVE CENTRES

As organizational behaviour studies have consistently shown, it is people who shape organizations and make them succeed or fail. This axiom certainly applies to the problems of 'coping management', yet surprisingly little attention has been paid to the particular set of adaptive skills which management may need.

Studies in the field of innovation theory concerning early acceptance of new ideas and tolerance of change illustrate some of the cognitive abilities. Other studies in the field of leadership indicate that successful leaders adapt their styles of management to cope with different circumstances and subordinates – illustrating a behavioural approach which adapts to different contingencies. It would be possible to extract other examples, but the point is clear: certain individual skills are of critical importance in successful adaptive behaviour. Table 3 offers a list of those (collected from various course members on a number of occasions) which appear to be relevant in defining 'the coping manager'

A RECIPE FOR MAKING ADAPTIVE MANAGERS

Given the need for managers with the skills identified above (Table 3), the question is raised as to whether such individuals actually exist? We believe that they do and that they contribute significantly to adaptiveness within organizations. But is it the same story as for other key individuals – that they are born, not made? We think not: we would suggest that such skills can be trained and developed within organizations. That is not to say that there is a single, simple

Table 3   Characteristics of the coping manager

Curious
Imaginative
Explores
Systematic (structural)
Many avenues/viewpoints
Positive
Decisive
Determined
Inventive
Confident
Good communicator (resource assembler)
Knowledgeable (in-depth and broadly)
Listening skills
Ambitious
Takes long-term view
Monitors progress
Prepared to change goals (especially in response to environment changes)
Resilient
Awareness of change
Positive attitude
Adapts to different people/circumstances
Has alternative strategies available
Influences change directly

---

prescription for adaptive skills. Rather, it is necessary to develop an open-ended approach which makes use of a synthesis of techniques, experience, and personal abilities coupled to a positive attitude to problem-solving. The basis for this approach lies in work which has been done on *open-ended* problem-solving, and it will be useful to consider this briefly now.

OPEN-ENDED PROBLEM-SOLVING

In a general sense, problem-solving involves:
● recognition of a need,
● a useful definition(s) of this need,
● exploration of possible ways to satisfy the need,
● assessment of these ways,
● evaluation and decision-making,
● action which may fulfil the need,
● repetition of the process if it fails to fulfil the need.

The most common types of problem-solving are system based; they seek to use prior experience and knowledge of systems, and make comparisons with prior solutions. (The Kepner–Tregoe method is a typically successful system-based approach – see Kepner and Tregoe, 1965, for details.) Approaches of this kind are essentially normative and retrospective. A hidden goal is that the process seeks to reproduce known solutions and to fit present circumstances to past models. Such problem-solving approaches are usually termed 'closed-ended' in that the problem as given is assumed to be sufficient and necessary, and that a solution is a fairly direct result of the application of known techniques on all the relevant information. However, problems vary in their characteristics and may not fit the above criteria; this implies the selection of a suitable strategy depending upon problem type. (For a detailed discussion of this see Johnson, 1972.) Clearly, the approach needed to tackle poorly defined problems, or those admitting of multiple solutions, will need to be far more flexible. Such *open-ended* problems differ considerably from *closed-ended*, as can be seen in Table 4.

Table 4   Closed- and open-ended problem-solving

Aspect	Closed	Open
Problem	All necessary elements understood and present	Inexplicable and missing elements
	Composed of discrete elements	Holistic and integrated
Solution	One 'right' answer	Many answers
	Validated/assumed correct	Requires proof
Process	Made up of rational steps	Discontinuous
	Normative	General heuristic
Knowledge base	Prior experience	Prior experience and intuition, gambling, hunches, etc.
Outcome	Predictable	Unpredictable
		Contingent upon many factors

An open-ended problem can be characterized as one in which not all the elements are understood, or even present; in which the precise nature of the problem is not necessarily clear; in which the type of solution sought is not necessarily clear; in which many solutions and definitions are possible; in which the method of solution is not necessarily clear; and in which the present phase of problem-solving is not necessarily clear (Rickards, 1974). Forecasting in and coping with a complex and turbulent environment are essentially open-ended problems.

The creative problem-solving literature stresses six important principles:

1. *Process awareness.* Although the problem may not be amenable to analytic methods, it is often amenable to a systematic approach (Gordon, 1961; Prince, 1970). Typically, problem-solving moves through a series of phases: recognition of the problem and elements; definition and re-definition; exploration for ideas to solve the problem (as now understood); development of ideas

towards practical and workable solutions; implementation, action, and acceptance-seeking of the potential solution; and review of progress. Like most such systemic models it is not expected that progress will be linear or uniform through the phases.

2. *Separation of activity*. Inherent in the notion of phases of problem-solving is that of separation of activity. Attempts are made to tackle the phases in an orderly manner. However, separation of activity is also to be found at a more profound level. Running throughout all the phases is an underlying process of generating alternatives and then closing-down to a few to be considered in depth (Gryskiewicz, 1976). The opening-out of alternatives is to be kept separate from the closing-down process to best options. The process is often likened to searching a maze or to exploring a relevance tree (Figure 1).

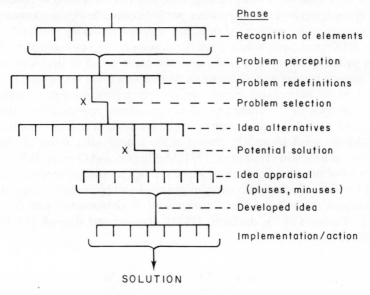

Figure 1. The problem-solving process modelled as a relevance tree

3. *Postponement of judgement*. Process awareness, both in terms of process phase and in separating the opening-up and closing-down processes, predicates the postponement of judgement. Deferment of judgement (note *not* the cancellation of judgement) is necessary in order for the problem-solver to maintain the focus of activity at the appropriate phase and not to move prematurely ahead. More significantly, the same principle applies to the generation of alternatives. Research has demonstrated that the generation of ideas is greatly enhanced by the deferment of judgement, both in terms of quantity of ideas and quality of ideas (Osborn, 1957; Clarke, 1958).

4. *Quantity*. Since the best solution, definition, or idea is not known, another important principle is that of 'quantity'. The more alternatives generated the greater the likelihood of arriving at a better quality solution. Research has established a clear relationship between the postponement of judgement, quantity of alternatives, and the quality of the eventual solution(s) (Clarke, 1958).

5. *Perspective shift*. The requirement for novel insight in open-ended problem-solving predicates a change in intellectual perception or construct system (Kelly, 1955). Quite a number of psychological, and other, theories of the mechanisms for perceptual shift have been suggested, ranging from Gestalt theories to psychoanalytic theories (Mackler and Strantz, 1965; Rickards, 1979).

6. *Positive attitude*. The foregoing three points have tended to concentrate on the opening-up aspects of a process, partly because the closing-down aspects are more generally understood in terms of decision-making and analytic approaches (Kepner and Tregoe, 1965). However, the open-ended problem-solving process has some special requirements in terms of decision-making. When assessing ideas and alternatives these alternatives are usually no more than an initial conception which are not yet robust enough to withstand rigorous analytic or screening procedures. A general approach has grown up which seeks to evaluate the young potential solutions in terms of why they will work (What's good about it?) instead of more destructive terms of why that alternative is deficient (Hamilton, 1974; McPherson and Guidici, 1978).

Within the broad framework of these six aspects of open-ended problem-solving (several of which also apply in general to all problems) a large toolbag of techniques, methods, and tips have evolved. An introductory sample is to be found in Parnes (1967), de Bono (1971), Koberg and Bagnall (1974), and Rickards (1974).

TRAINING APPROACH

Existing methods of 'futures scanning' largely rely on forecasting techniques (e.g. trend extrapolation) and systems models (e.g. cross-impact matrices). By contrast, open-ended forecasting emphasizes *process techniques* (e.g. divergence and convergence mechanisms) in order to maintain flexibility under many circumstances. The training for process skills acquisition necessary for open-ended forecasting cannot be prescriptive. The skills presuppose an open, flexible, and positive approach. Their application to a real-world situation presupposes a contingent response to the requirements of the moment. Similarly, response strategies practised by managers tend to rely most on reactive capabilities: a central requirement for effective coping management is that it is *proactive*. That is, able to anticipate change and to draw on a wide repertoire of skills to produce an effective and appropriate response.

This has led to a training programme, developing a mixture of *intellectual and affective* skills, which seeks:

● To deliberately let participants experience uncertainty and complexity in a supportive atmosphere.

● To build the course around general stages and tasks which are shared with the participants.

● To be contingent upon the participants' needs at that moment (a 'Chinese menu' of inputs has been our response in trying to reduce the design problems as we seek to maintain flexibility – see Table 5).

Table 5   Some techniques from the 'Chinese menu'

Crawford slip method	Relevance trees
What's good about it?	TABS
Goal orientation	'Here and there'
Brainstorming	Coping man
Itemized response	Reversals
'Patterns'	Wishful thinking
Consequences	Graduation ceremony
Killer phrases	5W : 1H
Top dog/under dog	Nominal group
Clock problem	Concensus cards
Headlining	Elephant
Construct reflection	Ball and bucket
Metaphor/analogy	Matches (introduction)
SWOT (strengths, weaknesses, opportunities, threats)	Checklists
Matrix work	Screening criteria
Morphological analysis	Greenlighting
Task analysis	Minimum game contract
Bankers and flyers	Blocks to ideas
'Threats to opportunities'	Blocks to change
'Now here's my plan'	Vulnerability analysis
Intermediate impossibles	Potential problem analysis
C.C. graph	Boxes and squiggles
Packing the luggage	Acceptance seeking
Living sculpture	The change sketch
'The God act'	Successive abstraction
Balloons and weights	Successive reduction
Future memory	Buzan
Anthropomorphism	Fishbone

● To establish routine skills which may assist the participants in doing their existing jobs, only more effectively.

● To provide a basic framework for trainee managers to examine threats and opportunities in the future (for themselves and their organizations) and to develop process skills associated with responding flexibly to those changes.

● And, most importantly, to build on participants' existing strengths (we do not teach anything new) and to let them reassess their own latent skills.

The training experience is, necessarily, of short duration and limited impact compared with job-time. We have enhanced its impact by building upon existing strengths and practices. Rather than exhorting participants to return to the workplace with new techniques and approaches (a common outcome of training) we have invited them to analyse their current activities and tasks. The aim is to ask: 'In what ways might you enhance your effectiveness by doing what you do already, only *better*.' This builds on existing routines within the workplace which are more likely to persist than new activities which may be in conflict with the work environment. A growth point which reinforces positive points and approaches is established for future development.

The practical application of the open-ended approach as a training tool is itself an important component in our activities. Since the problems confronting a given group of managers – the managers themselves and various other features will all be highly specific – it seems to us to adopt a non-prescriptive approach. Instead of trying to force-fit a set of techniques, etc. to a particular situation, we try and operate a 'Chinese menu' approach to the problem. That is to say, we offer a broad structured framework only, and fill the remainder with highly specific and relevant interventions and techniques linked to particular problems.

Examples of the range of techniques, etc. which may be used during this process are given in Table 5. Clearly, such an interactive training process depends on flexibility on the part of the trainer as well as the trainee. For the same reason, it defies definition in anything more than the general pattern described above. However, our experiences suggest that it does work – and in particular that it provides managers with a set of skills and an understanding of processes and techniques which:

(a) they have developed for themselves, and which is highly specific to their needs,

(b) have innate flexibility and will thus be applicable to other problem areas, and

(c) they can continue to develop and adapt for their purposes.

PROOF OF THE PUDDING?

We are aware that in trying to describe how our open-ended approach operates we have only partially succeeded. Whilst both the need for flexible and adaptive skills, and at least an outline definition of them can be identified, their training and development is less easy to measure. We try to provide an understanding of the way in which complex problems might be tackled and a set of tools with which to make a start; in this role – as 'quartermasters' – we can demonstrate success by taking an inventory of the techniques that trainees acquire and retain during the training process.

However, the real effectiveness must be measured in terms of the use to which the individual puts that experience – and that is a highly complex variable. Subjective feedback provides us with a partial source, but in the end our approach to the problem of optimizing our training effectiveness must be an open-ended one. Whilst it may be close to cliche to talk of 'mutual learning', we do try to monitor our own programme, to record new and improvized techniques, and to observe our success and failure in responding to particular needs in an overall attempt at improving our capability to responding to the open-ended training problem in a flexible and adaptive fashion.

REFERENCES

Ansoff, H. I. (1979) *Strategic Management*, Macmillan, London.

Argyris, C. (1971) Management information systems – the challenge to rationality and emotionality, *Management Science*, **17**, 275–295.

Ashby, W. (1956) *Introduction to Cybernetics*, Wiley, London.

de Bono, E. (1971) *Lateral Thinking for Management*, McGraw-Hill, Maidenhead.

Barron, I. and Curnow, R. (1979) *The Future with Microelectronics*, Frances Pinter, London.

Beer, S. (1974) *Platform for Change*, Wiley, London.

Bell, D. (1972) *The Coming of Post-industrial Society*, Heinemann, London.

Bessant, J. *et al.* (1980) *The Impact of Microelectronics: A Review of the Literature*, Frances Pinter, London.

Chandler, A. (1962) *Strategy and Structure*, MIT Press, Cambridge, Mass.

Child, J. (1975) Doublethink in our organisational society, Inaugural lecture, University of Aston, Birmingham.

Child, J. (1977) *Organisation: Problems and Practice*, Harper & Row, London.

Clarke, C. (1958) *Brainstorming*, Doubleday, New York.

Cole, S. *et al.* (1974) *Thinking About the Future*, Chatto & Windus, London.

Drucker, P. (1970) *The age of Discontinuity*, Heinemann, London.

Galbraith, J. (1977a) *Organization Design*, Addison-Wesley, Reading, Mass.

Galbraith, J. K. (1977b) *The Age of Uncertainty*, BBC Books, London.

Gordon, W. (1961) *Synectics – The Development of Creative Capacity*, Harper & Row, New York.

Gryskiewicz, S. (1976) *Fuelling Creative Communication in Groups*, Centre for Creative Leadership, Greenboro.

Hamilton, W. (1974) Screening business development opportunities, *Business Horizons*, **August 1974**, 13–24.

Holroyd, P. (1979) Some recent methodologies in future studies: A personal view, *R&D Management*, **9**, 3, 107–116.

Johnson, A. (1972) *A Systematic Introduction to the Study of Thinking*, Harper & Row, New York.

Kelly, G. (1955) *The Psychology of Personal Constructs*, Norton.

Kepner, C. and Tregoe, B. (1965) *The Rational Manager*, McGraw-Hill, New York.

Koberg, D. and Bagnall, J. (1974) *The Universal Traveller*, Wm. Kaufman Inc., Los Angeles.

Lawrence, P. and Lorsch, J. (1967) *Organization and Environment*, Harvard University Press.

Mackler, B. and Strantz, F. (1965) Creativity: Theoretical and methodological considerations, *The Psychological Record*, **15**, 217–328.

Macrae, N. (1975) The coming entrepreneurial revolution, *The Economist*.

McPherson, J., and Guidici, D. (1978) *Advances in Innovation Management*, SRI International Business Intelligence Program Report no. 609.

Osborn, A. (1957) *Applied Imagination*, Charles Scribner & Sons, New York.

Parnes, S. (1967) *Creative Behaviour Handbook*, Charles Scribner & Sons, New York.

Prince, G. (1970) *The practice of creativity*, Harper & Row, New York.

Rickards, T. (1974) *Problem-solving Through Creative Analysis*, Gower Press, Epping.

Rickards, T. (1979) *Creativity for managers*, Manchester Business School.

Rivett, B. (1979) Future literature and futures forecasting – a critical review, *Omega*, **7**, 1, 33–41.

Schumacher, E. (1973) *Small is Beautiful*, Abacus Books, London.

Sheane, D. (1976) *Beyond Bureaucracy*, Management Research, London.

Stopford, J. and Wells, L. (1972) *Managing the Multi-national Enterprise*, Longman, London.

Toffler, A. (1970) *Future Shock*, Pan Books, London.

Management Development: Advances in Practice and Theory
Edited by C. Cox and J. Beck
© 1984 John Wiley & Sons Ltd

CHAPTER 9

The Management of Creativity

*Iain L. Mangham**

> Come on ladies, puff out those feathers . . . really show us what it is like to be a
> down-trodden old biddy. Try to keep to the beat . . . 1, 2, 3, 4, . . . listen to it, listen
> to it! . . . Good, good. Now, let's try it again, and this time, really try to get it
> together. I know it's a massive creative leap from a draughty room on a wet Friday
> in Cardiff to a hen yard in Bohemia or wherever, but that's what it is all about. The
> magic of the theatre and all that stuff. Ready? . . . *And* . . . (Transcripts prepared by
> the author.)

Creativity has been given a great deal of attention over the past twenty years or
so. Some of the research has been centred on identifying forces within an
individual related to creative output, some has been concerned with factors
which may influence group creativity, and some, relatively little, has been
concerned with the management of creativity. Not a great deal has been done
in investigating the conditions of organization that may foster creative behaviour, and even less has been concerned with the process of management.

It seems to me that there are pressing reasons for studying such issues, since
it is arguable that without sustained creativity, an organization cannot survive.
Within commercial enterprises, creativity has to do with 'bottom-line' profit
and loss, for such companies are concerned with developing and producing new
products in order to compete in the market-place. Elsewhere, in national and
international organizations, in institutions of education, in prisons, hospitals,
unions – in every conceivable type of agency – creativity is at a premium if these
bodies are to respond effectively to the challenges which confront them.

The starting point for the research reported here was an image of the creative
individual: romantic, starving in a garret, giving all for his art, essentially a lone
figure (aside from occasional convivial binges with fellow artists), creating
masterpieces unacknowledged and – aside from his faithful model and con-
sumptive mistress – unloved. The one word that summed up the creative

*The research reported in this paper is supported by a grant from the Social Science Research
Council. I am grateful to my colleague, Michael Overington, for comments and advice, and to
Albert Natchkirk for his continuing interest in the project.

individual was non-conformist. This view of the creative individual is certainly not idiosyncratic; Barron (1969), for example, lists a number of traits common to all highly creative persons and terms such as spontaneity, relatively little interest in relations with others, independence, impulsiveness, self-assertion, and non-conformity occur throughout his analysis.

I recognized that my vision of the creative individual was no more than that: a portrait of the solitary creative individual. Furthermore, I was aware that my vision told me little of consequence, since contemporary organizations are set up so that there are *groups* of administrative, scientific, and entrepreneurial personnel, all of whom are involved in the creative process; scientific and technological creativity is, probably, much less of a solitary pursuit than is painting, literature, and the composition of music. In seeking to understand better the creative process and its management in order to attempt to generalize, I needed to study the creativity of a group rather than that of relatively isolated individuals. Furthermore, since my concern was discovery rather than verification, my approach had to be qualitative rather than quantitative, based upon observation rather than questionnaires. I was convinced familiarity would breed concepts. The obvious source was Research and Development (R&D) departments; the obvious shortcoming was the length of time it would need to identify, let alone follow through, the creative process. What I needed was an opportunity to observe that process within a group in a fixed location over a relatively short time, a circumstance where I could go seek the answer to the question: 'How do you go about managing people in a way that releases their creative efforts?'

And this is where the chickens come in. Despite their apparent glamour and air of frenzied improvization, opera companies, theatre groups, film and TV units, are work systems. In each phase of the production process a group of people collaborate (or not) to form a work organization which – like any other – has characteristic problems of planning, structure, leadership, motivation, and control in the pursuit of creativity. Unlike most other enterprises concerned with creativity (such as R&D departments), for Arts organizations, however, each phase represents a relatively temporary system, limited in time, space, and membership, in which personnel are selected, interact, create 'the product', and then disband. Such enterprises, therefore, are ideal settings for qualitative, longitudinal studies, the more so as throughout the various phases the director has to stimulate and manage different kinds of creative work under tight time schedules and intense budget pressures. The job of the director is not to be simply concerned with his art, it is also – and I would argue largely – concerned with management of the creative process.

I have been fortunate enough to have been given complete access to two theatre companies – the Bristol Little Theatre Company and the Bristol Old Vic – and one television company – an Arts unit working on a programme concerned with music and musicians. Since in the latter case I am still engaged in the fieldwork, my comments in this paper are derived from, and apply only to, the theatre and opera companies. In these cases my involvement (or that of my colleague Andrew Travers) was with a complete production from planning through rehearsal and into performance. Our observation entailed us being with the production full time, taking notes, in some instances making recordings, taking photographs, and interviewing participants, both formally and informally. Subsequently, field notes were written up and transcripts prepared, and these records form the basis for the rest of this paper.

Clearly, with such a mass of data – from one production alone I have some 600 pages of closely typed transcripts – the question of selection arises. There are a number of ways of considering the material and choice, obviously, depends upon particular purposes. Here I am concerned with the nature of group creativity and, in particular, its management, so I need a frame to organize the data that fits these ends. For the former – the characteristics of the effective creative group – I have chosen to draw upon the work of Pelz and Andrews (1966), who studied scientific groups, and upon that of Stein (1975), who devotes a whole volume of his studies on creativity to groups. To draw out parts concerned with the management of creativity, I have used the work of Steiner (1965), *The Creative Organization*, and have sought to adopt his ideas wherever and whenever it seemed appropriate. Imposing any frame, of course, has consequences, since a way of seeing is simultaneously and necessarily a way of not seeing; metaphors, models, and frames illuminate some features at the expense of others. What follows, therefore, should be taken for what it is, very much work in progress, rather than a finished statement; the creative process as seen through existing concepts derived from the literature (for the most part), rather than as illuminated by concepts deriving from observation. Such an analysis is the daughter of time, not the literature.

A final introductory word before we 'cut the cackle and get to the chickens'. A matter of definitions which, in the social sciences, are always contentious. Temporary system need not take up much space: a set of diversely skilled people working jointly on a task of some complexity over a limited time period. Creativity is much less easily defined. Stein (1975) defines creativity as a 'process that results in a novel product or idea which is accepted as useful, tenable, or satisfying by a significant group of others at some point in time'. Poggioli (1971), working from the standpoint of a literary critic, comes up with a similar view when he defines creativity as that element in the arts which goes beyond the existing corpus either by stylistic or technical development, stylistic variation, or revolutionary departure from existing canons or conventions. Others, not defined by him, determine whether or not the work has gone beyond the existing corpus. My measurement of creativity for the particular productions I have been concerned with has relied exclusively upon the judgement of professional critics; I have taken their views as to the value and creativity of the performance they observed as being *the* measure of artistic endeavour. They constitute the significant group of others whose judgement as to whether or not the ideas, styles, and techniques of any particular performance were accepted as 'useful, tenable, or satisfying'. In this respect, both of the major products commented upon in this paper – the production of *Edward II* at the Old Vic and *The Cunning Little Vixen* by the Welsh National Opera – were rated highly creative by the majority of significant others.

Back to the chickens and the characteristics of whether or not a group is or is not working creatively. How do factors such as group climate, patterns of communication, the composition of the group, group ageing, the nature of leadership, and the like affect the level of the group's contribution and its overall creativity?

PATTERNS OF COMMUNICATION

Stein (1975) notes that one of the frequent problems encountered between or within groups lies in the area of communication and claims that 'faulty dissemination of information can not only inhibit the group's creativity but can also undermine the members' morale and lessen the effectiveness with which they organize themselves for any cooperative or mutual endeavour'. He also notes that part of the problem in the dissemination of information may be attributed to the manner in which the patterns of communication between members are established and maintained. Following up the studies of Bavelas (1948, 1950), Leavitt (1951), and Shaw (1964), he argues that creativity may – in part – be a function of available channels of communication. The comparison he makes, put somewhat simply, is between highly centralized networks, that which Bavelas termed 'the wheel', and decentralized networks, imaginatively termed 'the circle', and he concludes, with Shaw, that when problems are simple, more errors are made when the network is decentralized; but when the problem is complex, more mistakes are shown in the centralized network. It would then appear, following Stein (1975) and Shaw (1964), that: 'centralized networks are good to collect information in one place. But if we expect to do something with the information, then decentralized networks are better.'

The direct application of ideas deriving from studies of patterns of communication is that, given the appropriate pattern, Stein *et al.* would argue, then the individual is encouraged to contribute to and to build upon others' ideas and suggestions, 'for none of them is the private property of any one participating member'. He further notes that in a truly effective group, 'the participants can use communication networks flexibly to meet the demands of problems and not get trapped by any specific network where the responsibility for solving the problem falls on one person to the exclusion of the others.'

What, then, of my chickens? What part did they play in the development of the production of *The Cunning Little Vixen*? From my observation, very little. The network was a classic wheel with the two directors – musical and stage –

constituting the hub. The majority of communication went from them out to the cast, the musicians, the set designers, and was directed back into them. There was little or no encouragement of individuals to make suggestions other than about their own specific contribution and, even here, the majority of the traffic was one way – from the director to the individual. For example, he demonstrated what he took to be the appropriate gait for the chickens, he told them where to stand, and he carefully coached them in the necessary gestures to accompany the music. Likewise, the musical director worked on the phrasing and intonation and indicated clearly what he took to be the appropriate interpretation line by line, beat by beat. A single sequence lasting some 5 minutes in performance occupied over 4 hours of rehearsal time, during which the balance of communication was some 90% hub to wheel, with virtually nothing going along the rim.

The impression of a strong centralized network may need some qualification in that the directors had a clear idea of what was needed, since they had both been engaged with some of the principal singers in an earlier production of the piece. Since I did not observe their early attempts to arrive at an interpretation which may or may not have been more collaborative (more of the circle pattern of communication), I am not in a position to claim that the wheel was the predominant pattern throughout. My conversations with the cast and with the stage crew, however, did suggest that, for the most part, they expected a highly centralized mode of communication. A finding confirmed in the structure of calls for rehearsal which rarely brought substantial numbers of the cast together; indeed, on a number of occasions singers rehearsed scenes without the presence of others who were also to perform in the scene, thus further reducing the likelihood of synergy.

The patterns of communication observed in the production of *Edward II* were much closer to Stein's ideal type. Here, as in the opera, the director was the central figure and for part of the time – some 60% – he acted as the hub and both received and radiated communication. For the rest of the time he encouraged, and most of the cast readily fell into, more of a circle pattern of communication. When faced with a difficult or complex piece of action, or a problem of interpretation, he sought ideas and suggestions from as wide a circle as possible and encouraged an atmosphere of building, of experimentation, and risk-taking. It was notable, however, that (with very few exceptions) he determined whether the pattern was to be wheel or circle and (again with very few exceptions) the actors did not discuss with each other individual characterizations; uncertainties in this area were nearly always handled one-to-one with the director. Conversations with the actors and the director confirmed that this somewhat more flexible pattern of communication was not necessarily usual; different directors adopted very different postures, some being completely and 'anarchically' participative (orientated to the circle pattern), others dictatorial (hub orientated). Most of the actors appearing in *Edward II* found the flexible approach adopted by the director both effective and satisfying, though one or two asserted that they much preferred a director who 'has a clear idea of where he is going and takes us there'.

GROUP COMPOSITION

In his attempt to answer the question as to whether or not creative groups should consist of individuals who have the same personality and attitudes or abilities, or should the individuals in the group be as different from each other as possible, Stein (1975) arrives at another of his 'it-all-depends-on-the-situation' conclusions. There is, he argues, an optimal mix of personal characteristics for any given group project. 'The optimal mix for simple routine tasks includes fairly similar kinds of individuals, whereas for complex tasks requiring creativity, the mix would be more diversified.' The problem, of course, which Stein and others carefully avoid, is that of defining the nature of compatible and incompatible personal characteristics. Not that this or any other element of composition appeared to be an issue for the groups I have studied. They had a wide age range and a broad span of abilities but were, of course, selected with such factors in mind; it is difficult to have a geriatric playing a juvenile lead and foolish to have someone of considerable technical ability playing a very minor part.

The director of *Edward II* indicated that he did pay attention to the composition of his group along other dimensions: 'Other things being equal, I prefer an intelligent actor, since he can make a contribution to the production as a whole.' He also mentioned that he liked a particular performer because 'he is quite likely to disagree with me and you need a few of those around to keep you on your toes'. He was more forthright about those that he did not 'need around': 'those without any real ability, you have to devote a disproportionate amount of time to resolving their problems', and 'those whose best perform-ances are left on the rehearsal floor or in the dressing room. Those who throw a tantrum at any opportunity. People have got to be able to work together, not against each other.'

The issue of compatibility was also touched upon by the opera directors who felt that decisions about casting *and* direction had to be carefully taken. For example, it was noted that for a projected performance of *Tristan and Isolde* they had been fortunate enough to secure the services of Goodall, 'Wagner reincarnate', and that, in looking for a producer, they were basically searching 'for someone who had the experience, who came from within the German tradition, and also wouldn't in any way go against what we knew Reginald Goodall was going to put into the music'. The Welsh National Opera Com-pany, I was told, 'unlike most opera companies, insist on the conductor being present at the majority of production rehearsals, so that there is a very close relationship. Elsewhere, often the situation is that the producer will do his work and then the conductor will come in at a fairly late stage of orchestra rehearsals, and of course tempi don't work to the movements and so on. The best work is achieved by building that relationship up over a long period and this we have tried to achieve – quite successfully so far.' Ability to 'fit in' also influences (but does not determine) the choice of singers. 'There are so many singers today who fly around doing as little rehearsal as they can, and give good performances, but ones which don't have much reference to their fellow artists – we're not in that market, largely because we don't want to be, and partly because we can't afford it. We go for singers who prefer to take a lot of time rehearsing a particular part and that, plus this ability to work reasonably well with others, tends to dictate the sort of person we have.'

GROUP AGEING

Groups, like individuals, age. Just as individuals develop rigidities in their characteristic responses to circumstances, so do combinations of individuals in groups. Stein (1975) notes that as a group of people ages, it may become less and less sensitive to new ideas, new processes, and creative developments. There is evidence that 'temporary' groups do better than permanent ones.

Torrance *et al.* (1957) found that temporary bomber crews performed better on a series of problems than did permanent crews; Shepard (1956) discovered that the most effective R&D teams were those which were relatively new; and Pelz and Andrews (1966), studying 83 research groups, came up with a series of findings which, broadly, appear to support the contention that beyond a certain age, groups assume a pattern of fixed behaviour which is detrimental to creativity.

Since the groups I observed were, by definition, temporary, I can add little to this debate, save the comments of the directors, actors, and singers who, unanimously, agreed that staying too long in one place, having a long run, or becoming part of a bureaucratic, state-supported theatre or opera company was likely to lead to 'a drying up of the creative juices'. Change of location, change of setting and colleagues, most of them appeared to think, was necessary if they were to keep their vitality. Clearly, in view of the success of such companies as the Royal Shakespeare and the National Theatre, the definition of 'temporary' and of 'ageing' is critical; no doubt, as Pelz and Andrews' (1966) data suggest, the relationship between creativity and group age is curvilinear; young groups do not effectively capitalize upon their resources, and beyond a certain age (clearer in R&D than in the theatre), effectiveness begins to decline.

GROUP CLIMATE

One characteristic technique for stimulating group creativity is to seek to make groups become non-evaluative. It is felt that if members of a group evaluate each other's responses, they will inhibit the free flow of ideas. In synectics (Gordon, 1961, 1971), for example, freedom is encouraged and criticism of any kind is banned, in order to create a freer, more easy group environment and climate in which the participants will be able to think up, verbalize, and develop ideas.

Such a climate was not, for the most part, evident in the rehearsals of *The Cunning Little Vixen*. Every movement of the chickens was scrutinized and evaluated, though usually the evaluation consisted of saying, 'Good. Good.' The real measure of success was whether or not the routine or sequence had to be gone through again; only very occasionally was something declared 'absolutely dreadful'. In this circumstance, as in the production of *Edward II*, the cast expected to be criticized and looked upon the comments as necessary for the development of their parts; indeed, lack of evaluation was deemed evidence of incompetence on the part of the directors. Comments to each other by the singers, however, were without exception complimentary, often effusively so; the absence of comments from peers was taken to indicate a degree of negative criticism.

The climate within the group rehearsing *Edward II*, although similar in some respects, was different in others. Actors were encouraged to make suggestions, to present ideas, and usually these were not evaluated without trial; for example, an actor may suggest a particular interpretation of a line or series of lines and, on most occasions, would be encouraged to 'give it a try'. He would then play through the sequence, embodying his interpretation in his performance, and would subsequently expect to receive some evaluation of it, primarily from the director but also, to a more limited extent, from his peers. Occasionally, a rapid and dismissive evaluation would preclude a trial: 'That is the silliest idea I have heard in a long time.' On other occasions, suggestions were pointedly ignored but, overall, the climate was one in which suggestions were put forward and tested out in expectation that they would be evaluated. Evaluation, itself, was apparently not a matter of concern; the form it took probably was, in that in this particular group the atmosphere had been created in which having a suggestion not taken up (either before or after trial) did not appear to inhibit the flow of further suggestions.

LEADERSHIP

Which brings us to the question of leadership. Stein (1975) argues that in 'real-life' situations, groups which are called upon to be creative are likely to have a leader who 'when the group begins to work creatively . . . must try to become a group member, or the group will not be able to function properly'. The evidence from my observations does not support this conclusion; indeed, it runs contrary to it, and thus contrary to much of the literature on leaderless groups and upon participative management.

In the case of the opera, at no time did the stage director or the musical director become group members, in the sense implied by Stein. In the case of *Edward II*, the role of the director remained differentiated from that of other group members throughout the rehearsal period and beyond. Whenever he chose to involve the cast in decisions about interpretation or in the resolution of particular issues, it remained clear throughout that the final decision would be his and his alone. He recognized that discussion was an important element of that decision process since, as he put it, 'in the final analysis, the actor has to make it work on the night, and if he is not convinced, it won't'. But equally, the final responsibility for co-ordination and overall interpretation was seen both by him and by the actors to be part of his role. In this sense, he never became simply a member of the group. Contrary to Stein, Pelz (1967) appears to agree that performance is good when people have a sense of belonging to a group headed by a competent chief.

The group characteristics cited and examined above serve to illustrate some of the more common factors which have been taken at one time or another to affect creativity in groups. Although the findings from my observations do not wholly support all of the findings derived from experimental groups, the discussion may have served to illustrate how factors such as channels of communication, group composition, ageing, group climate, and leadership may affect group effectiveness. The discussion of both climate and leadership leads us directly into a consideration of those organizational and management factors which may release or inhibit creativity.

CREATIVE ORGANIZATIONS AND MANAGEMENT

Underlying all of the previous factors, of course, is a pattern of organization which is created by management. In the theatre or the opera, management chooses the members of the group, chooses (other things being equal) how long to keep it in being, helps to set the climate, and has a hand in determining the patterns of communication. As indicated, a great deal of research has been done with regard to the characteristics of effective groups but there is a dearth of research on the conditions characteristic of highly creative organizations. Much of that which follows, therefore, is highly speculative.

Gary Steiner (1965), in his book *The Creative Organization*, provides the impetus for my speculation in his comparison of the creative individual and the creative organization (see Figure 1). The organizations I studied could certainly be characterized as able to produce a large number of ideas quickly; the ability to think creatively and 'to come up with something' was taken for granted in both institutions. It was accepted both at the Old Vic and at the Welsh National that once having defined the problem to the appropriate people, it would be resolved. The problem of engineering the killing of Edward II on stage became one of manufacturing some device for protecting

The creative individual	The creative organization

Conceptual fluency . . . is able to produce a large number of ideas quickly	Has ideas men
	Open channels of communication
	Ad hoc devices:
	    Suggestion systems
	    Brain-storming
	    Ideas unit absolved of other responsibilities
	    Encourages contact with outside sources

Originality . . . generates unusual ideas	Heterogeneous personnel policy Includes marginal, unusual types Assigns non-specialists to problems Allows eccentricity

Separates source from content in evaluating information . . . is motivated by interest in problem . . . follows wherever it leads	Has an objective, fact-founded approach
	Ideas evaluated on their merits, not status of originator
	Ad hoc approaches:
	    Anonymous communications
	    Blind votes
	Selects and promotes on merit only

Suspends judgement . . . avoids early commitment . . . spends more time in analysis, exploration	Lack of financial, material commitment to products, policies Invests in basic research; flexible, long-range planning Experiments with new ideas rather than pre-judging on 'rational' grounds; everything gets a chance
Less authoritarian . . . has relativistic view of life	More decentralized; diversified Administrative slack; time and resources to absorb errors Risk-taking ethos . . . tolerates and expects taking chances
Accepts own impulses . . . playful, undisciplined exploration	Not run as 'tight ship' Employees have fun Allows freedom to choose and pursue problems Freedom to discuss ideas
Independence of judgement, less conformity Deviant, sees self as different	Organizationally autonomous Original and different objectives, not trying to be another 'X'
Rich, 'bizarre' fantasy life *and* superior reality orientation; controls	Security of routine . . . *allows* innovation . . . 'philistines' provide stable, secure environment that allows 'creators' to roam Has separate units or occasions for generating vs. evaluating ideas . . . separates creative from productive functions

Figure 1. The creative individual versus the creative organization. From G. Steiner, *The Creative Organization*, University of Chicago Press, 1965. Reproduced by permission of the University of Chicago Press

the actor from the violence about to be wrought upon his personification and of masking the action from the audience in a manner which led them to believe in it. There was no doubt in the minds of all concerned – actors, director, stage management, and property construction – that a solution would be found.

Again, both organizations separated out 'idea units' from other responsibilities. The artistic director was differentiated from both financial control and administrative responsibility either by time (as in the Old Vic, rehearsal time and place were sacrosanct), or division of function, as at the Welsh National. Similarly, the television companies tend to keep artistic/creative functions separate from more routine duties.

Both organizations pursued 'heterogeneous personnel policies' in that eccentricity of personal appearance, dress, and behaviour appeared to be positively encouraged. Clearly, there were limits on this heterogeneity, but people were not excluded primarily – as may be the case elsewhere – because of their manifest failure to conform. Similarly, at the Old Vic, ideas were more likely to be evaluated on their merits rather than on the status of their originators, and there were more *ad hoc*, suck-it-and-see approaches than was evident at the Welsh National, but both organizations displayed a degree of flexibility well beyond that found in other commercial and industrial organizations of a similar size.

As I have indicated above in the discussion around group climate, the actors at the Old Vic were encouraged to experiment with new ideas rather than pre-judge them on 'rational' grounds; everything, or nearly everything, was given a chance and taking a chance was not only tolerated, it was expected. Here, but not at the Welsh National to anything like the same degree, employees were encouraged to have fun and given freedom to discuss ideas and problems. Dissent was actively encouraged by the director and time was taken out to play games of tag. Not to be recommended to staid institutions, but here taken to be a 'way of loosening up' preparatory to intense creative work.

Both the Welsh National Opera and the Old Vic are organizationally autonomous, although both have Boards of Governors who in a general way oversee the repertoire and the standards. In both cases, however, the directors appear to have considerable lattitude for deciding upon both artists and the works to be performed. Within this framework, directors and performers come together to create *ab initio* a product which will be acclaimed as unique; not another production of *The Cunning Little Vixen* or *Edward II*, but definitive versions of these pieces.

Finally, and arguably most importantly, each organization had a marked security of routine. The Welsh National Opera had a strong administration, very good planning and scheduling systems, and a tight routine of financial control. Creativity occurred within this framework and as a consequence of it, not in spite of it. Similarly, at the Old Vic the basic disciplines were anything but *ad hoc*. In both institutions, once a budget had been agreed upon, rehearsals scheduled and duties assigned, there was little or no room for manoeuvre and all concerned accepted that only by the provision and maintenance of such a secure environment could they be free to innovate. Administration was not seen as the enemy to be outflanked, but as the support to be relied upon.

ROLE CLARITY AND ROLE AMBIGUITY

Steiner (1965) does not directly comment upon one strategy for seeking to enhance creativity other than to imply – 'assign non specialists to tasks' – that clarity of role is *not* needed. In many temporary systems, but notably in the theatre, film, and opera production, the organization adopts an approach in which 'role clarity' is pre-eminent. As an example, the Welsh National Opera had a choreographer who created dance sequences to fit the music, as conducted by one specialist, and the set, as designed by another. His dancers had to be able to perform in the costumes designed by another specialist and within the overall mood as required by the stage director or producer, another specialist. Thus, here as in construction, for example, each specialist takes the other specialists as given and every person knows what they can and cannot do.

It is arguable that the adoption of a role clarity strategy does not make the best use of manpower, since it frustrates the potential synergy available from using the talents of the role occupants in areas or on problems which are interdependent with other talent. Goodman and Goodman (1974), for example, argue against role clarity and for what they term a 'role fuzzy' alternative. They claim that most of the literature 'seems to suggest that creativity and growth' are associated with various forms of 'organic "role fuzzy" strategies'. Their own research into the production of plays does not support these ideas, though notwithstanding this, they conclude by urging that a more creative product will result from less role clarity and, generally, more participation by all concerned.

My data do not support their ideas either. On the contrary, they stress that, for much of the time, most of the contributors are very clear about their roles and these issues of interdependence are handled by the director in his role as co-ordinator. Issues falling between roles are handled by direct discussion in which the contribution of the expert is given due weight; actors do not expect directors to tell them directly how to do something (there is evidence from some of our other data that actor/directors who transgress this role differentiation are resented), nor do directors expect to know how to design and produce the appropriate setting. Unlike industrial and commercial concerns, the demarcation is not written into the contract, but for most people the boundaries are clear and are only crossed by invitation. Thus, actors may become involved in matters of overall interpretation at the invitation of the director, but may not comment upon individual interpretations other than at the invitation of the performer concerned.

MANAGEMENT ACTIONS THAT FOSTER CREATIVITY

Steiner (1965) has identified five management behaviours that encourage the development of creativity.

1. *Values and rewards.* The creative organization prizes and rewards creativity. A style of management that stresses creativity at all levels will increase the chances of its occurrence.

2. *Compensation.* Creativity and not productivity should be measured and rewarded.

3. *Channels for advancement.* There should be formal channels for advancement and status within the area of creativity.

4. *Freedom.* Creativity is increased by giving creators freedom in choice of problem and method of pursuit.

5. *Communication.* Many observations point to the importance of free and open channels of communication, both vertical and horizontal.

To a greater or lesser extent, each of these management behaviours was observed at the Old Vic and the Welsh National Opera. Creativity was the goal of both organizations and every member accepted that as being the nature of the business they were in. The extent of creativity was crudely, if effectively, measured by a mixture of critical reaction from significant others, and the numbers of 'bottoms on seats'. A success with 'those that matter', the cognoscenti, was more important than the returns at the box office, though all concerned recognized that opportunities for further creative endeavour was more dependent upon this than upon the plaudits of the few. Both organizations provided advancement for success, from chorus through to principal, from walk-on to star, though, naturally, it was somewhat difficult to demonstrate creativity in the minor parts. And, as much of the previous discussion has indicated (with qualifications), both freedom and communication were in line with Steiner's prescriptions.

My own observations lead me to add some other management behaviours which may encourage creativity.

(a) Assign *leaders* to projects who have sufficient self-assurance to be able to encourage, support, co-ordinate, direct, and evaluate the efforts of all other members of the team, as and when appropriate.

(b) Select personnel for the team who have diverse ideas and skills, but who are neither compulsive 'joiners' nor compulsive 'dominators'. People with a marked ability to make their particular contribution clearly and undogmatically, with an ability to tolerate relatively high degrees of ambiguity, experimentation, and flexibility, are ideal members of creative groups.

(c) Limit participation. Synergy does not appear to be the product of everyone doing everyone else's job, but of invited and appropriate involvement in the resolution of difficult problems. Creativity may be more the product of clear assignment of duties and responsibilities than of extensive group interaction.

(d) Provide protection for the group. Assign clear budget and time limits, provide support staff to enable the group to monitor its targets, and seek to eliminate all other external pressures.

THE DEVELOPMENT OF ORGANIZATIONAL CREATIVITY

The average 'organization' man or woman has, through a process of personalization and socialization, learned to conform (Mangham, 1979, 1981); has learned that remarkable personal characteristics are unlikely to advance their careers. Most development programmes within organizations are concerned with the eradication of deviancy and non-conformity and nearly all promotion is based upon criteria that are devised to reward the person who 'fits in', who does not 'rock the boat' too much, who can be relied upon to meet the expectations of his colleagues and his subordinates. The rebels, the deviants, the nay-sayers, are unlikely to be rewarded for their efforts. Indeed, such people are either ignored, expelled, or sent upon a training programme to 'straighten them out'. A great deal of what passes for management development within organizations is concerned with the inculcation of what are taken to be the appropriate norms and, all too often, these norms encourage the suppression of deviancy, idiosyncracy, and, ultimately, of creativity.

Much of what currently passes for organization development appears to confirm this observation. Whatever the protestations to the contrary (and there are not that many), in practice, OD stresses allegiance to the group beyond all else. It is assumed that people need the warmth and acceptance of others and that they ought to reduce their 'dysfunctional' (read as deviant) behaviour in order to obtain such rewards. It is assumed that trust, collaboration, shared power, and the like are self-evidently good and a great deal of effort is often expended in enhancing these attributes within a team. In some circumstances, of course, such activities may be highly appropriate and in many, the process need not lead to 'group-think', nor to a form of sticky conformity, but for the development of creativity the process may be counter-productive; it must not be forgotten that it is the grit in the oyster that produces the pearl. Some irritant may be a precondition of creativity. In my observations of the theatre, opera, and film, some degree of irritation appeared to be actively encouraged; there was trust, collaboration, and reasonably good interpersonal relations, but these were *means* rather than *ends* in themselves which, in my observations, they all too readily become in many efforts at development within organizations. For actors and singers the team is an important vehicle for the realization of creativity, but the task – putting on a production on schedule – clearly and unequivocally is paramount; process is taken-for-granted.

In my own practice as a consultant, quite frequently my assessment of the circumstance is that those concerned do not need more trust, love, collaboration, and the like, but more deviancy and an incidence of idiosyncratic, even wild behaviour. Most organizations have well-developed, carefully rehearsed, and thoroughly constraining situational scripts (Mangham, 1978); members go on doing the same things in the same way long after such behaviour is appropriate and, as Kaufman (1972) notes, such people are *astounded* when someone suggests that there are other ways of seeing the world, and alternative ways of responding. Such organizations, and in my experience they are the norm rather than the exception, do not encourage innovation in either their form or their processes and, unless shaken out of their particular patterns by a crisis, continue to function as if there were no other way to function.

All revolutions begin in transformations of consciousness (Berger, 1963). Situational scripts which restrict creativity are socially created and socially sustained; it follows that they may be socially transformed:

> Established patterns of group life exist and persist only through the continued use of the same schemes of interpretation; and such schemes of interpretation are maintained only through their continued confirmation by the defining acts of others. It is highly important to recognize that the established patterns of group life do not carry on by themselves, but are dependent for their continuity on recurrent affirmative definition (Blumer, 1969).

The rehearsal process in the theatre and the opera is devoted to the discovery of an appropriate interpretation and to the establishment of patterns of group life such that they will be recognized by the audience. In so doing, the familiar is, in fact, made strange, since the very taken-for-grantedness of what passes for normal interaction is dissected, analysed, tried out, and re-assembled. This provides a clue to how patterns within organizations may be changed; if they can be rendered strange, if those who participate in them can be alienated from them, can become aware of them, change becomes a possibility. Putting the frighteners on established patterns of behaviour is at the heart of organization development. Creativity can be released to the extent that organization members can stand back from their everyday performances and allow *givenness* to become *possibility*.

A final caveat, however, needs to be entered. My observations strongly suggest that creative persons are not at their best unless they are working within a framework which they can take for granted while getting on with their own activity. The creativity of those concerned with the production of *Edward II* and *The Cunning Little Vixen* may have depended to a very large extent upon the routine observance of the norms in the organization by the finance people and the administrators; by most of the people most of the time. Within such a framework, the ordinary and the extraordinary co-exist and are necessary to one another. In terms of development, 'putting the frighteners' on everyone may be dysfunctional: organizations need those who stand for order and change, stability, and innovation. As Steiner (1965) notes, and as my data amply confirm, administrators can provide the stable environment in which irritating but creative people realize their potential.

REFERENCES

Barron, F. (1969) *Creative Person and Creative Process*, Holt, Rinehart and Winston, New York.

Bavelas, A. (1948) A mathematical model for group structures, *Applied Anthropology*, **7**, 16–30.

Bavelas, A. (1950) Communication patterns in task-oriented groups, *Journal of the Acoustical Society of America*, **22**, 725–730.

Berger, P. (1963) *Invitation to Sociology*, Penguin, Harmondsworth.

Blumer, H. (1969) *Symbolic Interactionism*, Prentice-Hall, New Jersey.

Goodman, R. A. and Goodman, L. P. (1974) Professional development and effective manpower utilization in temporary systems: The theatre case, Research Paper No. 22, Management in the Arts Research Program, UCLA, Los Angeles.

Gordon, W. J. J. (1961) *Synectics*, Harper, New York.

Gordon, W. J. J. (1971) *The Metaphorical Way*, Porpoise Books, Cambridge, Mass.

Kaufman, H. (1972) *The Limits of Organizational Change*, The University of Alabama Press, Alabama.

Leavitt, H. J. (1951) Some effects of certain communication patterns on group performance, *Journal of Abnormal and Social Psychology*, **46**, 38–50.

Mangham, I. L. (1978) *Interactions and Interventions in Organizations*, John Wiley and Sons, Chichester.

Mangham, I. L. (1979) *The Politics of Organizational Change*, Associated Business Press, London.

Mangham, I. L. (1981) The limits of planned change, in: *Organization Development in Europe*, Edited by K. Trebesch, Haupt, Bern.

Pelz, D. C. (1967) Creative tensions in the Research and Development climate, *Science*, **157**, 3785, 160–165.

Pelz, D. C. and Andrews, F. M. (1966) *Scientists in Organizations*, John Wiley, New York.

Poggioli, R. (1971) *The Theory of the Avant-Garde*, Harper & Row, New York.

Shaw, M. F. (1964) Communication networks, in: *Advances in Experimental Social Psychology*, Edited by L. Berkowitz, Academic Press, New York.

Shepard, H. A. (1956) Creativity in R/D teams, *Research and Engineering*, **October 1956**, 10–13.

Stein, M. I. (1975) *Stimulating Creativity: Vol. II Group Procedures*, Academic Press, London.

Steiner, G. (1965) *The Creative Organization*, University of Chicago Press, Chicago.

Torrance, E. P., Rush, C. H., Kohn, H. B., and Doughty, J. M. (1957) Fighter–interceptor combat effectiveness: A summary report, Air Force Personnel and Training Research Center, Larkland Air Force Base, Texas.

Management Development: Advances in Practice and Theory
Edited by C. Cox and J. Beck
© 1984 John Wiley & Sons Ltd

CHAPTER 10

Getting Management Development Started: The Manager as Trainer

C. F. Molander and D. Walton

INTRODUCTION

In many organizations, training, management development (MD), or organizational development (OD) specialists often regard themselves (or are seen by others) as holding the major responsibility for introducing and resourcing MD activities. This view may be taken because trainers doubt the capacity or willingness of line managers to get involved, or (perhaps more likely) as a response to the political systems operating within the organization, to establish a power base and source of influence/security from which they can fulfil what they see as an important and necessary function.

We believe, however, that the existence of 'central ownership' may actually hinder the development of managerial quality and significantly reduce the potential impact of such work on the systems and structure of the organization. If significant change on either is to be effected, the 'ownership' of development must rest with the line managers within the system, a theme well explored by Schein (1969). The primary responsibility for the development of staff within any function must be with the managers of that function, even to the extent of becoming their own consultants, diagnosticians, and trainers. Mumford (1980), amongst others, has argued that the function of the management development adviser (MDA) may be seen, therefore, as both compatible with, and indeed essential to, a manager's normal job performance.

This paper is based on the experience of one very large public service organization. It has tried to incorporate a management development activity into its operating processes by relating the nature of these activities to needs perceived by line managers at various levels within it, and by using the managers themselves as MD consultants.

THE NEED FOR STRATEGIC PLANNING

In previous years, numerous attempts have been made to provide traditional opportunities for management development:

- use of internal/external courses,
- consultants,
- action research programmes, at the levels of both individual education and systems development.

Whilst in some areas the benefits from these activities have taken root, others have rejected the approaches as 'academic', 'theoretical', or 'not relevant to our situation' – a common cry to be heard about many training events! In reviewing previous management training we found no obvious design faults, merely a generalized feeling within the culture that non-task-related activity was somehow 'unproductive' or somebody else's empire. The feeling may have been enhanced by the variety of courses which have been used in the past, and no clearly perceived rationale amongst line managers for the time and money invested.

However well-designed, programmes of individual or organizational change cannot hope to succeed if they are viewed by sections of the organization as superfluous to what they perceive as real needs. The need for adequate individual and organizational development processes within the organization is all too frequently something seen by trainers or consultants, rather than coming from the line manager. These processes will only be endorsed by the organization if, in practice, the original diagnosis was correct, and if the prescriptions which follow are relevant to the recipients' needs. We believe that for maximum effect, the major components of MD must be integrated into some form of coherent strategy to which line management is committed. Furthermore, an essential part of the strategy must be to involve line managers in determining priorities for change or development and, preferably, the methods through which it is to be achieved. This implies a need to plan the introduction/ development of MD using a coherent, contingency-based strategy.

The organization in which we have been working took this view and tried to involve a group of senior line managers in determining for themselves:

(a) what definitions of management development were useful to them;

(b) what special needs their particular part of the organization might have; and

(c) what forms of activity would be useful and who could resource them.

(N.B. The need to explore these questions provided the basis of a development programme referred to below.)

As a result of the work undertaken by the line managers, a new policy was adopted by the organization which had four significant elements.

1. It reflected interest in and, more significantly, activity towards making better use of human resources throughout the organization.

2. The three major elements of MD were included:
(a) individual training,
(b) developments in group or team settings, and
(c) improving organizational systems, patterns, or structures.
(Figure 1 shows these components as an integrated whole, any individual activity having an impact on the other two areas.)

3. Different parts of the organization prescribed action at different levels, with needs, goals, and priorities closely related to the 'real-life' situation perceived by the line managers involved.

4. The process used to define these goals and priorities resulted in a greater commitment of non-training staff for development of individuals and the organization, shown through their preparedness to become involved in further work.

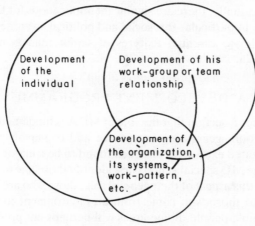

Figure 1. Management development – the integration of major components

ROLES OF THE LINE MANAGER/CENTRAL SPECIALIST

The policy or strategy devised for initiating MD had, as its cornerstone, the recognition that different parts of the organization would develop their own direction and impetus, pursue goals through their own efforts, and not be constrained by a central view of 'right' and 'wrong' approaches. Despite a strong corporate presence, the need for co-operation and forward planning of any corporate MD strategy was seen as simply a matter for good communication between managers and trainers. The line manager is primarily involved in setting standards, specifying priorities, acting as an effective trainer, and measuring achievement. The contribution of the central specialist is in resourcing the line manager – guiding, offering expert help, understanding, and clarifying – while the manager implements his version of what MD is about. His secondary role is in representing MD activity to the top of the organization as the need is more clearly recognized, and has a major responsibility for the generation of further internal consultancy skills within other line managers.

A fundamental question facing the central specialist seems to be: Who is his/her prime client? Is it really top management who initiates the need for change, its direction, and impetus, or is the process of changing an organization an essentially cumulative process which starts somewhere in the middle? Our experience suggests that the latter is the most appropriate level for initial diagnosis and this would suggest major role issues for the central specialist (Blackler and Brown, 1980). The use of MD as a tool for 'placating' movement for change without real commitment (resources and action) from top management hits at the heart of many unsuccessful MD activities. This emphasizes the importance of the Central Trainer/Specialist feeling able to represent MD activity without the confusion of personal ownership and the need to demonstrate 'success'. Equally, there are significant implications for the skills needed for this function, in particular for 'social and political awareness' and 'translative' skills which are essential features of senior management interaction (Kakabadse, 1982a, 1982b).

A DEVELOPMENT PROGRAMME

Despite our earlier assertion that the role of MDA is fundamental to every line managerial function, generating acceptance and ownership of this amongst busy, task-orientated executives has been found to be a major problem. As an initial strategy the MD specialist must first identify those line managers who are willing to accept this aspect of their general role; those who are likely to make a success of it; and those who come from an environment in which they are accepted as credible people. Some areas will perhaps not produce anyone. In our experience, it is better initially to have a piecemeal coverage of MDAs rather than try for blanket coverage with its attendant risk of having to bully managers into becoming MDAs or to cope with the consequences of developing some individuals who might do more harm than good.

Since the organization referred to in this paper adopted the 'contingency-style' approach in its MD activities, a number of specific development programmes have been run for line managers, helping them to adopt (and adapt to) the MDA role, and determine needs and prescriptions appropriate to their part of the organization.

By the end of 1983, six programmes had been completed, in which some eighty senior managers participated. Whilst each programme has been adapted to meet the needs of those attending, there has been a common modular basis. This is outlined below.

Stage 1. An attempt is made to introduce key concepts in the behavioural sciences which are relevant to MD. MD is, itself, explored, emphasis being placed on the scope of possible activities and the need to develop a strategy based on an analysis of the environment in which it will be introduced.

As much time as possible is spent in small groups using participants as resources, so they can test their assumptions and perceptions of their own working environment. By the end of the week, participants should have a common core of basic knowledge and a strongly-felt awareness of contingency theory. It is also expected that they will have adjusted to a trainer style which is designed to encourage a feeling of independence rather than traditional dependence and passivity.

Stage 2. This element concentrates on developing the personal skills that an MDA is likely to need. Great emphasis is placed on providing opportunities for participants to increase their level of self-knowledge, ability to understand and manage relationships with others, and their consultancy skills. Unlike the first stage, this stage is 'experience-based'. There are several major activities which continue throughout the stage. Instrumented learning methods are increasingly used to stimulate review of each other's behaviour and, at a different level, each other's organizational setting.

Another aspect of the programme is unstructured small-group work which has some similarity to the 'T-group', but is less intense. The programme also provides an opportunity to practise consultancy by working in self-managed groups of three, in which problems are explored. The roles played by the trainers in this part of the programme are concerned with developing sensitivity towards process issues. The techniques used are adequately explored by Casey (1976).

Stage 3. The emphasis of this stage is given over to strategic considerations relating to the participant's own role in his department. Where do managers' strengths lie as an MDA? What activities are likely to be most useful? What behaviour will be seen by others as credible? With the help of personality inventories and the like, some answers to the first question can be provided. With the help of fellow participants, as well as trainers, managers can answer the other two. Much time is given to the development of an action plan – developed and tested with the involvement of other programme members. As such, this stage falls into line with the general principles of training expressed by Lippitt and This (1966) and is based on the model described above.

Stage 4. An important element in the total programme is the project. By the end of Stage 3, participants will not only have developed an actionable plan for their longer-term role, but will have thought through the action necessary to carry out a short-term project. This is designed to be in line with the individual's overall strategy. Its purpose is to serve as a starting point for the participant's new role. A key element is an agreement between the participant and his head of department about the nature/extent/implications of the exercise.

Periodically throughout this stage, participants meet in 'sets' or self-managed work groups to review progress with projects. These meetings take place in the workplace.

Not all assignments are completed within a three-month period. For those who make significant advances, however, an opportunity is provided to discuss their approach and results to date with the management team.

DEVELOPING THE LINE MANAGER AS MDA

We have already said that, in our view, the primary responsibility for the development of staff within any function (and indeed of himself) rests with the manager of that function. However, studies by Gagné and Fleischman (1959), Schein (1969), and others, show what many trainers are often forced to recognize – success in individual training is substantially conditioned by the climate and norms established in the work-group from which the trainee comes. Furthermore, the relationships between training, team performance, and organizational systems indicate the complex nature of the development process. The line manager's perception of this process, his diagnostic skills, and his capability to intervene productively are therefore crucial. The ability of the line manager/MDA to assess accurately the possibility of change (its nature, implications, and alternative means by which it can be achieved) becomes a key issue in his extended role. It is dependent both on the manager/MDA's understanding of the notion of MD (its major techniques and goals) and his understanding of the system within which he is operating (the forces and pressures on him and on his surbordinate staff). These considerations were perhaps not fully taken into account in the work undertaken by Shell in conjunction with the Tavistock Institute (Blackler and Brown, 1980).

The ability of the line manager to intervene effectively in a complex set of systems highlights the need for clarity and reality of objectives. He must be fully involved, at both an intellectual and feelings level, in setting the purpose, and level of development activity and the approach to be adopted.

Whatever might or might not be achieved will also depend on the commitment of the manager/MDA. Two issues seem to be of fundamental importance.
1. *The question of 'ownership'*. His involvement in the overall strategy for bringing about change both in the organization and in his particular area; his understanding and acceptance of the aims and values which it represents.
2. *Himself*. The level of understanding of his own power (his role and the opportunities which are afforded to him); his skills – task knowledge, knowledge of MD, and his interactive skills for coping with his potential subsystem.

Figure 2 is an abstract of a model developed by the authors to illustrate the factors which the manager/MDA must take into account in developing a *personal strategy* for MD. The model is used as a major component in the

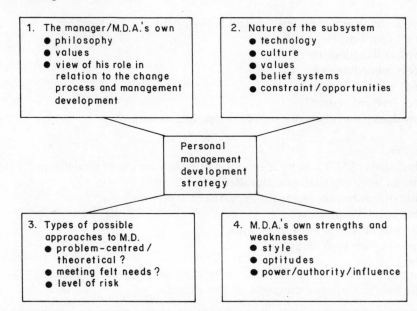

Figure 2. Personal management development strategy

development programme outlined in an earlier section. Its intention is to enable the course member to analyse his role, his view of the change process, his commitment to action on return to work, and the types of intervention which are likely to meet with some success in his particular work-unit. The model is supported by inputs on role-analysis and personal decision-making, but its fundamental significance is in the practical questions which stem from each section. He is asked:

Section 1
What has the development programme meant to you?
Has any significant change occurred?
In what areas?
What is your view of the goals of MD?
What should it be trying to achieve in your part of the system?
What effect does this have on you?
What part have you to play?

Section 2
What is your formal role in your department?
What other roles do you have at your disposal?
What indications are there of the need for change/development?
What opportunities for MD work exist?

Is your involvement in development activity helped or hindered by:
  (a) your boss (bosses)?
  (b) colleagues/others?
  (c) subordinates?
  (d) culture/climate?
  (e) reward system?
How does the system cope with MD-type interventions?

Section 3
Which area of MD activity seems most fitted to your goals? (See Figure 3.)
How do long/short-term needs differ?
What difficulties are facing the department at present?
What needs doing most?
Who would benefit most, from what?
How risky are your ideas?
Why?

	Individual	Group	Organization
Prescriptive	General management courses Qualification course T group etc.	Team-building, Project-based Learning, Some forms of management by objectives etc.	Management by objectives Some forms of organization development etc.
Diagnostic	Appraisal Self-assessment Needs analysis Counselling Coaching and career planning Specified experience, Job rotation, Task-related courses etc.	Analysis of problems Identification of needs, Assessment and appraisal Role negotiation, Team-building etc.	Organization analysis and feedback

Figure 3. Types of management development activity

Section 4
What are your strengths/abilities in:
  (a) understanding MD technology?
  (b) consultancy skills?
  (c) interactive skills?

How high is your personal commitment to implementing MD as a vehicle of change?
How will your style affect any approach you adopt?
What degree of personal risk can you accept?
What can't you do/need help for?

DIFFICULTIES AND DEVELOPMENTS

Since the introduction of the programme some five years ago great progress has been made in some areas, and from an external view, apparently little in others. A number of issues have arisen which warrant further comment.

Selection of the Line Manager/MDA

A critical task for the specialist must be to help the organization select which of its line managers are to be encouraged to develop their general role. During the initial programmes, some difficulty was experienced in that initial perceptions of the programmes tended to highlight traditional reasons for involvement in MD programmes: some inadequacies existed or improvement was needed for individuals or sections. For example, the need for new managers to 'know about handling people' or to develop particular skills, such as coping with conflict and change.

As awareness of the programme's implications for organizational change grew, some individuals responded to what they perceived as a considerable threat to their existing organization or management style. Some of them felt inadequate to deal with what they recognized as a needed, but difficult and wide-ranging, task. Issues about commitment of senior management, their understanding of OD implications, and ethical questions about participation in management were debated, in addition to personal fears and questions of worth. To some extent these issues have been raised on all subsequent programmes, but greater selectivity of participants has enabled these issues to be clarified, using criteria concerning:

(1) existing role and scope for change;
(2) relationship to policy-making levels; and
(3) previous management education or 'comfort' with conceptual tools.

One approach adopted was to identify line managers with major resource management responsibilities – who has to manage the most people/money/ equipment? Another approach was at a more subjective level – to identify managers who were already known for 'clear thinking' and sympathy toward new ideas.

Some participants were selected, unfortunately, for 'remedial' purposes or for political reasons. Such problems are only to be expected, however, for power, leadership and politics are frequently covert processes which cannot be ignored (Hill, 1972; Blackler and Brown, 1980).

The systems implications of MD/OD interventions are issues for both specialist and participants to resolve and is the essence of the model now in the development programme.

Trainer Style

The need to encourage interdependence between participants and trainers/ MD specialists poses many problems, particularly where line management have expectations of trainer-styles which lead to passive, lecture-type situations. In the programmes run to date, many participants have been previously exposed to that style only and introducing mechanisms for encouraging learner responsibility without trainer-rejection has had to be managed very carefully. A phased introduction into participants managing their own time has been adopted and norms established which rely on small group activity, instrumented learning, and peer-group counselling.

Success here is a major determinant of owernship of MD in the workplace. The greater the dependence which is retained after the programme, the less participants have been able to function as a facilitator or catalyst within their own organizations. Interdependence also encourages skill and understanding of the consultative process, the dynamics and realities of the change processes upon which the programme is based, and confidence in 'handling' behavioural science applications.

Setting Targets

Participants must set targets for themselves within the development programme, as a means of increasing the level of 'ownership'. It is equally important that managers learn to establish their own targets for MD generally – targets which will be seen by those they affect as being relevant to the needs of their part of the organization. The identification process is started by the involvement of top management in the development programme, is continued by means of the model outlined previously, and subsequently in support networks gradually being established within the organization as a whole. In reality, MD (or OD) is a question of movement. From what starting point, however, and reaching what goals – these are questions the central MD specialist may be unqualified to answer and can only be effectively tackled by those at the 'coalface', i.e. the manager. A major success in the programme has been the progressive focusing of objectives by line managers and the need for review of departmental action plans.

Role of the Internal Specialist

External facilitators working with organizations must inevitably rely on the participants in their programmes to demonstrate vicariously their real contribution. They may have difficulty (though some do not!) in breaking the relationship, but in the end the link is broken. The internal specialist can have a continuing role to play which, if an effective internal OD network is constructed, can be of immense value. His role is essentially at two levels.

(1) Representing the MD/OD process to the top of the organization. Whilst rarely in a top management position himself, access to top policy-makers and those who control resource allocation is essential. Political skills for dealing with that situation are required and the specialist must demonstrate through his own behaviour that the MD/OD process has much to offer, despite the variety of activities in which he may be involved. The process must be seen as a worthy competitor for priority. The extent to which the specialist can work on questions of relevance, as well as awareness and understanding at the top, will determine his success, and what resourcing he can expect.

The ability to work within a political system and affect the decision-making/ resourcing systems of the organization is crucial both for the internal specialist's acceptance and, more importantly, the success in MD/OD achieved by line managers/MDAs.

(2) Resources. Working with line management who have developed clearer perceptions of organizational ills and the need for development can create problems of expectations which cannot always be met centrally. The developments on which this paper is based have created a 'grass-roots' realization of the need for change and willingness to find ways of achieving it. Some managers/MDAs still view individual development as the 'trainer/specialist's patch' and the workload in terms of basic skill-training (including management skills) continues to grow. A much greater involvement on the part of the manager/MDA is seen, however, and the skills for which help is sought are noticeably those requiring deeper, more fundamental reflection, often only possible in an off-job setting.

Support networks have now been established within each departmental setting, and line managers are now co-operating in reviewing the capacity of the organization to achieve its goals. The establishment of these groups was negotiated by the staff themselves with senior managers at top level.

A consequence of this has been the demand from line managers to establish an appraisal process, to meet their needs for clarity of purpose and direction.

Besides this strategic development, the key improvements which are taking place are in the approach which managers/MDAs take in the day-to-day work situations and the extent to which the underlying values in MD/OD work are being translated into practical experience. Consultation, participation in targeting, involvement in decision-making, conscious effort in team-building, are all conscious behaviour on the part of manager/MDAs and one of an enabling and synergistic nature. This type of activity is now seen by ex-participants to be part of their normal role. The skills acquired during the programme in counselling and consultancy have proved useful both in diagnosing needs and helping managers to respond.

CONCLUSIONS

The organization referred to in this paper is typical of many where the history of MD is sending staff on courses with the subsequent complaint about difficulties of transferring the skills acquired back to the work situation. The use of a contingency-based strategy has enabled the programme:

(a) To deal with general principles – but with the specific situation in focus.

(b) To work towards managers becoming MDAs using self-resourcing networks for follow-up and reinforcement.

(c) To reduce dependence on outside consultants, thus enabling the organization to build its own expertise.

(d) To offer participants freedom in diagnosing what is to be done and what is to be gained from it; asking them to take over responsibility for the MD process.

(e) To help participants face the challenges and risks which are necessary if they are truly to be involved in facilitating change in their part of the organization.

One thing is clear: an overall strategy such as this, or individual strategies adopted by particular line managers, must be tailored to the culture of the organization receiving it. The extent to which any line manager will accept the trainer/MDA role is likely to be governed by a complex web of decisions which must be clarified and related to the expectations which his senior managers have of him. In this, the programme described has its roots: asking managers what they believe MD is about and should achieve, and asking them to take ownership of it. In essence, the programme asks the manager to re-define his task and concept of the organization by re-thinking his two basic commitments – meeting his job performance standards and protecting/developing human resources within the organization.

The strategy is a task-oriented, group focus model which sees management or organizational development as an open system, interacting in many diverse ways within other systems, technologies, and environments. The initial risk involved is largely for the specialist in coping with his need for ownership – '*Can I let go?*'

REFERENCES

Blackler, F. H. M. and Brown, C. A. (1980) *Whatever Happened to Shell's New Management Philosophy?* Saxon House, London.

Casey, D. (1976) The emerging role of the set adviser, *Journal of European Training*, **5**, 3.

Gagné, R. M. and Fleischmann, E. A. (1959) *Psychology and Human Performance: An Introduction to Psychology*, Henry Holt, Rinehart and Winston, New York.

Hill, P. (1972) *Toward a New Philosophy of Management*, Barnes and Noble, New York.

Kakabadse, A. (1982a) *Politics in Organisations*, MCB Publications, Bradford.

Kakabadse, A. (1982b) *Culture of Social Services*, Gower.

Lippitt, G. L. and This, L. E. (1966) Learning theories and training, *Training and Development Journal*, **April/May 1966**.

Mumford, A. (1980) *Making Experience Pay*, McGraw-Hill, Maidenhead.

Schein, E. H. (1969) *Process Consultation: Its Role in Organisation Development*, Addison-Wesley, Massachussets.

Management Development: Advances in Practice and Theory
Edited by C. Cox and J. Beck
© 1984 John Wiley & Sons Ltd

CHAPTER 11

Helping Self-development to Happen

Paul Temporal

INTRODUCTION

The concepts involved in self-development are now quite well known and industry has begun to show considerable interest in this field. Unfortunately, there are few guidelines for practitioners who wish to apply these concepts in an industrial setting. The issues which confront the practitioner are:

1. How can they translate theory into practice?
2. What kind of self-development do managers want?
3. What type of self-development activities are most appropriate for managers in industry who are faced with pressures on their time and resources?
4. What is the role of the management development practitioner in facilitating self-development?
5. How can the practitioner sell the concepts to his directors?

All these questions and more have not been answered by exponents of theory; instead they are left as problems for those in industry who want to take up new ideas, to solve in the best way they can.

This paper tries to answer many of these questions, and outlines one way in which self-development techniques have been implemented in a multi-site company. It is written from the point of view of a practitioner in industry.

My story is concerned with some of my experience gained over the last three years, having made the transition from the academic world to industrial life. As an academic I admired greatly (and still do) the concepts, values, and beliefs of those who concerned themselves with helping managers to learn, and I tried also to make some contribution in this very important field. The more I got involved in the work, the more I found the urge was present in me to leave the academic life and enter industry, first in order to further my own learning and development, and secondly – and equally important – to try to make my ideas work in a real setting. I was always conscious of the fact that industry seemed slow to pick up new ideas arising from educationists, and yet I wanted to apply my thoughts, and those of others, in a constructive way. My curiosity was aroused and I had to get in there and find out the answer to many questions in the area of self-development, none more important than that which asks: Can self-development work in industry?

The company I joined was a well respected one and yet it had fairly traditional views on training and development, and I wondered how successful I would be in getting the company to listen, and to let me do what I wanted to do. I quickly found that new ideas had to be fought for and 'sold' to the decision-makers – and opposition had to be overcome. I found that I had to sell myself too, and prove that I was more than a 'bloody academic'. That process did not come easy to me, and it took time, but within a year I had made some progress by giving presentations to senior people, encouraging the interested to sell my concepts, persuading the powerful to give them a go, dissuading opposition from squashing embryonic activities, and generally pushing for commitment at director level. My ambition was to implement self-development activities for managers in some way and test their effectiveness; I had to become a salesman. What, then, did I sell to top management?

The message was contained in the following statement:

Why self-development?

Because of a belief in *one* simple fundamental premise:

'That any effective system for management development must *increase* the manager's capacity and willingness to take control over and be responsible for events, and particularly for himself and his own learning.'

I then had to go a stage further and explain why self-development activities could provide what other forms of management development could not. There were three main points here:

Why self-development activities?

1. Companies have a responsibility to help people learn and develop, but individuals should take control over and be more responsible for their own learning and development.

2. Normal training and development programmes do not cater fully for the self-developing manager, who needs to make things happen (I gave here an example of the transfer of learning problem often associated with training courses, where application of learning is very difficult back at work).

3. Self-development activities give managers time to reflect on past experiences, experiment with new learning, and plan their own development and the application of their learning.

After achieving acceptance of the underlying philosophy of self-development. I had then to outline what possible benefits I thought there could be arising from self-development activities. The points had to be acceptable to industrialists who look for returns on investments.

Benefits for companies in promoting self-development

1. The encouragement and practice of self-development contributes towards the climate of participation that is being encouraged in industry, and this increases the commitment of individuals who see that they do have some responsibility for, and control over, their destiny.

2. Once established, the self-development philosophy enables organizations to keep up with the dynamics of change as it affects the organizations and the individuals in them, because managers are encouraged to think about change and improvement.

3. Management development and succession planning are made easier and are brought into sharper focus by discussions that take place with individuals concerning their strengths, weaknesses, expectations, ambitions, preferences, and learning and development experiences.

4. Selection and promotion decisions are likely to be more effective as a result, and more readily accepted by individuals who have contributed towards evaluating their own achievements.

5. Self-development activities are probably the most cost-effective way in which an organization can develop its human resources. They produce positive results in an economic way – DIY.

These were my basic arguments for implementing self-development, but I had not as yet said what kind of self-development activity I wanted to put into action. I now had to say what I wanted to do, and I chose self-development groups as my starting point. I opted for this route because I think group activities can be much more meaningful than individual ones, as individuals can develop themselves within a group context, and others can help them do this. They, in turn, can help the others who form the group with them.

What do self-development groups do?

1. They identify individual and group development needs, problem areas, and issues of concern, and members help each other to identify solutions and select the resources necessary to achieve these solutions.

2. The resources selected may be internal or external to the groups, and the groups assess and monitor how effective they are in achieving individual and group goals.

In conjunction with this statement and a verbal description of how I saw group formation, it remained only to outline the likely benefits that the self-development groups would hold for the people involved in them.

Benefits of self-development groups for individuals

1. The sharing of experience and abilities between people who have different roles, experiences, backgrounds, status, futures, ambitions, etc.

2. Groups deal with *real* development problems and issues and generate *real* solutions to them.

3. Group activities are adaptable to the contingencies affecting different individuals in different parts of the organization.

4. Group cohesion and motivation should help towards the achievement of group and individual goals.

5. They should result in improved work performance and individual behaviour.

6. They give individuals the time to step out of the work environment and reflect on past experiences, current issues, and future plans concerned with their development.

The board of directors agreed to the setting up of two self-development groups to start with and accepted certain fundamental principles associated with their operation. First, what each group or the individuals did when they met was up to them – there was to be no direction from outside. Secondly, the groups could keep their activities confidential if they wished (although later this was to be a problem that each group felt needed managing in terms of the interface between the group and the organization). Thirdly, the company expected no *short-term* benefits for itself or individuals. It was generally hoped that the company would have better managers in the long term as a result of the activities. Fourthly, the time spent on self-development activities was to be left to the group members, and fifthly, all self-development group meetings were to take place off-site, mainly to avoid interruptions and produce a more relaxed atmosphere.

THE COMPOSITION OF THE GROUPS

What we were aiming for in order to create opportunity for maximum learning was a complete mix of people in terms of ages, industrial experience, length of time in the company, status levels, disciplines, and functions. Nominations were obtained from senior executives, who were fully briefed on all the concepts involved and asked to put forward people, who they thought would be most likely to benefit from this kind of activity. Many nominees were classed as being in the 'high flyer' category, but others of lower potential were also put forward and were included in the groups.

Participants (all were accepted, none refused) were briefed by their bosses and myself, but they were given a choice of whether they wanted to take part in the activities or not. No pressure was applied, and they were told that anything they wanted to do in the groups would be regarded as being legitimate. The two groups each contained seven people; no one opted out.

THE START-UP EVENTS

Each group met for the first time over a two-day period off-site with two trainers (whose role will be clarified below). After these events each group decided when, how often, and for how long it met. The main purpose of the start-up events was:

(a) to help individuals explore the concepts involved in learning and development by reflecting on their past experiences;

(b) to allow each group to establish its own rules and the climate it felt necessary for activity to continue; and

(c) to let members diagnose the issues, at which, they wanted to look.

EXAMPLES OF ISSUES LOOKED AT WITHIN THE GROUPS

Below is a short list of examples of issues that members have been concerned with looking at, but it is important to emphasize that for each group there were 40–60 issues regarded as being important, from which priorities had to be chosen. The issues were very wide-ranging covering organizational, group, personal, work-oriented, and non-work-oriented aspects.

● Managing the tension between work and home life.
● Help in modifying 'firefighting' behaviour at work.
● Improving site and inter-site communications.
● Sorting out short- and long-term career goals.
● Help in developing presentation skills.
● Help in motivating a subordinate bored with his job.
● Help in solving a problem concerning my relationship with my boss.
● Starting my own business – is it worth the risk?
● Improving management development for technical people.
● Why do people view me as a miserable bastard?
● The need to learn about pricing and costing.

The groups went on after the start-up events to meet, on average, once every 5 weeks, off-site, for between 4 and 6 hours. However, in addition to full group meetings, subgroups have met quite frequently in order to continue to work on certain issues of interest.

ONE YEAR ON. WHAT HAD BEEN LEARNT?
HOW HAD PEOPLE DEVELOPED? A CRUDE EVALUATION

After about a year, I had no doubt that members had learnt quite a lot and developed in many ways, but there was a need to qualify this in some way. After talking with the two groups, it was agreed that a relatively formal evaluation of learning was appropriate, the results of which I can now tell you about.

The sources of data were:

(a) the individuals, and

(b) other people who work with them (mainly bosses).

Data from Individuals

With regard to the 14 individuals (7 each group) who took part in the evaluation, two methods of data collection were used – one closed-ended and one open-ended questionnaire.

(1) With the closed-ended questionnaire, each person was asked to identify if they felt that they had improved at all with regard to 13 managerial skills/ qualities as a result of being in the self-development group. Rating scales were used as a measure of perceived improvement. The results were analysed to give a profile for all 14 participants as a group (Figure 1).

The profiles show that, on average, the participants felt that they had improved on all 13 items, although there were differences between individuals and between the two groups. It is important to note that no individual felt that he had regressed in any way on any item. Also important is the fact that there were greater improvements on some quality dimensions than others. For instance, items 1 and 13 showed large increases (Situational Facts and Self-Knowledge) and this indicates that there appears to be a balanced learning taking place – in this case regarding organizational and personal issues.

(2) With the open-ended questionnaire, participants were asked how and in what way they thought they had developed or learnt something – if at all – as a result of being a member of the groups. The written replies brought forward a large quantity of information which was subsequently analysed and categorized, as shown in Table 1.

Learning items concerned with the company were the most referred to, and were wide-ranging in nature, and they tended to be knowledge- rather than skills-based. However, participants felt also that they had learnt many things about other people and themselves, and this learning was skills- rather than knowledge-based. Overall, this aspect of the evaluation shows evidence of

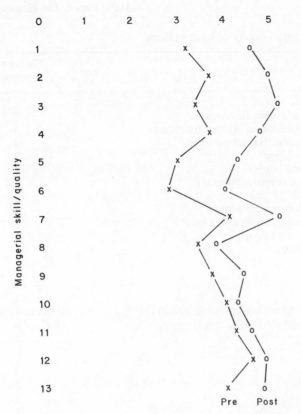

Managerial skill/quality

Pre Post

Key to profiles:

Item 1. *Situational facts* – knowledge of the business organization, all aspects of the company, the environment affecting it, etc.

Item 2. *Relevant professional knowledge* – knowledge of technical aspects of job and background, e.g. relevant legislation.

Item 3. *Continuing sensitivity to events* – sensitivity to all situations including figures, facts, feelings, methods, opinions.

Item 4. *Analytical, problem-solving, and decision-making skills.*

Item 5. *Social skills and abilities* – leadership, influencing, communicative skills.

Item 6. *Emotional resilience* – ability to cope with stress and pressure while still remaining sensitive to feelings and issues. Flexibility, adaptability.

Item 7. *Proactivity* – goal-oriented behaviour. Responding purposefully to events. Making things happen rather than waiting for them to happen.

Item 8. *Imagination/creativity* – ability to come up with unique, new approaches to situations, etc.

Item 9. *Mental agility* – Mental capacity for understanding complex situations, and speed of doing this. 'Juggling' skills. Thinking on one's feet.

Item 10. *Balanced learning habits and skills* – ability for abstract, concrete, practical thought, capacity for observation, reflection, ability to learn by discovery, etc.

Item 11. *You and your job role (1)* – extent to which your role is seen clearly by yourself, how well you have negotiated it.

Item 12. *You and your job role (2)* – the amount of commitment you have to your job role.

Item 13. *Self-knowledge* – goals, ambitions, strengths, weaknesses, ideals, values.

Figure 1. Movement on management skills/qualities. Combined data from both groups. (The managerial skills/qualities listed above are based on those to be found in Pedlar, M., Burgoyne, J. and Boydell, T. (1978) A Manager's Guide to Self-development, McGraw-Hill, London.)

Table 1   Self-reports analysis – range of learning items

	Number of references
A. *Company*	
More integrated view of the whole company	7
Understanding and appreciation of other functions	4
Understanding other people's work problems	4
Specific company knowledge	3
Overcoming hierarchical barriers	2
Better understanding of corporate strategy	2
Internal political skills	2
Better relations with senior management	1
Closer working relationships with colleagues	1
Identifying more with other people	1
Costing/Pricing knowledge	1
B. *Other people*	
Interpersonal skills	4
Listening skills	1
Coaching/counselling	1
Awareness of how others see me	1
More tolerant of others	1
C. *Self*	
Greater self-awareness	3
Better communications	2
Greater self-responsibility	1
Learning how to learn	1

substantial learning, especially about the business, which in some way reflects the composition of the groups, with individuals from various functions and levels of authority within the organization taking part.

Information from Other People (Mainly Bosses)

Interviews with people who worked closely with the participants resulted in various answers being given to the following question: 'What changes have you noticed in .... since he started attending the self-development group and to what extent are these attributed to the group?'

Typical information given is summarized in Table 2.

The results here appear to confirm what the participants themselves had thought regarding their learning and development, being a mixture of gains in knowledge and skills to do with the company and themselves. Two points are of particular importance, however:

(1) The managers responsible for group members actually said that work

Table 2 Reports from others (mainly bosses)

A. Company
　Greater knowledge/understanding of other departments
　Greater company knowledge
　Greater understanding of his role in the company

B. Self
　Greater self-confidence
　Increased maturity
　Development of latent ability
　Doing a better job
　Improved use of initiative
　More prepared to speak his mind
　Better at problem-solving
　Broader outlook

C. Negative
　No change
　Disappointed at lack of development

Note: Comments from people who thought that certain improvements might have occurred irrespective of the self-development group activities are excluded from this table.

performance had improved in some cases as a direct result of attendance at group meetings.

(2) Two comments were negative, and suggested no change in individual behaviour at all.

WHAT ELSE HAD HAPPENED IN THE GROUPS?

Both groups had spent a great deal of time in looking at the issues they had diagnosed in the start-up event, and new issues also came to the fore from time to time. The good thing, I believe, about their activities was that they spent time not only on personal and often very private discussions, but also on matters in the organization that concerned them. This helped them achieve balanced learning and also gave the organization some benefits and an idea of what they were doing. Time spent on discussing Pricing and Costing, for example, led to both groups and staff from two sites visiting each other, giving talks on related matters, and discussing problems related to their different needs for financial information. This helped improve inter-site communications and resolved differences of opinion between functional groups of managers.

A further example of the interface between members of the groups and the company was seen when one group came to the conclusion that the key to their group's success and the incentive for others to be formed, lay in the giving of information back to the company about its activities, and somehow involving other people at work. Individual members agreed to talk periodically to their bosses about what they were doing, but the group as a whole decided to tackle one large corporate issue that all had raised early on as an area of concern and which affected all levels of management.

The idea was to improve site communications, particularly through strengthening the existing briefing structure in the company, together with the introduction of other policies and procedures. The group eventually wrote a report and gave a presentation to the board of directors on the problem area, together with recommendations for a solution. The managing director's reaction was to ask the group to implement their report in full. The group gained tremendous motivation from the exercise, succeeded in involving others in the organization in the exercise, learnt a lot about how to present ideas to top management, and the company gained clarification of a problem area and the action-plan to solve it from an objective source.

There are other examples of group activities which could be mentioned in connection with benefits for the company, especially in the area of appraisals and corporate strategy, but the main message, I think, is that self-development groups can benefit the individuals in them in a variety of ways, and provide the company with learning managers who are highly constructive in their relationships with the business, being motivated to improve themselves and the working environment that affects their day-to-day performance.

THE ROLE OF THE TRAINER

Depending on how the groups are set up and briefed, and the decisions made by the groups early on in their lives, the role of the trainer could be minimal or highly involved. I found myself highly involved in the groups I set up in the company mainly because they asked me to fulfil many roles as well as asking me to participate as a member. I was thus required to attend every meeting and take part in individual group, and subgroup, activities, including sharing my self-development issues and problems with them, and over time I found myself acting in the following additional roles:

As a catalyst   There to help self-development to happen.

As a resource   A source of expertise for groups/individuals to draw on.

As an adviser   On issues associated with the groups and the organization.

As a co-ordinator   Of group activities and events.

As a trainer   When asked to give direct training inputs in certain areas.

I found the flexibility demanded of me to switch between these roles difficult at times, the biggest dilemma of all being taking decisions regarding when to operate in the conflicting roles of trainer/facilitator and group member. I was helped, however, by being fortunate enough to use another person from outside the organization to help run the groups. He provided a great deal of objectivity and fresh thought during difficult times, and continuity when I could not be there.

CONCLUSIONS

In conclusion, I will summarize a few points which stand out to me as being important in assessing the effectiveness of self-development groups.

1. It appears from the formal evidence collected that participants learn a lot in terms of knowledge and skills, especially on corporate aspects – they get a wider, more integrated view of the business as a whole. They also learn a lot about themselves and others through the group processes.

2. This learning tends to be different to that gained on courses – it is well balanced and precisely geared to their own needs and to their work if they want it to be. Because managers can choose their own learning goals, the application of that learning becomes easier, and is more helpful to them in improving their work performance. Their self-confidence is enhanced accordingly as they realize that they can influence the organization and contribute towards change.

3. The company itself will certainly get better managers in the long term because of the above points, but it is also probable that the company may gain some short-term benefits which could be of strategic importance.

4. Reflection is a very important part of the self-development process. Many members commented on this, and being off-site helps them to reflect as they are taken out of the firing line for a few hours. If the groups are to work well, this time must be given high priority.

5. It would not be fair to say that self-development groups are a panacea to the field of management development. There are drawbacks, in particular I have seen one or two cases where self-development groups have not helped people – they just have not worked for them. They are also moderately time-consuming, both for the managers and for myself as a trainer.

6. Taken overall, however, in this company the groups have proved to be highly successful. They still continue to function (and others have started) and directors are highly committed to them – because they bring results and are cost-effective. I would not close, though, without saying that more evaluative evidence is needed in this relatively new area.

Finally, I would like to say that I have enjoyed working with the groups immensely, and hope that others will be encouraged by this story to try something new in industry. If my experience is anything to go by, they will benefit enormously in terms of their own learning and development.

Management Development: Advances in Practice and Theory
Edited by C. Cox and J. Beck
© 1984 John Wiley & Sons Ltd

CHAPTER 12

'Just Tell Me What To Do' – *Some Reflections on Running Self-development Training Programmes*

S. Fineman and A. J. McLean

INTRODUCTION

This paper is an account of the design and running of a new management development programme. It is also a discussion of some of the broader questions raised by programmes concerned with heightening levels of awareness and facilitating personal growth. We begin by describing the intentions behind the new programme and explaining key features of its design, and follow this in the second half of the paper by outlining our experiences, together with some of the dilemmas that we encountered.

BACKGROUND: A REASON FOR CHANGE

Approximately three years ago, at the invitation of an organization's Head of Training, we began designing a management development programme to supersede their current activities. As far as we could see there were four main reasons why they saw the need to change. The first three were based on apparently sound intellectual reasoning, and the fourth, probably the main impetus to change, was primarily emotional.

First the Training Manager felt that the time was right for a training programme more specifically designed to meet the needs of his organization; one that allowed more time to dwell on particular organizational issues and one that took foci other than the current ones of 'team effectiveness' and 'individual styles'. In short, something that was more tailor made. For example, the issue of union power, and attitudes towards the union generally, was especially crucial in the day-to-day activities of most managers. Similarly, the role boundedness of many organizational members was a key feature of the culture to

177

which the trainers wished to draw the attention of course participants, and to encourage them to explore further. The second reason for developing a new course had to do with the trainers' doubts concerning some of the implicit values and judgements that they considered to be inherent in their current 'package' – for example, the implication of 'one best way' to manage seemed to fit less and less comfortably with their growing belief in a contingent approach to management. The Training Department was looking for a programme that heightened awareness, but in a variety of directions and through the use of a *variety* of theoretical frameworks, and away from a pervasive and seductive core model.

Thirdly, the internal trainers were uneasy with one aspect of their current programme's reputation within the company: namely, that of being like a managerial assault course because of its intensity and pace. Word had spread through the organization that it was 'gruelling', that it could 'break you', that people 'take each other to pieces' during it, and that, like a spell in the army, the more uncomfortable the experience, the more good it was doing you. Some course members would arrive having been thus briefed in a mood of grim stoicism, prepared to 'get stuck in' right from the word go. Others were exceptionally cautious and guarded. An even more extreme reaction was to seek to avoid becoming seriously involved. According to the mythology, this last group often 'came off worst', being the subject of intense group pressure and unwelcome scrutiny. This leads us to the fourth, and we suggest major, reason for their decision to replace the programme.

There had been an evident, and seemingly growing, concern on the part of the Training Manager and his staff at the deeply disturbing effect that the T-group type features of their programme had had on a small number of participants. In particular, the trainers had been alarmed by the disturbed and abnormal behaviour of some course members. To our knowledge, these extreme reactions were rare and probably totalled no more than three or four individuals in the entire five-year history of involvement with the programme. However, judging by the frequent occasions when these episodes were mentioned, the impact of such cases on the trainers was clearly disproportional to their quantity.

Over a period of approximately 18 months and in close consultation with the Training Department, we gradually developed our own programme.

Our overall objectives were as follows.

1. To enhance managers' skills of handling work relationships by extending their understanding and their range and level of inter-personal skills.

2. To encourage them to take increasing and eventually ultimate responsibility for managing their own learning, so decreasing their dependency on the trainers, and indeed on training events.

3. To move from a highly structured series of events, designed and administered by the trainers, towards a far more contingent set of activities aimed

at meeting the specific work-related needs of participants; the latter events to be collaboratively negotiated and designed both by trainers and participants.

Our means of attempting to meet these objectives was to use both processual and structural devices. Processually, we proposed to adopt standard techniques such as structured reflections, personal feedback, gentle confrontations, periodically drawing attention to processual issues, and encouraging people to explore the intended and unintended consequences of their own and others' actions.

Structurally, we wanted to encourage this process of transition by leaving more and more opportunity for the participant to influence the content of the programme. We decided to begin in a relatively traditional fashion in the first part of the course, with trainers as experts accepting the major responsibility for content, design, and success or failure. Thereafter, we wished to shift the emphasis towards the trainees with a correspondingly diminishing role for the trainers, until ultimately the trainee was managing his own learning almost completely independently.

We constructed a four-part programe to achieve this transition.

1. *Pre-course work.* We began by asking participants to read (before attending the course) an introductory booklet written by ourselves. It contained four substantive topics – motivation, conflict, leadership, and stress – to be used as the vehicles for raising awareness about relationship issues. Participants were also asked to complete a series of self-administered questionnaires which were designed to relate the theoretical ideas in the booklet to their own job situation. These instruments provided further data for use later in the programme.

2. *Structured experiences and reflections.* This aspect of the programme comprised five days of pre-planning, tightly scheduled, experiential exercises with periodic and structured reflections together with lecturettes.

The first four days were designed around the topics in the pre-course booklet. The final day was taken up by a day-long organizational simulation which served to integrate each of the subject areas into the context of a living complex production organization. It also acted as an ideal device to draw attention to key aspects of the organizational culture, and to provoke a questioning of many taken-for-granted assumptions regarding the organization functioning.

3. *Interim period – 4–6 months.* Following the first part of the programme, course members were asked to review and note down key aspects of their relationships at work in the light of their experiences on the course, and hopefully with a new awareness. They could then use this information as a basis for designing events specifically for themselves in the final phase of the programme. They were asked to send us their thoughts and observations some weeks before we convened again.

4. *Developing inter-personal skills.* This part of the programme represented the sharp end of the self-development philosophy we were adopting. It was

conceived as essentially a skills development workshop whereby individual participants would bring with them a personal agenda of items they wished to work on. Given the probable strangeness of this approach to our course members, we introduced the event by describing self-management through a 'swamp' model of responsibility for management problems, based on an idea put forward by John Adams of Case Western University. The essence of this view is that one can define the locus of responsibility for an issue or problem (in total or in part) as within oneself, or outside of oneself (e.g. '*They* are responsible', or 'it's the organization's fault'). Similarly, one can see responsibility for action as in the immediate present, or sometime in the future. The more the responsibility is projected outside of one's self, into the future, the more 'swampy' and unmanageable it becomes. Our aim was to focus on those issues that could be defined and owned *personally* and worked on in the here-and-now. We could do little with swamp problems in a training session.

We anticipated that a variety of learnings could follow. At one level, new inter-personal skills, perhaps in terms of handling a disciplinary interview, or possibly experimenting with new ways of communicating with a superior; skills of negotiating, counselling, influencing, self-assertion and so on. The possibilities were endless and limited only by the extent of individual requests. At another level, we aimed to encourage participants to internalize the approach to learning and skill development that we were using, so that they would end up able to manage their own learning independently of the trainers. The familiar notion of encouraging them to learn how to learn. We also believed that the process of negotiating and managing this part of the programme would in itself generate many 'real' issues concerning the ways in which individuals manage their relationships with each other.

This, then, was our thinking and the key intentions behind our design decisions. How did it work out?

WHAT HAPPENED

Structured Experiences and Reflections

Participants engaged actively and, generally enthusiastically, in all our exercises and events. They were clearly *most* comfortable when the exercises had a tight format with a clear outcome – such as winning or losing. So, for example, when we ran the organizational simulation with an organizational hierarchy and a product to make, they eagerly grasped the opportunity to compete. They loved involvement in a leadership exercise, again with very specific instructions including a nominated leader, a task, a required solution, and a time limit. The atmosphere was electric during these events.

But of course we were aiming to move them away from the games. Self-development required *learning* from the exercises; *reflecting* on one's personal behaviour and how the things one did in the exercises affected self and others; and ultimately *building* on any insights for future practice. 'Are there other ways of doing it which I haven't tried before?' Consequently, each exercise or event was followed by a detailed debrief and discussion in three small working groups. Participants were asked privately to record their experiences soon after an exercise, and these were used, together with tutor feedbacks, in the groups. In these sessions, where parts of self were being presented and analysed for the first time, we encountered a range of reactions. A number of people appeared threatened and responded by denying the validity of the exercise: 'Yes, it was great fun, but of course I wouldn't behave like that at work.' These people, and others, would be very reluctant to turn observations on themselves. They would react defensively and would happily accuse another party of fouling things up or behaving inappropriately. In one group, a person refused to say a word because he 'didn't like people watching him'. This contrasted with someone else who was very busy trying to convince us that the autocratic leadership style he had enacted in an exercise was *not* really like him at all. Yet reactions were not all so entrenched. Another group displayed a mass of energy and seemed to listen and reflect. While ownership of problems varied across members, there was indeed some recognition of 'self' and of differences between people.

So our initial consciousness-raising did just this – but not always consciousness about self. Nevertheless we recognized that the process had to take its natural pace for different individuals. The 6 months break before the final phase would provide a necessary period for consideration and cogitation.

Developing Inter-personal Skills

The three syndicates took to this phase of the programme in three very different ways. One group was utterly bewildered. The little work that they had done in the 6 months interim period was declared in terms of broad generalizations; and from there they would not budge. They turned on the tutor in anger and resentment. *He* had the expertise to help them. *He* could construct exercises. *He* could tell them what problems they should work on. Why didn't he do that? The tutor's valiant attempts to show them what they were doing, and encourage them to free themselves from dependency on him, failed. He met a tough, collusive block of disenchanted people.

The second group was in a different world. They had masses of energy. They had met during the interim period and had drawn up a list of things they identified as problems. They were very 'tasky', and looked like a trainer's dream come true. Yet it turned out to be rather more complicated. Their most important objective appeared to be wanting to be 'good trainees', and this meant doing what they were asked to, literally. Consequently, the problems they declared were again impersonal, and vaguely defined (e.g. 'The organization needs to improve communications', or 'My department should sort out its grievance procedures'). Few would take personal responsibility or ownership for what they had declared. Their task, compiling their list of issues, had been completed, and it was an end in itself. They had been seen to be performing. In this way all was OK and acceptable, like the earlier structured exercises. But moving away from generalizations and getting in touch with their personal side of the problem was another story; one they found very hard to swallow. The trainer pressed the message hard and eventually succeeded in getting it home. Group members did begin to realize that they were, perhaps, evading the issue of their own personal responsibility for problems. But this was no 'ah ha!' experience; far from it. They became disillusioned and depressed. It had left them denuded and helpless. Their props had gone and they did not know where to go next.

The third group was relaxed, easy-going, and humorous. Over half of the group declined to present any issues or problems that were bothering them, even at an abstract level. They would tend to ramble on about anything, ranging from the economic situation to the quality of the hotel rooms where they were staying. They had, in effect, withdrawn from the proceedings, but would stay around for the beer. A few wanted to *do* something, and for these people the programme worked well. One, for example, was anxious to gain feedback from the group on his career strategies in the organization, and on how he was managing his bosses. He declared a lot and received a lot back. Another was very concerned about his ability to make public presentations in his work which would effectively persuade clients or superiors. For him we structured, together, a tailor-made simulation, followed by intensive feedback, and then another simulation run.

Yet, for the remainder of this group, the validity of the session was fuzzy to say the least. The trainer's moves to involve them more personally were evaded. So he ended up by backing off and colluded with them in 'having a nice time'.

SOME IMPLICATIONS

What conclusions can we draw from our efforts at self-development? Two areas strike us as important. The first concerns our own skills as trainers. The second relates to the psychological model and values which underpin programmes of this sort.

Trainer Skills

Could we have achieved a more satisfactory outcome, in self-development terms, if we had done things differently? Was our approach misconceived? Certainly our first response to our difficulties was to look for different ways of achieving the self-development ends. We restructured exercises, integrated parts of the programme, and compared our different trainer styles to look for an 'ideal' style. We looked more carefully at those who were selected for the programme – maybe some people were more receptive than others to self-development?

The net outcome of all this reshuffling was the expenditure of a lot of energy for little gain. While it may be that *how* we are going about it can still be improved (as trainers we can certainly improve our skills), the thing that we constantly found ourselves querying was *what* we were doing.

Models of Behaviour

The self-development concepts are essentially humanistic. They reflect a belief that man can, and should, be self-determining and self-actualizing. He should be proactive rather than reactive. Feelings, and the whole person are all important. In organizations this recognition is said to free people from being simply role-labelled and role-dependent, and so releases a lot of creative energy. Well, that is the theory.

But our course participants seemed to operate at a very different level. They had lived their organizational lives by principles which were more reminiscent of behaviourism than of humanism. They had developed a repertoire of responses which had served them well. They had an intuitive, unquestioned understanding of 'the score' at work. They knew what worked and what did not work, from past failures and successes. Few had self-consciously examined their motives. They had no need to. A pragmatic philosophy was an effective one. Indeed, many of the course participants had survived well on it, and were judged as successful managers, or 'good potential' for inclusion on the course. In brief, our clients' value system served them well. What was there in ours for them?

We can show diagrammatically the position in terms of the simple model of behaviour portrayed (Figure 1). Basically, our humanistic philosophy centres us upon the 'person'. That is where self and self-development lies. But we were dealing with people whose organizational culture and beliefs were far more locked into stimuli and responses which characterize behaviourism. Rules, procedures, hierarchies, and job descriptions were essentially controlling stimuli to which to respond. They expected and sought directives. That is how the organization worked, and that is how many of them wanted *us* to work. 'Tell us what to do – provide us with the stimulus.' To be self-reflecting, proactive, and declaring feelings were all in the 'person box', a black hole which was inappropriate for them to enter.

Our games and exercises were much more consistent with the stimulus-response culture: exercises, rules, points, winners, and losers. (In behavioural jargon: stimuli, responses, schedules of reinforcement, and feedback.) All these skip around the person box; no self-questions asked.

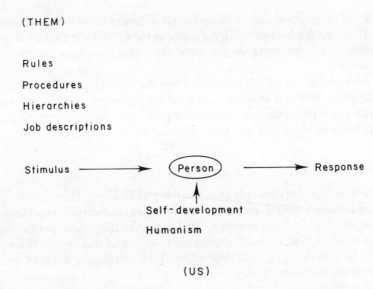

Figure 1. Behaviour models – theirs and ours

If our analysis is correct, when we keep directing trainees towards the person box, some will eventually begin to see over the boundary into a different world. But a weird and confusing world where stimulus–response structures no longer work very well. Consequently, feelings of helplessness – not liberation and insight. In a sense we are presenting a counter-culture which is contrary in premise and value to all that is held dear. We are throwing into question mechanisms that work for them. Like many trainees, ours did not volunteer for the programme. They had no strong reason to want to search for alternative models of action. The humanistic values were indeed ours. For us they work – or at least we like to believe they do – Why should they be good medicine for others?

SOME QUERIES AND CONCERNS

We are now left with some nagging questions and concerns.

1. We may indeed achieve greater self-awareness and self-development in managers by pressing home our humanistic views and technologies (something of a paradoxical process, in itself). So we can spend more time, more intensely on the self-development process. But should we? What is our role in a culture where often the ends justify the means and where this is an effective, satisfying process for those involved? Do we have the right to challenge existing attitudes and beliefs on the assumption that this process is, *per se*, a good thing?

2. Traditional OD consultants would contend that such an instrumental culture is full of rigidities and will fail when it needs to change. Maybe so, but

certainly not with our company. It has survived, apparently very healthily, under severe government and market pressures.

3. Humanistic philosophy is essentially multi-faceted at its core, reifying individuality. Yet for those who are established within a very different philosophical and psychological system, it can appear confusing and threatening, and can create exactly the opposite effect to that anticipated. This is particularly ironical for us, as we were encountering reactions not unlike those we were trying to avoid from their old programme.

4. In many other senses, self-development is as unitary and value laden as any training activity. In this we should not delude ourselves. If there are any deeper wisdoms buried amongst the paraphernalia of self-development, perhaps they suggest a greater tolerance of attitudes and styles which deviate from what is, possibly, a questionable ethic of 'self-awareness'.

Management Development: Advances in Practice and Theory
Edited by C. Cox and J. Beck
© 1984 John Wiley & Sons Ltd

CHAPTER 13

Maximizing Managers' Day-to-Day Learning: Frameworks for the Practice of Learning Interventions

Roger Stuart

INTRODUCTION

This paper is about helping managers to maximize the learning they derive in and from their day-to-day work experiences. My interest in this area derives its impetus from three significant developments in thinking on management training, development, and education.

1. The identification of different types or 'levels' of skills. Specifically the notion of 'meta-skills' and their relationship to managerial effectiveness.

2. The recognition of the value of and need for more 'self-managed' learning by managers.

3. The growing awareness of the opportunities for learning present in managers' on-job work activities as well as on off-job, formalized learning events.

The first of these developments is captured by the work of Burgoyne and Stuart (1976), who identified a key factor to effective managerial behaviour – the ability to develop what they called situation specific skills. Situation specific management skills are those skills required of an individual manager if he is to be effective in a particular work situation. As Katz (1955) and Stewart (1975) confirmed, dependent upon their situations, particular managers will have particular and different skills demands made upon them – for example, varying requirements for types of technical and social skills.

The ability to develop these situation dependent skills resides, however, in skills of a different nature, namely the higher level meta-skills. Moreover, research (Burgoyne and Stuart, 1976) has indicated the possession of *these* meta-skills to be an important ingredient in effectiveness *across* a whole range of managerial situations. The more a manager's work situation changes – whether from job-to-job or within a job – resulting in changing situation specific skills demands, the more frequently will the manager's meta-skills be called upon and used to maintain and improve work performance. Burgoyne and Stuart have described the meta-skills under three headings or categories, to which Pedler *et al.* (1978) have added a fourth, namely:

(a) mental agility,
(b) creativity,
(c) balanced learning habits, and
(d) self-awareness.

Of these, balanced learning habits appears to be the most ubiquitous across managerial situations. I have subsumed these and, indeed, many aspects of the other three categories under the broad heading of 'learning skills'. A key ingredient, then, of managerial success, particularly in times of change, is the manager's learning skills – his ability to learn the specific skills demanded by each new and changing situation.

Burgoyne – in association with Boydell and Pedlar – has again figured prominently in the second area of growing interest, namely managerial self-development (1978). In a recent personal communication, Burgoyne identified a number of emerging trends which have supported the recognition of the need for management development to be 'by self'. These trends include the shifting current of opinion in Behavioural Science thinking, and in changing attitudes to work. At the fore of the trends or pressures for management development by self are, I would suggest, the following.

1. The heterogeneity of managerial work (mentioned above), which coupled with the increasing level of organizational complexity, flux, and change, is making it more and more difficult for traditional training approaches to keep up with an individual manager's emerging training and development needs.

2. The promotion of self-development indicates a gain in efficiency, not least in labour and cost terms (though indirect costs of managers' learning being achieved through making mistakes for real, may alter the balance of this particular equation!).

Whatever the cause of this push towards greater development by self, there is a basic and significant implication – that fundamental to the success of development by self is an ability to learn. Burgoyne *et al.* (1978) cite managers' learning to learn from their practice and experience as 'one of the central goals of self development'. In attempting to improve managerial skills and effectiveness, *and* in attempting to promote greater development by self, we come, then, to a common and important concern – to help/equip managers to learn.

A third pertinent development in thinking on management development concerns the context and the sources of managers' learning – in particular whether this learning is 'on-job' or 'off-the-job'. Research into the nature of managers' learning (Burgoyne and Stuart, 1976) has re-affirmed that the bulk of a manager's learning takes place in the workplace, as a result of the manager carrying out his work-role activities. Furthermore, not only does on-job learning appear to be the most prevalent, but also, if one accepts the argument of management development practitioners like Casey (1980), Hague (1979), and Revans (1977), it is the most effective form of learning. Thus, it is claimed that whilst on-job learning is 'real' and useable, much off-the-job, formalized learning activity (e.g. on courses, seminars) tends to be far removed from the real world. Moreover, when off-the-job learning does occur, it presents the manager with major difficulties in transferring it back to his work activities.

In accord with such thinking, it would seem that attempts to help managers to learn will pay higher dividends if they are focused upon developing managers' abilities to exploit the full potential for learning offered by their on-job activities. Such a concern is also consistent with fostering managers' abilities to learn 'by-self' and, through their meta-skills development, to become more effective in their work roles.

Stimulated by such noble thoughts, I decided to develop my own training and development activities towards that of a 'learning consultant'. Unfortunately, my initial enthusiasm was somewhat stilled by the confusion which overcame me when I embarked upon venting my ambitions in practice. In common with a number of fellow aspirant practitioners in this area, and what Mangham (1978) has reported experiencing as an Organisation Development practitioner, the problem was (to quote Mangham out of context):

> . . . not that there is a shortage of ideas, or a dearth of research. It is that the existing theoretical fragments . . . are either not appropriate or not sufficiently integrated to provide a useful handle for the practitioners . . . .

The intention of developing a useful handle for my own and others' practice as learning consultants provides the starting point of the work I wish to describe in this paper. The work represents a synthesis which is enabling me to move from confused chance-directed activity towards informed action as a learning consultant. I have drawn together a wealth of ideas, theories, and experiences – some my own, the majority other peoples', including clients – into a series of frameworks which I feel clarify and help make more effective attempts to practise learning consultancy, that is, to help others to learn.

Development of these frameworks has been based upon four propositions:

1. That managers can, and do, learn, and not just in formalized, contrived learning activities such as seminars and courses, but as part of their informal, non-contrived, day-to-day work and life activities.

2. That whilst day-to-day experiences are an important source of managers' learning, and that managers have developed skills in enacting appropriate learning processes and behaviours, managers *do* have learning 'problems' in the sense that they can derive further pay-offs from this experience – they can further maximize their learning.

3. That a manager's learning problems have their origin in two sources:

(a) *Intrinsic* – internal to, 'owned by' the learner-manager (and concerning his knowledge, skills, feelings, attitudes, and beliefs about learning), and

(b) *extrinsic* – external to the learner-manager – his learning milieu (and comprising those physical, structural, and psychological factors which may collectively be viewed as his 'opportunity to learn').

4. That learning consultancy is a useful activity, in that something *can* be done to help managers overcome their learning problems. By drawing together knowledge and experience from different fields – principally those from what Knowles (1973) has termed androgogy ('adult learning' rather than pedagogy which involves assumptions of the learner as a child rather than adult) and those from the world of consultancy – it is possible to develop an understanding of the range of consultancy practices which can help resolve learning problems, and which will enable managers to maximize their day-to-day learning.

THE ROLE OF THE LEARNING CONSULTANT

Cunningham and Burgoyne (1980) have presented a model describing the range of facilitator roles. At its core the model presented four different intervention roles that a trainer or developer could adopt in helping a manager work on a task or solve a work problem (Figure 1).

The first role identified was that termed 'expert consultant'. Here the trainer works directly on the manager's task, and *solves* his problem for him. Acting in the second role, that of 'expert teacher', the trainer gives the manager not a solution to his problem, but a means of arriving at a solution – *a problem-solving methodology*. The manager is then able to work on and solve the problem for himself. The trainer carrying out the role of 'learning process manager' takes one step further back from a direct intervention 'at the coal face' and sets up and *manages a learning situation*, or 'event'. Within this

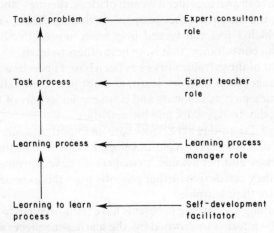

Figure 1. Four facilitator roles

learning event the manager, either on his own, or more commonly in association with fellow participants, discovers and develops problem-solving methodologies which he then applies to the resolution of his work problem (assuming, of course, transferability of learning!).

The fourth main trainer role identified in the model was that of 'self-development facilitator'. Here, rather than solving the problem/working on the task, or giving problem-solving methodologies, or managing a learning process from which these methodologies may emerge, the trainer instead focuses his attention upon the process of learning to learn. Here he is concerned with *helping* the manager to structure up and manage *his own learning* situations (from which problem-solving methods may emerge, etc.). He is following Revans (1971) in valuing the worth of helping the manager 'raise his awareness of his own learning processes'. He is concerned with helping the manager to learn how to learn; with helping the manager to develop his learning skills. What Cunningham and Burgoyne (1980) have called the 'self development facilitator role', I wish to call the role of the 'learning consultant'.

In identifying the role of learning consultant we are not, of course, precluding at this point any of the range of styles by which this role is enacted. Like all roles, the nature of the role behaviours enacted will be dependent upon the various parties' expectations both of the acceptability of that behaviour and its perceived and actual appropriateness and effectiveness. As will be discussed below, the appropriateness of a particular learning consultant's style will be contingent upon the client manager's particular learning problem. Adoption of a style most condusive to resolving these problems will therefore depend upon the clarity and sophistication with which the manager's learning behaviours are identified. Frameworks for considering these form the next section of this paper.

HOW MANAGERS LEARN – KOLB'S MODEL

Kolb and Fry (1975) described a model of experiential learning which is finding growing useage in the management development world, not least because it is both simple and yet penetrating in its descriptions of how people (including managers!) learn. Kolb identified a *cycle* of learning behaviours which together describe how an individual may learn not only by experiencing the situations which make up his daily life, but also by making sense of these experiences.

The cycle of behaviours has *four components* or stages (Figure 2).

1. *Experiencing* – Immersion in, getting in contact with 'here and now' concrete experience, followed by:

2. *Observing* – Observation and collection of data about that experience which he uses in:

3. *Conceptualizing* – Formation of abstract concepts and conclusions about his experience, which leads to:

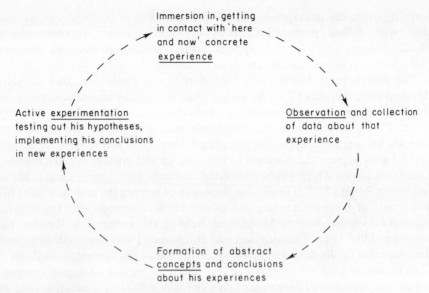

Figure 2. The Kolb learning cycle

4. *Experimenting* – Active experimentation, testing out his hypotheses, implementing his conclusions in new experiences.

Each stage of the 'Kolb learning cycle' requires different and *distinct skills* of the learner. The learner, if he is to be effective in learning from a range of learning situations, needs to be able to call upon four different kinds of abilities.

1. He must be able to involve himself fully and openly in each new experience; to be able to get in touch with his experiencing; to experience anew.

2. He must be able to stand back from his experience and reflect/think back/draw out his recollections and observations of that experience and what happened.

3. He must be able to bring his observations together in his mind; to make sense of his experience; to create concepts which integrate his data into logically sound theories.

4. He must be able to translate his thinking into action; to actively test out his hypotheses; to use his theories as a basis for action.

Kolb's research points to the fact that every individual comes to develop a *learning style* – he utilizes his particular learning abilities in emphasizing one or more of these stages in the learning cycle. Each of us, then, has developed a learning style that has some strong and some weak points. Our styles of learning, and the skills developed within them, coupled with the availability of learning opportunities and the appropriateness of our preferred styles to them, do much to determine whether, how, and what we learn.

Though each of us may have developed significant skills in certain learning behaviours, our learning can be viewed as 'problematic' in the sense of the limited range of these skills. For as Mumford (1980) suggests:

> . . . the really effective learner would be effective at all stages of the Kolb cycle, and in all main learning styles. Rather than allow any individual to retain a rigid treatment of opportunities for learning, it would seem to be desirable and necessary to try and increase flexibility in order to increase the options for learning open to him . . . .

To maximize learning it is therefore necessary to have developed skills in all four modes of learning – experiencing, observing, conceptualizing, and experimenting. Here then, is the *raison d'être* of learning interventions.

THE NOTION OF LEARNING INTERVENTIONS

In their book entitled *Consultation*, Blake and Mouton (1976) point to the essentially cyclic nature of much human behaviour, seeing 'a sequence of behaviour' as repeating 'its main features within specific time periods, or within specific situations'. For example, a manager who goes to work around the same time every day, has meetings with the same people, working on the same, recurrent problems; or the group of managers who are unable to finish their meetings, however much the time allowed for them is increased. This cyclic, almost habitual behaviour is seen by Blake and Mouton as providing the purpose for and the functions of an interventionist, which is to 'help a person (or group) to identify and break out of damaging cycles of behaviour'.

In the previous section of this paper we considered one form of cyclic behaviour – the learning cycle. Limiting learning styles and limited learning skills means that cyclic learning behaviours also may be habitually wasteful, ineffective, and suboptimal. Alternatively, an individual's range and depth of learning skills may be such as to enable him to take full advantage of, draw maximum learning from each of the learning opportunities presented by his work and, indeed, life situations.

Disadvantageous cyclic learning behaviour provides an appropriate entry point for a particular type of intervention, the learning intervention:

A learning intervention is an intervention into someone's learning cycle, the purpose being to help him/her to break out of/improve upon disadvantageous cyclic learning behaviours.

The person making such an intervention – the interventionist – is what I call a 'learning consultant'. Whatever the particular style the learning consultant adopts in his interventionist role, the outcome of his intervention is:

(a) a diagnosis of the client's learning problems, and

(b) the reduction of these learning problems, as evidenced by the client's modified learning behaviours and a move towards maximal learning.

The remaining parts of this paper present frameworks for understanding the nature of individuals' learning problems and for identifying the types of interventions open to the consultant trying to reduce these problems.

CAUSES OF SUBMAXIMAL LEARNING

If people learn by enacting the four learning behaviours which make up the Kolb learning cycle, then it follows that people fail to maximize their learning if they suffer *blocks* to engaging in, and *barriers* preventing learning from, the processes of experiencing, observing, conceptualizing, and experimenting.

Work carried out by Temporal (1978) has identified a categorization of blocks and barriers to learning. These blocks and barriers are of two kinds:

(a) *intrinsic* or internal, i.e. 'belonging to', 'owned by' the learner, and

(b) *extrinsic* or external, i.e. 'environmental' forces, pressures, factors acting upon the learner.

Within these two kinds of blocks and barriers, it is possible to identify a range of seven further categories (as summarized in Table 1).

Table 1   Blocks and barriers to individuals' learning

Nature of block/barrier		Effect
Intrinsic	Perceptual	Unable to see what's happening in potential learning activities
	Cultural	Precluded from potential learning behaviours
	Emotional/ motivational	Adverse reaction to potential learning situations
	Intellectual	Unable to extract potential learning from situations
	Expressive	Learning limited by inept communications
Extrinsic	Physical- structural	Opportunities availing themselves to learning are limited
	Psycho-social	Non-supportive of learning behaviour

Intrinsic Blocks and Barriers

(1) *Perceptual* – where the learner is unable to grasp, to recognize what is happening in a situation.

(2) *Cultural* – where the learner cuts himself off from a range of activities through his acceptance of norms regarding what is 'done' or 'not done', is right or wrong.

(3 *Emotional/motivational* – where the learner is reluctant to enter into certain learning activities because of various negative, unhelpful feelings and reactions held towards such activities.

(4) *Intellectual* – where the learner has not developed the necessary mental capability, does not possess the mental 'tools' required for learning.

(5) *Expressive* – where the learner is unable to communicate effectively.

Extrinsic Blocks and Barriers

(1) *Physical/structural* – where the learner experiences blocks and barriers to his learning which are rooted in the tasks he is given to do, the structure within which they are located, and the physical setting in which they are carried out.

(2) *Psycho-social* – where the learner experiences blocks and barriers to learning which arise from the prevailing climate and relationships of which he is a part.

At this stage in the development of my work I have concentrated on intrinsic factors acting as blocks and barriers to an individual's learning. This is not to suggest any allocation of priority or greater significance of intrinsic over extrinsic factors. In some situations, quite the reverse is apparent. Rather, I have found that working on learning problems owned by the individual presents a convenient first step in developing the practice of learning interventions. As will be discussed in the concluding section, diagnosis and reduction of learning problems having their roots in environmental factors represents an important next step in the development of this work. The remainder of *this* paper is, however, concerned with blocks and barriers owned by the learner himself.

In seeking to describe my own and others' observations and experiences of intrinsic factors preventing maximal learning, I have found Temporal's categories of great help in avoiding being swamped by the scope and diversity of such factors. A further move towards organizing data – and thus facilitating diagnosis – on individuals' learning problems comes from the construction of a series of matrices plotting the categories of blocks and barriers against the four learning behaviours of experiencing, observing, reflecting, and experimenting. The resultant matrixes are reproduced in Tables 2 to 6.

Space forbids full elucidation of the contents of the matrices in this paper. It is hoped that the format and the wording are such as to enable the tables to speak for themselves. Construction of the matrices is based on the assumption (which accords with my own observation, but which has not yet been subjected to rigorous research) that each of the categories of blocks and barriers acts in influencing each of the learning behaviours. Furthermore, each of the categories seems to assume more or less importance and has different implications for each of the different learning behaviours. Frequently a particular reaction to a learning situation may be identified which is beneficial to one mode of learning but detrimental to another. For example, an inclination towards being involved and at the heart of 'where the action is' may be seen as a favourable response in terms of learning through experiencing, but as a barrier to learning

Table 2   Blocks and barriers to learning (Focus: individual; Source: intrinsic; Category: perceptual)

Learning behaviour	Perceptual blocks/barriers
Experiencing	Failure to see opportunities for action; Distanced; Detached from own experience; Blind to himself; Not in touch with what's going on inside him; Unreceptive; 'Eyes are closed'
Observing	Involved; Insensitive to what's going on around him; Undiscerning; Indiscriminate; Non-reflexive; Seeing only that which he expects
Conceptualizing	Bogged down in detail; Unable to see the whole – 'can't see the wood for the trees'; Closed mind; Paucity of concepts/frameworks to interpret data; Mental set, doesn't apply different viewpoints; Unable to detach himself from his experiences, see them is a clear light
Experimenting	Lack of vision; Unable to see alternative ways of doing things; Failure to recognize opportunities for experimentation

Table 3   Blocks and barriers to learning (Focus: individual; Source: intrinsic; Category: cultural)

Learning behaviour	Cultural blocks/barriers
Experiencing	Norms about 'not getting one's hands dirty', 'mucking in'; Status and position related norms about 'being above that sort of thing'; Norms like 'don't get involved', cut him off from experiences and prevent him learning by experiencing
Observing	Observations and feedback data are limited by norms of 'let's get cracking'; 'What's next'; 'That's history'; 'Live for today'; and norms concerning level of disclosure 'Keep your opinions to yourself'; 'Don't wash your dirty linen in public'
Conceptualizing	Cut off from learning through conceptualizing by norms like 'Theorizing is for academics'; Trapped by existing paradigms; 'Ignorance is bliss'
Experimenting	Experimentation precluded by norms about 'Toeing the line', 'Sticking to the rules', 'Fitting in'; Conservative; Conformist. Learning valued for its own sake (rather than for its application)

Table 4 Blocks and barriers to learning (Focus: individual; Source: intrinsic; Category: emotional/motivational)

Learning behaviour	Emotional/motivational blocks/barriers
Experiencing	Fear of exposure; Insecurity; Doesn't involve himself in his own experience; 'Doesn't let himself go'; Emotionally withdrawn; Not open to experiences; Feeling suppressed; 'Heart is closed'
Observing	Insensitive/oversensitive; Impatient; Picking up only that which he wants to hear; Fearful that 'all may not be as it seems'; Inability to handle feedback
Conceptualizing	Obsessive need to be busy, to be seen doing things; Fear of understanding, of 'opening up a can of worms', revealing the 'awful truth'; Inability to view dispassionately
Experimenting	Plagued by inability to cope with uncertainty and ambiguity; Non-enquiring; Inflexible; Fear of taking risks, making mistakes, 'putting his ideas on the line'; Self-satisfied

Table 5 Blocks and barriers to learning (Focus: individual; Source: intrinsic; Category: intellectual)

Learning behaviour	Intellectual blocks/barriers
Experiencing	Lacking mental agility – inability to 'think on his feet', in the 'here and now'
Observing	Poor analytical ability; Inattentive; Low recall
Conceptualizing	Mentally non-acrobatic, 'rusty'; Unable to hold several things in mind simultaneously; Inability to concentrate; Rigidity of thinking; Unable to think in depth, logically, rationally; Inability to relate practice to theory
Experimenting	Unimaginative; Lacking creative ability – inability to come up with, take on board, utilize new ideas/approaches. Unable to relate theory to practice

Table 6 Blocks and barriers to learning (Focus: individual; Source: intrinsic; Category: expressive)

Learning behaviour	Expressive blocks/barriers
Experiencing Observing Conceptualizing Experimenting	Inability to express himself clearly, communicate with others; Limited vocabulary; Limited repertoire of behaviours; Unable to put his hunches, feelings, observations, thoughts, ideas into words and behaviour; Hearing only what he expects to hear; Poor listening skills; Socially inept

in the observation mode, where rather than involvement an ability to detach or distance oneself from the action is of the essence.

RESOLUTION OF LEARNING PROBLEMS

The matrices presented in Tables 2 to 6 represent the field of work, the constituents of the diagnosis, and the focuses of activity of the learning consultant. These matrices have, in my experience, high utility value, and meet our initial criterion of bringing together existing fragments of knowledge and integrating them sufficiently to provide a useful handle for the consultant's diagnostic practice. Of course, the data still needs to be collected. Data collection and formulation of a diagnosis, as we will see, is a process entwined in the other part of the consultant's activity – the resolution of his client's learning problems.

In identifying the scope and nature of intrinsic blocks and barriers to learning we drew heavily upon our understanding of learning processes. This body of knowledge underlies the diagnostic phase of learning consultation. In moving on to outline and consider frameworks for depicting the nature of the subsequent problem resolution phase, the accumulated wealth of knowledge in the field of consultation, and in particular the work of Blake and Mouton (1976), assumes greater significance.

Types of Learning Interventions

We earlier identified the role of the learning consultant as being equated with the role described by Cunningham and Burgoyne (1980) as the 'self-development facilitator'. It was pointed out, however, that adoption of this particular intervention role did not preclude any of the range of styles by which the role may be enacted. Blake and Mouton (1976) identified five styles or types of consultative activity which, with comparatively little modification, are translatable into a categorization of five basic types of learning intervention.

Thus learning consultative activity may be:
- Acceptant.
- Catalytic.
- Confrontational.
- Prescriptive.
- Theory/Principle based.

Acceptant Learning Interventions

In acceptant learning interventions, the predominant consultant activities are those of sympathetic listening and provision of empathic support. The client with a block or barrier to learning is helped to relax his defences and to sort out and work through his learning problems for himself. The acceptant type of intervention calls for the consultant to seek to understand the situation from the client's point of view, but whilst being sympathetic he is not partisan. The purpose of the intervention is to help the client identify and break out of his current learning behaviour, not, for example, to consolidate this behaviour by colluding with the client in 'ain't it awful games'.

Catalytic Learning Interventions

A learning consultant operating in the catalytic mode of intervention accepts his client's point of view as the frame of reference within which to work. Having understood this frame of reference, the consultant engages in active collaboration with his client, helping him, for example, to seek out data and to develop a wider understanding of his learning problem situation. The consultant seeks to help his client to formulate action steps aimed at reducing his identified blocks and barriers to learning. Decisions about which steps to pursue are made by the client, and are broadly in line with the direction he would wish to pursue under his own steam.

Confrontational Learning Interventions

Here the learning consultant does not take the client's view of his learning problems, nor does he respond to the client's felt needs. Rather, the consultant presents his client with alternative views on his learning behaviours. Using Argyris and Schon's (1974, 1978) terminology, the consultant may, for example, challenge the client's 'espoused theory' of how, and with what effectiveness, he learns, and confronts him with facts revealing his theory-in-use. By making the client aware of alternative interpretations of his learning behaviours, the client is then faced with rejecting the consultant's viewpoint (and a major limitation of this intervention is that it can easily degenerate into win–lose arguments), or with taking it on board and modifying his learning behaviours, or continuing in the face of a recognized inconsistency and evidence of submaximal learning habits.

Prescriptive Learning Interventions

In prescriptive learning interventions the relationship between consultant and client is closely akin to that traditionally described for a doctor and his patient. The prescriptive learning consultant activity is based (whether implicitly or explicitly) on the assumptions that the learning consultant is 'the expert' and is thus able to identify the client's actual as opposed to his felt learning problems and needs. The learning consultant engages in a diagnosis of the learning problem area, and recommends the actions required for the client to break out of his disadvantageous learning cycle. The client is deemed to lack sufficient knowledge, skills, or objectivity to be able to take any responsibility for this himself.

What the client receives from a prescriptive learning intervention is a 'best' solution to solve his ills. Consequent lack of client ownership and dependency on the consultant are commonly encountered drawbacks of prescriptive interventions. Nevertheless, as will be described below, prescriptive approaches are certainly useful in working on certain blocks and barriers to learning, and hence are a valuable part of the consultant's repertoire of intervention types.

Theory and Principle Learning Interventions

In contrast to prescriptive approaches, the theory and principle type of learning intervention places a great deal of responsibility on the client to break out of his own submaximal cyclic learning behaviour. The consultant operating in the theory and principle mode is concerned to put the client in touch with, and help him to acquire, a theoretical basis for his learning behaviour. Thus, the consultant teaches his client the theories and principles of learning and allied behaviour, and equips him with the (consultant's) knowledge and skills needed to become aware of and to overcome his learning problems for himself.

Relating Learning Problems to Types of Learning Interventions

Individual learning consultants and, indeed, their clients, may have expectations about, and preferences for, particular kinds of learning interventions. These favoured approaches may be rooted predominantly in one type of intervention, or may be rather more eclectic. Particular inclinations and preferences will be important influences on the learning interventions strategy adopted. This is not to suggest that particular dysfunctional, submaximal learning cycles can be equally well addressed by all five of the interventions types described in the previous section of this paper. In fact, following Blake and Mouton (1976), it would appear that some types of interventions may be more appropriate than others for particular intrinsic blocks and barriers to learning. My conclusions at this point, whilst requiring considerably more exploration before they can be offered as anything more than tentative guidelines, may be summarized as shown in Table 7. The suggestion here is not that there is a neat relationship between learning problems and learning interventions, but rather that there are varying degrees of appropriateness. Thus, *acceptant* learning interventions appear particularly helpful in enabling a client to work through the intrinsic, emotional blocks to learning. The process of catharsis would represent an extreme instance, and captures the essence of acceptant interventions – release of pent-up feelings and emotions. Through providing a supportive relationship in which the client is freed up to talk things through and to put his thoughts and feelings into words for perhaps the first time, not only may emotional, but also previously experienced perceptual and expressive blocks and barriers be overcome.

Catalytic learning interventions may be appropriately used when perceptual blocks are preventing the client achieving maximal learning. By assisting his client to collect data which is additional to, and/or helps verify data already held, the learning consultant enables his client to develop a wider view of his learning situation. Thus, the catalytic intervention is most appropriate to working on perceptual blocks, particularly to learning through observing. Should the intervention call for the client to *actively* seek out data from others, the client may be assisted in working on some of his expressive barriers to learning, such as listening skills. If the intervention is more concerned with drawing out data already in the client's head, then active probing can help develop a client's intellectual skills.

The *confrontational* mode of intervention, whereby a client is exposed to his own values, beliefs, and accepted perceptions and is called upon to justify them, is an approach which is appropriate to helping the client to break out of a number of causes of submaximal learning behaviour. Thus, perceptual ('lets stop kidding ourselves, what's happening is') and intellectual ('how, logically

Table 7. Appropriate learning interventions.

Learning intervention type	Nature of intrinsic learning block/barrier
Acceptant	Emotional Perceptual, (Expressive)
Catalytic	Perceptual (Expressive) (Intellectual)
Confrontational	Cultural Perceptual, (Intellectual)
Prescriptive	Emotional/ motivational, intellectual
Theory and principle	Perceptual (Expressive)

can you reconcile those two points of view?') blocks and barriers may be exposed and resolved. In particular, however, confrontational approaches are congruent with helping a client to overcome cultural blocks and barriers to learning. Indeed, confrontational approaches represent the only truly effective way of dealing with a learning situation where the values held by a client are manifestly inappropriate and unjustified – for example when the client is strongly prejudiced against the worth of taking time out to reflect upon an experience.

Prescriptive learning interventions – where the client is presented with both a diagnosis of his learning problem and a prescription for resolving the problem – may be used to help clients' overcome a broad range of sources of submaximal learning, including self-doubt, lack of confidence, lack of resources, and generally being 'at his wit's end'. The prescriptive approach seems to be especially useful when dealing with learning problems in the emotional/motivational and intellectual categories, and is justifiable in getting a client back on his feet and actively learning. As was mentioned above, prescriptive interventions can have longer-term drawbacks if the client becomes dependent upon the learning consultant for continued direction.

As a result of *theory and principle* interventions, the client is equipped with the theories and principles he needs to resolve his own learning problems, that is, to be his own learning consultant. The approach is apparently applicable across the whole range of blocks and barriers to learning. For example, expressive blocks to interacting with others and learning from them might be overcome by the client internalizing the theories of transactional analysis (e.g. James and Jongeward, 1978) or theories might provide the vehicles for expressing hitherto unarticulated thoughts and ideas. My early experiences, however, indicate that theory and principle interventions are most effective in dealing with perceptual problems, particularly to learning from conceptualizing, where a client possesses a paucity of concepts and frameworks with which to interpret his experiences.

Taken over all, each of the intervention modes has its uses in the repertoire of the learning consultant. Some modes seem more appropriate than others for particular categories of learning problems. The least clear-cut relationship between intervention mode and type of intrinsic block or barrier to learning are for the expressive category. This is almost certainly a consequence of the broad range of learning problems subsumed in what at this point in my work is almost a catch-all category.

In practice, and as was discussed above, the particular approach actually adopted by the learning consultant will be coloured by both the consultant's and the client's expectations and preferences – which may even be explicitly embodied in a formal contract. Furthermore, just as it would be simplistic to suggest a series of neat relationships between the various types of problems and interventions, so it would be misleading to suggest that the most effective interventions are necessarily 'pure' in the sense of being based on one intervention type only. For example, an acceptant mode may be followed by a phase of catalytic consultative activity: as emotional fears are released and blocks to getting into action removed, perceptual barriers to observing may be tackled, enabling the client not only to learn by experiencing but also to collect feedback data on his actions which will assist towards maximization of his learning.

The intervention modes used in an intervention will depend upon the nature of a client's primary and perhaps secondary blocks and barriers to learning, and also the difficulty encountered by the consultant in discriminating symptoms from causes. Hence, following a theory and principle intervention intended to remove apparent perceptual blocks preventing a client from maximizing his learning from conceptualizing, a consultant may come to realize that the block lies not in his client's lack of frameworks and insight but in his adherence to values and norms which devalue the importance of conceptualizing as a learning process. A confrontational intervention may then be deemed the most appropriate next step.

The comparatively non-prescriptive nature of this account of the relationship between learning problems and types of learning interventions is a stance dictated, then, by the number of intervening contextual variables and also a congruency with professional norms pertaining to work at this early stage of development. However, in concluding this part of the paper, it does not seem out of place to identify what is emerging as the author's preferred style of intervention. A pattern of intervention strategy is emerging which starts with theory and principles as a means of getting clients tuned in to the topic of learning; then the intervention progresses to a catalytic mode in which clients are helped to seek and generate data about their own learning behaviours (Kolb's Learning Interventory – Kolb *et al.*, 1974 – is a useful first step). A review at this stage may then lead on to interventions of any of the five types described.

CONCLUDING REMARKS AND FUTURE INTENTIONS

By drawing together pertinent knowledge and experiences from the fields of andragogy and consultancy, this paper has set out to provide a useable handle for future intervention practice designed to help managers to maximize their learning from day-to-day experience. As has been indicated, the work is at a comparatively early stage of development. A number of potentially fruitful areas for future exploration can be identified. Thus, a particular need is seen to be the diversification of methods used as vehicles for learning interventions, to include not just coaching and counselling activities – carried out in a one-to-one format – but also small group activities and self-administered exercises. Furthermore, the scope of the learning problems tackled needs to be broadened out from intrinsic blocks and barriers to learning to extrinsic influences. Preliminary observations as to the nature of these extrinsic blocks and barriers are summarized in Tables 8 and 9.

As before, these tables represent matrices obtained by mapping the mode of learning behaviour against the category of blocks and barriers to learning. Though far from complete, the tables do serve to indicate the scope and range of blocks and barriers to learning which have their origin largely in sources

Table 8. Blocks and barriers to learning (Focus: individual; Source: extrinsic; Category: physical/structural)

Learning behaviour	Physical/structural blocks/barriers	
Experiencing	Activities are routine, ritualistic, low in variability, predictable, undemanding, uninvolving, unstimulating	*Overall* The range of *opportunities* for learning; the *time* to avail himself of these opportunities, the *conduciveness* of the physical conditions; and the *incentive* to take up the opportunities, i.e. the nature of the reward system
Observing	Poor communications, information flow; Inadequate feedback; Isolation: 'solo' role	
Conceptualizing	Emphasis on results; Interruptions; Disjointed, short time scale, activities; Lack of 'post mortems' / review / policy-making / planning / 'think tank' procedures	
Experimenting	Prescribed duties, methods; Rules, procedures, 'red tape'; Closed systems (not open to outside ideas, developments); Low slack; High cost of failure	

Table 9. Blocks and barriers to learning (Focus: individual; Source: extrinsic; Category: psycho-social)

Learning behaviour	Psycho-social blocks/barriers	
Experiencing	'Ivory-tower', theory oriented; Reserved, non-expressive, impersonal	*Overall* The value attached to, the *legitimacy* of the various learning behaviours, and of learning itself
Observing	Present-oriented; Secretive, Mistrustful; 'Keep cards close to your chest'	
Conceptualizing	Action oriented; 'Hairy chest'; Pragmatic; 'Feely' (or 'that's thought bullshit!' – Amis, 1978)	
Experimenting	Cautious, 'non-error embracing' (Mirvis and Berg, 1977); Low or high felt security – lean/ miserable or fat/happy; Conservative; Traditional; Conforming	

'outside of' the individual learner. As shown, these factors do much to determine the opportunities that a manager has to learn as part of his day-to-day work, and also the value or legitimacy that others (implicitly or explicitly) attach to that learning. Given condusive physical, structural, and psycho-social conditions for learning, however, the individual manager still requires the skills to recognize the opportunity for learning, to be motivated to take up this opportunity, and have the skills to maximize his learning from it.

Another exciting direction for development of learning consultancy activities would be to move from interventions at the individual level to work on learning at the group and organizational level. Hence, it is possible to conceive not only of individual learning behaviour, but also group and organizational learning behaviour though reification may be seen as a problem (Silverman, 1970). The work of Carlsson, Keane, and Martin (1976), and of Argyris and Schon (1978), is pertinent here.

Given these possible and important future developments, in the immediate short term there is an obvious need to consolidate the work described in this paper. In particular, more extensive experience is required to refine and validate the suggested relationships between type of block/barrier to learning and intervention mode. Opportunities for such work will depend upon a more widespread recognition of the basic and fundamental importance of developing managers' skills to maximize their day-to-day learning. The ability to learn in and from everyday experience appears to be at the root of, not only self-development and growth, but managers' effectiveness in changing work roles. To quote from Mumford (1980), the practice of a learning intervention is an attempt to help a manager 'not merely to get closer to the ideal' maximal 'learning cycle, but to get closer to full effectiveness as a manager, by becoming a better learner'. It is hoped that the work presented in this paper will assist movement towards this goal.

REFERENCES

Amis, K. (1978) *Jake's Thing*, Penguin, Harmondsworth.

Argyris, C. and Schon, D. A. (1974) *Theory in Practice: Increasing Professional Effectiveness*, Jossey-Bass, London.

Argyris, C. and Schon, D. A. (1978) *Organisational Learning: A Theory of Action Perspective*, Addison-Wesley, London.

Blake, R. R. and Mouton, J. S. (1976) *Consultation*, Addison-Wesley, London.

Burgoyne, J. and Stuart, R. (1976) The nature, use and acquisition of managerial skills and other attributes, *Personnel Review*, **5**, 4, 19–29.

Burgoyne, J. G., Boydell, T. H., and Pedler, M. J. (1978) *Self Development: Theory and Application for Practitioners*, A.T.M., London.

Carlsson, B., Keane, P., and Martin, J. B. (1976) R. and D. organizations as learning systems, *Sloan Management Review*, **17**, 3, 1–15.

Casey, D. (1980) Transfer of learning – there are two separate problems, in: *Advances in Management Education*, Edited by J. E. Beck and C. J. Cox, John Wiley, London.

Cunningham, I. and Burgoyne, J. (1980) Facilitating behaviour in work centred management development programmes, in: *Advances in Management Education*, Edited by J. E. Beck and C. J. Cox, John Wiley, London.

Hague, H. (1979) *Helping Managers to Help Themselves*, Context, Oxford.

James, M. and Jongeward, D. (1978) *Born to Win: Transactional Analysis with Gestalt Experiments*, Addison-Wesley, London.

Katz, R. L. (1955) Skills of an effective administrator, *Harvard Business Review*, **January–February 1955**, 33–42.

Knowles, M. (1973) *The Adult Learner: A Neglected Species*, Gulf, Houston.

Kolb, D. A. and Fry, R. (1975) Towards an applied theory of experiential learning, in: *Theories of Group Process*, Edited by C. L. Cooper, John Wiley, London.

Kolb, D. A., Rubin, I. M., and McIntyre, J. M. (1974) *Organisation Psychology. An Experiential Approach*, Prentice-Hall, New Jersey.

Mangham, I. L. (1978) *Interactions and Interventions in Organisations*, John Wiley, London.

Mirvis, P. H. and Berg, D. N. (1977) *Failures in Organisation Development and Change*, John Wiley, New York.

Mumford, A. (1980) *Making Experience Pay*, McGraw-Hill, London.

Pedler, M. J., Burgoyne, J. G., and Boydell, T. H. (1978) *A Managers' Guide to Self-Development*, McGraw-Hill, London.

Revans, R. W. (1971) *Developing Effective Managers*, Longman, London.

Revans, R. W. (1977) An action learning trust, *Journal of European Industrial Training*, **1**, 1, 2–5.

Silverman, D. (1970) *The Theory of Organisations*, Heinemann, London.

Stewart, R. (1975) The manager in his job: A behavioural viewpoint, *New Behaviour*, **24 April 1975**, 20–22.

Temporal, P. (1978) The nature of non-contrived learning and its implications for management development, *Management Education and Development*, **9**, 93–99.

Management Development: Advances in Practice and Theory
Edited by C. Cox and J. Beck
© 1984 John Wiley & Sons Ltd

CHAPTER 14

Rethinking Experience Based Events

Richard Boot and Michael Reynolds

INTRODUCTION

Experience based approaches to learning have their origins in war games, drama, and in psychotherapy. The form they take has been influenced by developments in the fields of social psychology, systems theory, and decision theory and by the application of computer technology. Since the early 1960s the use of such experience based approaches as role plays, games, and simulations has become widespread, particularly within management education and training but also within teacher training colleges and in schools.

More recently still, there has been a trend towards the use of more structured exercises. Many teachers and trainers regard this as an improvement over less structured designs because the participants are involved in less ambiguity. The assumption which underlies this development is that structure, direction, and control are necessary if specific learning goals are to be achieved and if the confusion and frustration often associated with more anarchic models is to be avoided. This point of view is consistent with the description of structured exercises by Bradford and Eoyang (1976) as 'a bounded activity having its own rules and procedures with predetermined learning goals and involving all members'.

Our concern with such descriptions is not that they are completely untrue but that they fail to do justice to the essential nature of experience based learning events and the complexities involved in taking part in them.

Abt (1968) summarizes the choices confronting the teacher in deciding on the degree of structure as being those of realism or simplification, concentration or comprehensiveness, melodramatic motivation or analytic calm. We intend in this paper to develop this idea in demonstrating the many aspects of learning, educational and social, personal and moral, in which the use of this type of learning involves teacher and student. Specifically, we pose the question: *Can a learning event be both experientially involving and at the same time*

207

bounded and predictable. The following are examples of experiences which cause us to question that assumption.

Example One

One trainer, working with a group of five participants, introduces an exercise by stating that its aims are to 'increase understanding of group processes' and to 'provide material for developing a tool for group process analysis'. He places a folded paper boat on the table and instructs the group that they are to make as many identical boats as they can in two minutes from the time of first touching the original. The group spends approximately fifteen minutes discussing how they should set about the task and eventually decide to operate individually. They produce nine in the allocated time. When asked after the event what their feelings are arising from the exercise and what, if anything, they have learnt, one man replies: 'very frustrated and rather inferior. It reinforces the view of myself as manually incompetent. It's the story of my life. I never manage to get anything done properly.'

Example Two

A one-day industrial relations simulation run by a female trainer has as its objectives 'to explore the problems of negotiating and bargaining and to develop skills in the area'. Roles in the simulation are allocated by the trainer. A man and woman taking part in the exercise, although using different surnames, are, unbeknown to the trainer, a married couple. The man is given the role of a shop steward and the woman the role of a manager. At the end of the exercise the couple approach the trainer and state: 'How clever of you to give us reversed roles so that we could explore the gender issues in our relationship.'

Example Three

Sixteen managers attend a residential course on Human Relations in Management. They are presented with a 'fishbowl' exercise during a session on inter-personal and group communications. One group is to discuss a back-at-work problem for twenty minutes and the others observe. In a second run the roles are reversed and the session ends with discussion of observations and experience of the exercise. The exercise is lively and the feedback of observations enthusiastic and rich in content. The discussion period begins with a surprising and awesome silence. The course staff, in attempting to discover what this signifies, are angrily asked why they had set up an exercise clearly designed to make the course members appear foolish to each other.

Example Four

An exercise in intergroup behaviour for students of social administration is based on one group designing a task for the other group to carry out. In the discussion period which follows, a small group of male students declare that in their opinion no aspects of group behaviour worth talking about were generated during the exercise. The staff member comments that as this same subgroup appeared to exert considerable influence during the exercise, that at least might be a point to start from. The staff member is informed by the student group that this distribution of influence has been a dominant feature of the year so far and as they have found ways of coping with it, they do not wish the issue to be opened up again.

In setting out to answer the questions which these illustrations raise, it is important to consider the reasons why experience based events are used in the first place. Intentions vary from instrumental to ideological. Which rationale applies to a given teacher or trainer is likely to influence their response to the questions we raise and the implications we draw.

Incorporating the students' direct experience into the process of learning acknowledges that in more conventional methods experience is usually divorced from the ideas and theories which make up the course content. In experience based methods ideas can be generated, tested, and developed: variables can be manipulated in the classroom to discover 'what happens if?' and the validity and the limitations of concepts can thus be explored. Ultimately, as Coleman (1968) puts it, the advantage of experience based learning is that it 'allows a way to translate a set of ideas into a system of action rather than a system of abstract concepts'.

A further advantage over more conventional approaches is that active participation in the classroom procedures means that the content is more likely to reflect the students' perspectives and the learning to be more personally related to their interests and aspirations. In testing out ideas or practices related to and simulating work, political, or social settings, there is the opportunity to make mistakes with the minimum cost (Rockler, 1978). In short, the experience based approach meets the frequent demand for socially related material to be used in education (Taylor and Walford, 1978).

A different rationale is one based on values held by teachers or trainers about their role, the role of course members or students, the preferred nature of their working relationships, and on beliefs about the developmental function which the educational process should provide for the people who are involved in it. For such people experience based learning events imply that value is being placed on students' ideas and respect shown for their needs and interests. Furthermore, because of the nature of the method, the teacher is in a more facilitative and less judgmental role and it is legitimate for students to learn from each other. More remotely, 'taking part' in such educational settings provides the students with the confidence and experience which will enable them to take a more active and responsible role in work and other social affairs within the community (Pateman, 1970). The processes which let this development happen are not always overt, models of social and political behaviour are mirrored in the instructional system adopted (Joyce and Weil, 1972) and in the social structures created or evolved within the classroom (Reynolds, 1980).

So far we have considered educational and ideological rationale but many authors advocate the use of experience based methods on purely 'motivational' grounds. The students' role is seen as less passive and more involving: the interest and excitement which results increases the students' commitment to the work and therefore they learn more. This is a contentious rationale and its implicit instrumentality avoids the questions raised by the method about responsibility and control. Its added interest for those of us working within management education is that it is an exact parallel of rationale which is at the root of so many 'participative' approaches to management and human relations in the workplace.

OUR ARGUMENT

In questioning the validity of assumptions about the predictability of structured exercises we would like to develop the following points.

1. Because the role which experiential approaches demands of participants is more active and involving than that demanded by traditional methods, it is unrealistic to assume that participants' experience can be predicted or their learning outcomes prespecified.

2. Usually, only a proportion of participants' experience of learning events of any kind is made explicit, making it more difficult for the trainer to judge the full range of experience which an exercise elicits.

3. When this hidden content of participants' experience is discovered, it demonstrates that even the most 'straightforward' exercise can generate a range of reactions of considerable complexity. Anyone who doubts that need only try the stimulated recall method to find out what the content of people's thoughts and feelings during an exercise has been.

4. Given the first three points, it is questionable whether it is either realistic or desirable for trainers to imagine that they could or should decide unilaterally which aspects of the participants' experience will be salient or which should be made public.

5. Given this potential complexity, the skills and understanding available to those taking part need to be broader than the prespecified purpose of the exercise, however limited that may be, in order that what is actually taking place in the learning event may be engaged usefully and with sensitivity.

6. What implications follow for trainer development? Management educa-

tion already has available methods of developing the range of awareness and skills which are required (e.g. Tavistock 'conferences' or sensitivity training). But if there is a decline in the application of these methods within management education, it becomes less likely that trainers and teachers will have had the benefit of such development.

Before continuing with our ideas in detail, there are some general points to be made about our approach.

A limitation of this discussion is that there is no way in which we can confront the significant gap which can frequently be observed between what trainers like to think they do and what they actually do. That can only be explored in practice. Specifically, central to any discussion about experience based events is the notion of participation and the processes of control, responsibility, and choice. Yet many of those who would purport to be using a participative approach are not. They are creating an opportunity for course members to be busy, which is not the same thing. So often is this the case that it has become necessary to make a clear distinction between the idea of participation as being about having some significant influence over choices and direction, and 'participation' as it is often used in the context of management and management education.

This underlines two fundamental aspects of our argument. First, the dilemmas we are exploring are not simply or even primarily technical in nature. They are psychological and ideological questions. We are talking about the roles of trainers and of participants and of the relationships between them. How these roles and relationships are understood will be affected by the ideas we hold about men and women, teaching and learning, and whether those ideas are based on technological or anthropomorphic assumptions. Secondly, and given the importance we attach to the first, a simple contingent approach is untenable. It is an avoidance of the questions involved to claim that the degree of control adopted should depend on situational factors alone.

THE NATURE OF EXPERIENCE BASED EVENTS

Having outlined our argument we shall now look at it in more detail. In essence we are saying that the 'systematic' approach to the design of structured exercises which can be represented as in Figure 1 is so simplistic as to be misleading in that it denies the inevitable complexity of experienced based learning events.

We would regard Figure 2 as a more appropriate representation. Such a view stems not only from our own experience of such events, which collectively is in excess of two decades, but also from the exploratory research we have been carrying out in the last few years. In this research we have attempted to increase our understanding of such events by exploring the perspectives of tutors who 'run' them and also of 'learners' who have been involved in them as participants. We shall look at each of these perspectives in turn.

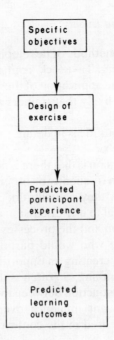

Figure 1

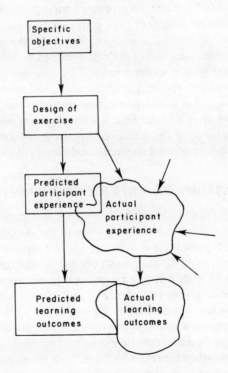

Figure 2

Exploring Tutors' Perspectives

Our starting point for the first was an attempt to identify the essential nature of experienced based events. We did this in collaboration with a number of colleagues with experience of using such approaches in a range of different settings. The way we went about this part of our exploration was based loosely on the 'triadic construct elicitation' technique associated with the repertory grid and described in Fransella and Bannister (1977). In effect we asked each trainer to consider various experience based events they were familiar with in groups of three and to state on what basis they would differentiate between them. It soon became obvious that the conventional manner of distinguishing them in terms of a single structured–unstructured dimension was at best unhelpful. We generated a very large number of distinct characteristics in which these events were considered to vary and it was difficult to reduce these down to a small number of dimensions without losing much of the meaning.

When we tried to group or cluster them, however, we did find a definite pattern emerging. Figure 3 is intended to give the 'flavour' of this process, both in terms of the kinds of distinction being made and in terms of the way they seemed to group together.

In trying to make sense of, or find some meaning in, these groupings we were aware of two important factors. The first was that, in this exercise, we were dealing with the way tutors, as opposed to participants, viewed experience based events. The second was that we were not asking them to consider specific cases or occurrences of such events in practice but to consider them in general. In other words we were not dealing with the 'essential nature' but tutors' beliefs about, expectations of, and intentions for such events. With this in mind, therefore, in order to make the loose groupings represented in Figure 3 more intelligible, we formally summarized them as in Figure 4 under the general heading of 'Tutors intent to influence learning'. We were also able to provide each grouping with a heading summarizing what we believed it represented. Referring back to our earlier comment about loss of meaning through reduction of data we think it is important to emphasize that this diagram and the explanation of it should be viewed as our attempt to make sense out of the complexity contained within the extensive and rich material with which we were provided, rather than as a 'model' summarizing our 'findings'.

Tutor's General Aims

This cluster contained statements about the purposes for which the various events might be used. We have already mentioned reasons for use earlier in the paper but it is worth mentioning here that there seems to be a general contrast between open-ended uses on the one hand, represented by such terms as 'exploration', 'generating personal knowledge', and 'personal growth', and

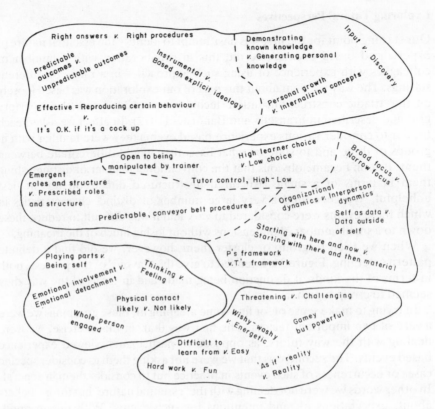

Figure 3

closed-ended uses on the other hand, represented by terms like 'demonstration', 'skill development', and 'internalizing concepts'. This cluster appeared to us distinct from, but closely related to, the next one.

Tutors' Beliefs

Here we seemed to be dealing with more fundamental beliefs not only about what is or is not desirable, possible or allowable, when using these events, but also about the essential nature of mankind in general and of learning in particular. So, for example, there are those who believe it is important that learning objectives be clearly stated in advance and those who do not. Some believe that, irrespective of whether it is desirable/possible to predefine objectives, it is important to have clearly worked out procedures in advance. Some approaches are associated with a single fixed theory for explaining the behaviour of individuals and groups, which for others theories are open to discussion, development, and change by all those involved. Contrary to what

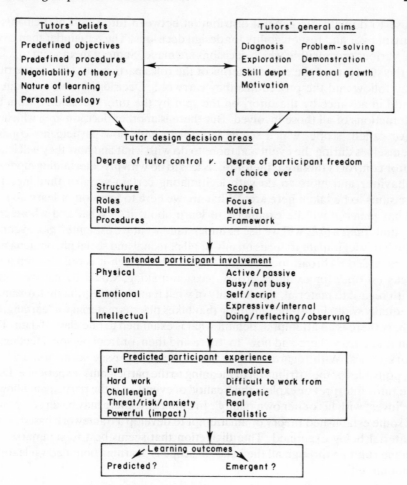

Figure 4. Tutors' intent to influence learning

other writers have suggested (e.g. Burgoyne and Stuart, 1978) it seems that experience based events can be associated with or even justified by a wide range of different learning theories and ideological stances. These beliefs combined with the tutors' general aims are likely to influence the decisions he or she makes whether implicitly or explicitly with regard to event design.

Tutor Design Decision Areas

This cluster seemed to us to be at the heart of the issues conventionally blanketed by the simple structured–unstructured dimension. We found it easiest to make sense of the characteristics it contained by placing at a first level those to do with the general distribution between tutors and participants of control over and responsibility for design decisions. The remainder then cover the various areas within which decisions are made. Some of them seem to relate to the structure of the event in terms of the roles participants take or the rules they follow and the procedures they carry out. Decisions in this area can be made in advance by the tutor, on the spot by the tutor, or emerge from the interactions of all those involved. But there is another decision area which we have called 'scope' which seems less to do with how participants conduct themselves during the event and more to do with what and how they will learn. Tutor control in this area, therefore, is less to do with predetermining modes of behaviour and more to do with legitimating certain ways of thinking. The decisions to be taken here are: 'What are we here to focus on or learn about?' 'What *material* will be examined to learn about it?' 'What and whose conceptual *frameworks* will we use to understand what we examine?' So, events in which it is legitimate to focus on any or all personal and social phenomena may be regarded as broad focus, while those within which it is only legitimate to focus on one, for example group decision-making, would be narrow focus. With regard to material, the diversity of what it might be legitimate to examine is equally wide. For some, anything that takes place is material for learning, for others there is an attempt to delimit what is examined to one class of data. This can range from 'here and now' to 'there and then' or from personal feelings to work topics. With regard to frameworks the crucial issue seems to be who is responsible for the attribution of meaning to the participants' experience. Does the tutor interpret or explain the 'reality' of events or is the participant allowed to 'invest with his or her own reality'. In either case there may be an acceptance of some established theory or an attempt to develop a framework based on the material being examined. The distinction that seems best to summarize the theme running through all the issues of scope is 'learning bounded vs. learning unbounded'.

Intended Participant Involvement

If the previous cluster represented decisions the tutor might make in an attempt to influence the learning, then this one represents assumptions he or she may make about the likely or possibly even desirable nature of the participants' involvement in the event. They might be any or all of physically, emotionally, or intellectually engaged in what is going on. So in some events it was thought that 'physical contact is likely' while in others it was 'not likely'. Some events demand 'emotional responsibility' while in others it was thought 'easy to cop out'. Some events seem more associated with 'affective problem-solving' while others with 'cognitive problem-solving'. Some were considered to 'engage the whole person' while others encouraged 'fragmentation'. Other characteristics that fitted this grouping seemed applicable to any of the three dominant modes just mentioned. So, depending on the event it was assumed that the participants would be active or passive, busy or not busy. It is worth mentioning here that a number of people saw these two dimensions as quite distinct. 'Busy' seems to do more with the frequency and pace of activities engaged in, whereas 'active' implies initiating own activities and creating own meanings. Presumably therefore some events might require a passively busy involvement in the same way that many production lines and much clerical work are thought to. Other distinctions made were between those events that require participants to 'play a part' or 'act out a script' and those that allow them to be themselves; between those that involve 'internalizing data' and those that involve 'externalizing thoughts and feelings'; between the 'private' and the 'public'; and between 'thinking and observing', and 'saying and doing'.

Predicted Participant Experience

This large cluster contained statements which seemed to have in common the tutors' attempt to characterize the different events by predicting the various ways in which participants are likely to experience them. The diversity of the statements was very wide. There were a number to do with threat, risk, and anxiety; a number to do with immediacy, power, and impact; a number to do with fun, boredom, and hard work; and a number to do with energy and challenge.

Learning Outcomes

This is not in fact a separate cluster but we included it in the diagram because it could well contain all those characteristics contained in the first two we described. That is to say, depending on the tutors' beliefs and general aims, he or she is likely to intend that all the design decisions, participant involvement, and participant experience will lead either to predicted or to emergent learning outcomes. One thing, however, we think will have become clear. The field is highly complex and for predictions about learning to have any claim to validity they will have to acknowledge and incorporate that complexity.

Before moving on to the next aspect of our research which examined the relationship between tutors' intentions and actual participants' experience, we should mention two other smaller groupings we identified in the tutor statements, neither of which seemed to relate to those in Figure 4 but were of a different order altogether. One was broadly concerned with logistics and contained statements about length of time taken, number of people involved, amount of preparation required, and so on. The other could be loosely categorized as public image and contained such distinctions as 'wierdo vs. conventional', 'way-out vs. not way-out', and 'associated with cult/charisma vs. not associated'.

Exploring Participants' Actual Experience

In the previous section we looked at tutors' beliefs about, expectations of, and intentions for experience based events. But we have also been interested in how such events are experienced in practice. To find out about this we have not only observed and recorded incidents but have also used a variation on the stimulated technique described by Bloom (1953). We found little trouble in building up a 'case file' of examples in which the resulting experience was different from that intended by the person setting up the exercise. So an exercise limited in intent to focus on organizational factors may result in quite personal preoccupations. One designed to illustrate concepts in psychology may surface the immediate politics of the participant tutor relationship, and so on. The examples we described earlier in this paper are extracted from that 'case file'. Figure 5 is our attempt to summarize some of the influences that have

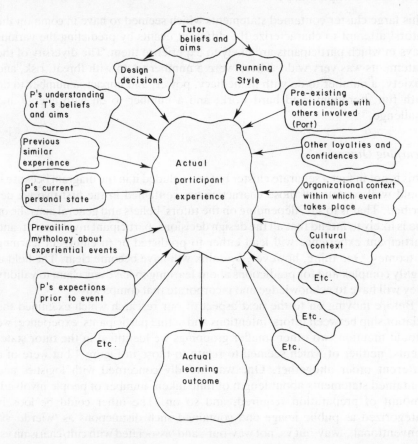

Figure 5. Influences on participant's experience and learning

been at work on the participants' actual experience and presumably therefore on the learning outcomes in the cases we have examined.

Two things need to be said about this diagram. First, it is not intended to be an exclusive list of all the influences on participant experience. Secondly, and more important, the experiences related to these various influences will not necessarily have been discussed or even made explicit during the course of the exercise. This will have been determined to some extent by what has been regarded as 'legitimate', as we have suggested in the previous section.

DISCUSSION

Our main point so far has been to demonstrate that although the trainer can *intend* to limit what goes on 'in class' or within a structured exercise, the participants' resulting experience may well be different from that. What are the implications of this? Are we advocating that trainers should resign themselves to chaos as the only alternative to structure and control? At its most extreme we do see a fundamental choice in practice between rigorous sterility through ever increased control and vigorous fertility with the attendant risks of some confusion. From our standpoint, however, as users of both structured and less structured approaches, it is as much malpractice to constrain participants' opportunity to acknowledge and reflect on the richness of their experience as it is to stand by and watch them drown in an intellectual or emotional morrass.

Experience Based Events, Trainer Control, and Participant Responsibility

What is different about experience based events and why are they special? One approach to this question is to work out what distinguishes, educationally or socially, an experience based event from a lecture. Superficially, a commonly cited difference is whether the participants' involvement is primarily intellectual or emotional, as is implicit in this description of a simulation exercise:

> They did not just talk about how to solve the problems as is done in a case study; they actually solved them. They experienced fears, doubts, satisfactions, they became tired and frustrated, but most of all they became the person with the job to do and the problem to solve (Tansey and Unwin, 1969).

The problem with the intellectual–emotional distinction is that while it contains some truth in practice it is a simplification and therefore misleading. This is equally true for generalizations in terms of 'active or passive' participant roles and for discriminating between different teaching methods as being based on cognitive or affective learning processes. Experiential approaches such as the Sensitivity Training Group contain a significant intellectual component as well as opportunities to deal with values and emotions. Equally, a lecture or seminar is never wholly devoid of emotional content. People can feel strongly about ideas, one way or another, and make emotive connections between the content of a lecture or discussion and other aspects of their work, personal, or social lives.

More substantially, it appears to us that what distinguishes an experience based event from more conventional approaches like the lecture has to do with the certainty or uncertainty attached to the roles of student and teacher and to the nature of the relationship between them. In a lecture, assumptions and expectations are made about the role of the student, the conventions which govern the relationship between teacher and students within the boundary of the lecture, and the material which is legitimate; which usually means that material for learning originates from a body of public knowledge. Both teacher and students are aware of the rules or understandings which determine what is publicly legitimate even though inwardly experience may deviate more broadly from those limits.

But as soon as students or course members are invited to make their experience available, there is some question as to whether these rules or conventions still apply. What are the rules now – and who is to make them? More to the point and the first of the implications which we draw – *in an experience based event the material for learning which the trainer has invited belongs to the participant*. So who now has the responsibility for how it is to be dealt with? In our view participants must be involved in these decisions and should have the final say over which aspects of their experience are made public. Otherwise there is not only a moral question about who should decide how personal material is managed but also a question of how much potential learning relevant to the participant is lost because it is unfacilitated.

A further distinction between experience based events and other approaches to teaching and learning is that the boundaries of time set by the tutor are more problematic in experience based events. An exercise followed by discussion seems a simple enough format but because the experience of the student has been formally engaged, emotional involvement may not terminate just when the exercise timetable says that it should. To illustrate the point: the discussion planned to follow an exercise to demonstrate conflict behaviour and strategies for resolving conflict may depend on the students' collaboration with each other and with the tutor. But what may actually happen is that conflict generated by the exercise may continue long after that part of the session is over. Similarly, and as a general rule, attraction or dislike is more likely to develop quickly between members of a role play than amongst the audience of a lecture. Those feelings will not disappear simply because the exercise is over.

Control and the Educational Context

How do we take account of these ideas in deciding which is the appropriate context in which to use structured exercises, whether to demonstrate particular points or to accelerate discussion on particular themes? It follows from our analysis that the clearest place for structured exercises is in the context of a course or programme in which questions of responsibility and control have been openly explored and where control is shared between trainer and participants. Conversely, the most doubtful application is in the context of a course or programme where this is not the case: for example, an exercise inviting interpersonal feedback in a tightly tutor-controlled course, with a background of conventional assessment methods and where attendance is not voluntary.

As educational technology has been refined, users and designers seem to lose sight of the fact that complexities of authority and responsibility on the course and in the classroom remain. Bradford and Eoyang (1976) observe that if they are too powerful, exercises can be damaging. But it is relatively simple to design an exercise which, because of the material it generates, plunges students in minutes into a personal confrontation which is more appropriately handled in a climate which may take three or four days to build in a less structured group event. A further problem is that the structured nature of design and the directiveness of the tutor results in the students or participants abrogating responsibility for what happens, what happens to them, and for the use to which their personal experience is put. Alternatively, within a context where these matters have been clarified and negotiated and where understanding and mutual trust is already evolving, a structured exercise can be most useful as a calalytic device.

A further implication of our analysis is that for course members to take responsibility within an event or exercises they will need to know something of the rationale that went into its design. Tutors will need to share the ideas on which the design was based. Taking part in events in this way seems appropriate if the participants are or will become managers, coping in their work with responsibilities under technical and social conditions of considerable ambiguity. Is not development of that kind consistent with the overall function of management education?

Implications for Trainer Development

Trainer development should be interdisciplinary and cover a wide range of conceptual frameworks because neither psychology, social psychology, nor sociology alone can offer an adequate explanation of the dynamics of the classroom. Management Education has unfortunately had an unbalanced background dominated by popularized psychology.

Furthermore, if trainers are to use experiential approaches, then their own training should include both structured and unstructured work from exercises to learning communities, hierarchic and anarchic. The effects of different degrees of structure, direction, control, and all other aspects of complexity within experience based designs are not only worth understanding in their own right, but because of the interpersonal, group, and organizational processes which such approaches allow to be studied.

Trainers and teachers need all their wits about them in being aware of, and skilled in helping participants deal with, the processes within the 'classroom' during the use of experiential exercises, however 'structured' they appear to be. Especially useful is the ability to work out which of all that is going on is the process which needs dealing with most urgently.

CONCLUSION

Our title was consciously phrased in the present tense. The aim of this study has been to start for ourselves a process of re-examination and to share those ideas with others, rather than to pre-empt further thinking by presenting some all-embracing 'model'. Experience based events are complex. Ideas free of the strait-jacket which models often seem to impose are, we believe, more likely to provoke or illuminate, even though they may need further refinement.

REFERENCES

Abt, C. C. (1968) Games for learning, in: *Simulation Games in Learning*, Edited by S. S. Boocock and E. O. Schild, Sage, Beverly Hills.

Bloom, B. S. (1953) Thought-processes in lectures and discussions, *Journal of General Education*, III, 3, 160–169.

Bradford, D. and Eoyang, C. (1976) The use and misuse of structured exercises, in: *Developing Social Skills for Managers*, Edited by C. L. Cooper, Macmillan, London.

Burgoyne, J. and Stuart, R. (1978) Management development programmes: Underlying assumptions about learning, in: *Management Development: Context and Strategies*, Edited by J. Burgoyne and R. Stuart.

Coleman, J. S. (1968) Social processes and social simulation games, in: *Simulation Games in Learning*, Edited by S. S. Boocock and E. O. Schild, Sage, Beverly Hills.

Fransella, F. and Bannister, D. (1977) *A Manual for Repertory Grid Technique*, Academic Press, London.

Joyce, B. and Weil, M. (1972) *Models of Teaching*, Prentice-Hall, New Jersey.

Pateman, C. (1970) *Participation and Democratic Theory*, Cambridge University Press.

Reynolds, P. M. (1980) Participation in work and education, in: *Advances in Management Education*, Edited by J. Beck and C. Cox, Wiley, Chichester.

Rockler, M. J. (1978) Applying simulation/gaming, in: *On College Teaching*, Edited by O. Milton, Jossey-Bass, San Francisco.

Tansey, P. J. and Unwin, D. (1969) *Simulation and Gaming in Education*, Methuen Educational, London.

Taylor, J. and Walford, R. (1978) *Learning and the Simulation Game*, The Open University Press, Milton Keynes.

Management Development: Advances in Practice and Theory
Edited by C. Cox and J. Beck
© 1984 John Wiley & Sons Ltd

CHAPTER 15

The Gestalt of Action Learning

Ronnie Lessem

> Each man's identity is an emergent of the myths, rituals and corporate legends of his culture, compounded with the epic of his own personal history. The paradoxical interstice of power and vulnerability, which makes a man most human, rests on his knowing who he is right now, because he can remember who he has been, and because he knows who he hopes to become. All of this comes of the wonder of being able to tell his tale (Kopp, 1976).

INTRODUCTION

Learning about Myself

I can well remember my colleague, Tony Morrison, saying to me 'of course we must use "action learning" '. Back in 1978 I had read Revans' early books on management and warmed to his approach. I respected Tony's judgment and was always open to new ideas. Most important of all, we were engaged in entrepreneurship. The Urban and Economic Development group had recently become involved with the economic regeneration of the inner city. As part of that group I was set to launch a New Enterprise Programme, with the blessing and sponsorship of Manpower Services. We were making things happen for people who make things happen. Action learning had a good ring to it.

My own background was in economics, strategic planning, and corporate responsibility. Wait, I tell a lie. I was reared before that in a zone of transition: Rhodesia becoming Zimbabwe. I was born a middle child in Central Africa of European parents in an African setting. My skin was white and I affiliated with blacks. At the local university I formed a bridging group. We sat in a row in the communal dining room. Black, white, . . . like a chequered table cloth. I devoted most of my early years to playing sport, and the later ones to reading books. My grandfather on one side was a mining engineer, and on the other a rabbi. I seemed destined to move from action to vision and back again.

When I came to the United Kingdom I thought I was leaving class conflict behind me. What I discovered instead was that black and white were replaced by the artisan and the scribe. As a well-trained scribe myself, with fine qualifications from the London School of Economics and Harvard, I launched into corporate planning. Putting pen to paper I drew up all kinds of analyses and future scenarios. I was yet to realize that nothing was further from the business of business.

I returned to business through an indirect route. I say 'return' because my father was your proverbial self-made man. I had chosen to close myself off from that reality. I could only begin to open my eyes when, via the community arts, I came across some 'social entrepreneurs'. So I began to play with the right side of my brain. Mind you, I had been playing around with business games and other fancy educational exercises for years.

From play I was led on to work and creativity. The connection between creativity and entrepreneurship became ever more apparent. As my 'luck line' would have it, I got involved in urban economic development via the Turning-point network – a group of people concerned about mankind in general, and Britain in particular, at a 'Turningpoint'. The inner city was calling for 'indigenous entrepreneurs' and the Manpower Services for new jobs. So I became the intermediary, the middle man, helping to create new enterprise through training programmes. My vision was to turn self-employment into 'employment of the self', and in so doing to bring together the scribe and artisan. So I turned to Grael Associates and to action learning.

Moving from Vision to Action

I had come across Grael, and its Centre for Human Communication, in the mid-seventies. Kevin Kingsland, its founder, had developed an organization and approach to life that brought together Eastern mysticism and modern physics. Grael started off with Yoga courses in the West Country and branched out into printing and publicity, initially to serve its own needs. As student numbers grew, Kevin Kingsland decided to establish his own wholefoods restaurant. This led Grael naturally into the wholefoods business. So the thing grew like Topsy until very recently when the holding company was formed and its constituent 'facets' – publishing, wholefoods distribution, and environmental design – reformed. Printing has been lost in the evolutionary process.

Before he left for India and America, Kingsland devised a programme on 'Developing Guts in Business'. It has its origins in the seven paths of Yoga, and in the 'chakras' of the body. In Table 1 the basic model is outlined, together with the corresponding colours of the rainbow; from violet to red, from vision to action. Whereas, on the one hand, these colours are appealing mnemonic labels, on the other they have physical relevance. For, whereas violet light is of a very high frequency, red light is made up of very low-energy protons.

Table 1 Paths of yoga and personality function

Colour spectrum	Type of yoga	Path of yoga	Personality function
Violet	Tantra	Imagination	Creative
Indigo	Raja	Meditation	Intuitive
Blue	Mantra	Power	Conceptual
Green	Bhakti	Devotion	Emotional
Yellow	Gnana	Psychological discovery	Perceptual
Orange	Hatha	Health	Social
Red	Karma	Activity	Physical

Application of the model
In the first instance, the model is a vehicle for PERSONALITY assessment and inter-personal communication. The following key questions apply to the respective types:

Colour spectrum	Type	Key question
Violet	Imaginative	How do you image the future?
Indigo	Intuitive	How do you experience harmony and beauty?
Blue	Conceptual	What principles do you operate by?
Green	Emotional	What is the threat and how do you defend against it?
Yellow	Perceptual	What change or exciting things are happening?
Orange	Social	Who are you in with?
Red	Physical	What are you physically doing?

Our seven-level model can be used to describe and enrich group, organizational, and management processes. Each level, or energy centre, is in fact some combination (greater or lesser) of the 'three wise men' of psychology: thought (cognitive, C); emotion (affective, A); and action (behavioural, B). Thus, we have:

- Vision – C A B.
- Harmony – C A b.
- Concept – C a B.
- Commitment – c A B.
- Perception – C a b.
- Interaction – c A b.
- Activity – c a B.

In our entrepreneurial programmes we were interested in applying the model to the business process. For, like action learning, we are concerned with the whole man. Moreover, complementing Revans' concern for the whole manager, we are interested in the whole entrepreneur. In this paper I shall be moving back and forth between action learning and self-business development, using the Vision to Action model as a conceptual framework.

THE VISION: DOERS OF THE WORD

But be ye doers of the word and not hearers only, deceiving your own selves. For if any be a hearer of the word, and not a doer, he is like a man beholding his natural face in the glass. For he beholdeth himself and goeth his way, and straightway forgetteth what manner of man he was St James, Epistle 1.22.

Anybody who has read Revans' work is aware of innumerable quotations from the Bible. Whether or not this makes Revans a religious man, there is no doubt that a spiritual element shines through. By 'spiritual' in this context I mean a concern for the essence of man, and for his moral obligations to himself and others. Revans seems to have an almost religious *commitment to action* as opposed to book learning. For, he says, doing or action calls for commitment or true belief, while talking, or argument, calls only for intelligence or quickness of wit. Education has a role, Revans argues, in helping the manager build bridges between his *subjective self* and the world out there. For, he says, human experience remains only partially accessible to external observation. Deep within the manager: is the darkness of his subjective world. Education should play a part in helping him explore that darkness, so that he may find his own way through the solitudes of conscious experience. Doubtless Revans himself has spent many years exploring his own inner world.

But the self is incomplete without the other. Revans alludes to learning situations in which there are neither Chiefs nor Indians. In such a context each, in seeking to enrich and enlarge his own subjective self, helps, reciprocally, to enrich and enlarge the subjective selves of others. Revans even refers to a process of 'spiritual barter', whereby our latent capacity for warm and genuine exchanges manifests itself. Revans is constantly referring to *comrades in adversity* learning from and through each other's moving experiences.

In dealing with 'Vision' on our entrepreneurial programmes, we ask our students to respond to the following questions:
● What is your mission in life?
● How has the mission evolved?
● What business are you therefore in?
● How will it affect the world?
● How will it affect your own life?

Revans' mission may well be reflected in his quote from Toynbee's study of History:

Real progress is found to consist in a process defined as 'etherialisation', an overcoming of material obstacles which releases the energies of society to make responses to challenges which henceforth are internal rather than external, spiritual rather than material.

Revans' vision has evolved through a lifetime of action learning, undoubtedly shaped by his experiences as athlete, scientist, manager, and coal-face worker. It has had a dramatic effect, for many years, on management education in Belgium, and possibly in that country's whole economy (Revans, 1979). In a more diffuse way, action learning has filtered through to Australia, Egypt, India, and the United States; and, recently, into this country. It has always skirted the educational establishment as an overtly subversive influence. Revans himself has devoted some thirty years to developing his ideas and testing them in companies, the hospital service, in government, and education. Perhaps, more than anything else, he has fought to close the gap, particularly in this country, between the artisan and the scribe.

HARMONY: LINKING ARTISAN AND SCRIBE

It is a virtue of action learning that, like truth itself, it is a seamless garment; with its help all parties alike, scribe and artisan, manager and workman, should tackle their common foe, the external problem. Their own opinions of each other, personal and interested, stained by the antipathies of unforgettable tradition, teased and ex-accerbated by every civilising process of the educational establishment, reinforced by every decision of our industrial tribunals, may be, pretty intransigent; advance will not be easy (Revans, 1980, p. 240).

Action learning, at a meta-societal level, digs at the root of our nation's problems. Mant (1977) has put the matter very succinctly. He describes a schizoid person or nation as one whose parts remain split, feeding off and sustaining each other, but essentially unintegrated, incapable of resolution into a whole because of fear of some fantasied destruction. Such a person is, literally, without integrity. The obvious split in Britain, Mant says, is that between owners and workers. Revans addresses the question of integrity simultaneously in both personal and social terms. Action learning is there to link thought and action within the person, as well as artisan and scribe within the nation. Mant describes this social process extremely vividly in the book to which I have already referred:

People in clerkish roles do not have an experience of, and cannot therefore properly comprehend, the three dimensional world of bulk, lumpiness, weight and unpredictability while lies outside their immediate preview. . . . If there were two ingredients I most wanted to inject into clerkish veins, they would be inspiration and panic (Mant, 1977, p. 157).

Revans' 'market niche', as it were, is the no man's land between artisan and scribe, on the one hand, and the gap between learning and the rate of change on the other. Those who cannot keep up with what is new, he maintains, will lose control of their surroundings, while those who take innovation in their stride will profit by being able to turn it to advantage. In other words, in epochs of convulsion, like our own, the advantage lies with those able to learn. This need to develop a 'learning society' has been argued most eloquently, in the Club of Rome publication *The Limits to Learning*, by Botkin and two colleagues. Botkin, in a very similar vein to Revans, claims that we are facing a growing human gap between complexity and our capacity to cope with it. Moreover

> . . . it is not only our capacity to cope which is in question but also our willingness or ability to perceive, understand and take action on present issues, as well as to foresee, overt and take responsibility for future ones (Botkin *et al.*, 1979).

The Limits to Learning distinguishes between what is termed 'maintenance learning' and 'innovative learning'. Whereas the former is needed to cope with what is known, the latter is required to meet the unknown. Innovative learning, then, is first characterized by *anticipation*, i.e. preparation for possible contingencies and future alternatives. It is secondly associated with *participation* which involves co-operation, dialogue, and empathy. It means not only keeping communications open, but also constantly testing one's operating rules and values, retaining those that are relevant, and rejecting those that have become obsolescent. The right to participate, Botkin maintains, is integrally linked to the right to learn. Individuals learn by participating in interactions with society. Society learns, in turn, from the participation of groups and individuals in its activities. Thus, two capacities emerge as particularly important for innovative learning. On the one hand, individuals have to be able to enrich their contexts, keeping up with the rapid appearance of new situations. On the other hand, they must communicate their variety of contexts in ongoing dialogue.

Revans' orientation towards self and other is complemented by Botkin's focus on autonomy and integration. Botkins argues, on the one hand, for individual and societal autonomy as a necessary goal of learning, which can only be achieved when learning itself becomes a process of exercising autonomy. On the other hand, he demonstrates that autonomy involves the assertion of one's right to belong to the whole, to make linkages with others, to understand larger systems, and to see the whole of which one is a part. This is what is meant by integration.

'Harmony', as implied in our own model From Vision to Action, is reflected in the fitting together of parts within a whole. This is what sensitive marketing is all about – finding out how to plug a gap, or fulfil a need, or harmonize one's product with the customer's requirements. The key questions we raise are:

● What are the signs of the times?
● How can you harmonize with them?
● What market niche can you therefore fill?
● Who is willing and able to pay for your product or service?

Revans recognized, way back in 1952 while at the Coal Board, how management–worker relations were impairing the nation's economic performance.

At the same time he recognized that the potential of management science was largely going untapped. Initially in the hospital service, where tensions between nurses and doctors as well as between medical and administrative staff were rife, he was able to bring together social science and statistical methods to research, and act on the problems. Thereafter, in the sixties, Belgian industry seized upon Revans' product. Belgian managers realized that, since they lived in a resource poor, landlocked country, they had to learn faster than their richer European counterparts if they were to keep up. In the United Kingdom Sir Arnold Weinstock, an action centred leader, became receptive to the product in the mid-seventies. He was also willing and able to pay for it.

What, then, was, and is, the market niche being filled? The hospitals, in the action research project, were interested in improving both personal relationships and productivity. The Belgians were probably sold on the prospect of business and economic development. In our own case, in running entrepreneurial programmes, five needs are being fulfilled. First, we have a need to engage in a form of education that meets our values as human beings; secondly, we need to foster independence, initiative, and self-business development amongst our participants; thirdly, we need to create a supportive climate for people in a state of economic and social transition; fourthly, we wish to construct a platform across which the entrepreneurs and their supportive institutions can engage in dialogue and reciprocal exchange. Finally, it is critical that we, as educators, keep close by the entrepreneurs' side so that we can continually learn from their variety.

CONCEPTS OF MANAGEMENT: SYSTEMS ALPHA, BETA, AND GAMMA

Management

Professor Revans distinguishes between two kinds of learning, 'P' and 'Q'. P refers to the acquisition of existing, programmed knowledge, while Q refers to the acquisition of the ability to ask fresh questions. . . . Both types of learning are necessary for managers. They need to keep up to date with their technical work, and also to develop the skill to cope with the ambiguities and uncertainties of innovation and policy making (Boddy, 1980)

From what we have seen so far, the action learning 'concept' is a much richer one than is conventionally considered. Because most of its advocates are either humanistically or pragmatically inclined, the wider social significance of the approach is often missed. Moreover, because of the OD bias of many of its interpreters, the 'management science' aspect is often watered down, if not ignored.

In his early writing on 'Science and the Manager', Revans cited four major forces bearing upon management in the sixties. The first arose through a need for economy in managerial time and effort. For, in an age of science, economy, prudent thought, precise design, and *exact calculation* were each important. Secondly, there was the *analytic method*. While intuition, or the un-remembered urges of the past, must always be the first weapon of the manager, he must be able to grasp the underlying structure of the situations that challenge him, and know of any new methods that may help him in modifying it. Thirdly, the study of variability through the language of *statistics* had brought to the manager a means of describing the unexpected, the capricious, and the random elements of his task. Fourthly and finally, the *social sciences* had thrown a little light on the human forces that, in the final analysis, determine whether or not any enterprise will succeed.

Arising out of these four fields of knowledge is a taxonomy of six subjects of managerial concern:

● The nature of *values*.
● The nature of *information*.
● The logic of *systems*.
● The theory of *decision*.
● The extension of *uncertainty*.
● *Learning* and adaptation.

Whereas the first and last draw primarily upon the social sciences, all the others lend themselves to mathematical, statistical, and intellectual analysis. All six could form a basis for the acquisition of programmed knowledge. It must be pointed out, however, that Revans has always been extremely re-luctant to separate the 'subjective' person from 'objective' knowledge:

> A real *decision*, firstly, is always that of a particular person, with his own ends not to be neglected, his own fears to amplify his problems, his own hopes a mirage to magnify his resources, and his own prejudices, often called, to colour the data in which he works. A choice of *goals* (values), secondly, so much bound up with decision theory, is yet distinct from it, in that the ends for which one strives, deliberately or subconsciously, as an individual or with others, are but partly determined by the calculations of economic strategy. Behind them jostle the egocentric drives of the individual. Thirdly, the relevance of *information*, that product of which the raw material is data and the manufacturing process the personal sensitivities of the individual. . . . Fourthly, the theory of *systems* describes the web in which the world-line of a particular manager is entangled. The assess-ment of *probability* (uncertainty) is, fifthly, that farrago of mathematical statistics and simple guesswork . . . by which we attempt . . . to assess our forgotten experience, our present wishfulness and our future hopes. . . . And, sixthly, the *learning* process . . . integrating everything that one has so far become, and one's sole hope for further improvement (Revans, 1974).

What we see here is a blurring of the scope for programmed (P) and unprogrammed (Q) knowledge. In our taught courses on starting up a business we also began with a formal programme which, we believed, contained the appropriate knowledge base. Our one-week induction course was divided up between marketing, finance, administration, and business planning. However, we soon realized that the person and the knowledge base could not be separated. At the same time we were unwilling to dilute the substantive and necessary content by merely substituting personal problem-solving methods. So we have evolved a structure that brings together business, psychology, and common sense. This is portrayed in Table 2.

Table 2   Entrepreneurship induction programme

Common sense	Psychology	Business
Creating a business	Imagination	Strategy
Finding customers	Intuition (harmony)	Marketing
Getting organized	Conceptualization	Accounting
Doing deals	Involvement	Negotiation
Planning ahead	Perception	Finance
Getting people together	Interaction	Social science
Making things happen	Activity	Action learning

Management Systems

The three principal influences on management may be represented by systems based on the use of information. We call them system alpha – the use of information for DESIGNING objectives; system beta – the use of information for ACHIEVING these objectives; system gamma – the use of information for ADAPTING to experience and to change (Revans, 1971, p. 33).

Probably the best known of all Revans' concepts is what he terms System Alpha. A course of action, he says, to be flexible, demands first that the manager VALUE what he anticipates will be the outcome of the action; secondly, that he be aware of the EXTERNAL DIFFICULTIES he will need to surmount in order to achieve this outcome; and thirdly, that he can find INTERNAL RESOURCES enough to deal with these difficulties at a cost consonant with the value of the outcome. In more everyday terms, Revans therefore raises the following questions on the manager's behalf:

● By what values am I guided?
● What is blocking their fulfilment?
● What can I do against the blockage?
    or
● By what set of values am I guided?
● What is the chance to fulfil them?
● What can I do to seize the chance?

So management objectives should be designed to reflect pervading values, to take into account external difficulties, and to utilize internal resources. Where then does System Beta come in?

System Beta is concerned with achieving objectives. I shall have much more to say about it below, when we deal explicitly with the learning process. Suffice to mention now that, at its simplest, it involves four stages: a survey during which an event is observed; an hypothesis – through which a relation is perceived; an action – in which a trial is made; and an audit – through which the results are analyzed.

System Gamma, finally, which deals with aspects of learning, brings together the person and the situation. The manager, a unique person, confronts a problem in the field and takes in the facts in a particular way. In effect, they are processed by his 'predisposing mental set'. It is his perception of values, the external problem, and the internal resources which condition both his decision and his learning.

In summary, in business or in management, the conceptualizer wishes to know:

● What are the key activities involved?
● How do they relate to each other?
● How do they relate to the outside world?

In management, Revans claims, you need to design objectives, work towards their achievement, and learn in the process. The media through which you work consist of values, information systems, decisions, probabilities, and learning processes. The key individual relationship is that between the manager and the problem, mediated by his predisposing mental set. The key organizational relationship is that between the internal resources and the external environment, mediated by the manager's own goals and values. In business, we claim, you need to formulate an idea (vision), link it with a need (harmony or intuition), and then give it tangible form (comprising money, people, and things). The key individual relationship is that between the entrepreneur and the enterprise, mediated by his motivational style. The key organizational relationship is between the enterprise and the environment, mediated by the entrepreneur's goals and values. This is made apparent when we commit ourselves to action.

COMMITMENT: KNOW, CARE, DO

. . . to enable every enterprise to make better use of its existing resources, by trying to engender within it a social process of learning calculated to help it identify its internal strengths and weaknesses, to understand better its inertias and dynamics, and in other ways to make more effective use of its stored experience (Revans, 1980).

Action learning is not only a vehicle for management development but also, and at the same time, it is a route to organizational learning. One cannot proceed without the other. Because of this characteristic, it is critical that the organization as a whole subscribe to the learning objectives. For as Powell (1980) has pointed out, if the problem is seen as requiring a project report, this does not interfere in any way with the day-to-day operations of the company.

However, if the organization is going to examine procedures, operations, and methods, and then, at the action learner's behest, change them, there is a substantial threat of disruption to present operations that must be anticipated and negotiated. How then can organizational commitment to learning be developed?

Revans (1978) has itemized 15 matters for consideration in any dealings between educator and institutional client:

- The choice of problems around which to form projects.
- The role and responsibilities of clients.
- The qualities and selection of participants.
- The monitoring of projects.
- The development of set (small group) advisers.
- The representation of the firm in any consortium of learning organizations.
- The monitoring of projects.
- The role of training staffs.
- The induction of fellows into their projects.
- The continued academic support for participants.
- The continued role of line management in projects.
- The supply of appropriate technical knowledge.
- The extension of one project into another.
- Issues of cost and benefit.
- The concept of the whole organization as a learning system.

One of the participants in the G.E.C. action learning programme highlighted three considerations as being critical for both participating organization and manager:

> Participants should be given projects that are *major business problems* – simple problems involving tedious clerical work will not train future senior managers. They must also be *important problems* for the client, so that they are determined to get them fixed. [Participants] should be told that there will be *new jobs* at the end of the programme, and these should be arranged as soon as possible (Casey and Pearce, 1977, p. 56).

Two other managers on the same programme listed eight points which determined, in their eyes, the success or failure of the learning activity – for both individual and organization:

1. Certain fundamental *issues* need *clarifying* in the early stages between client and participant (e.g. the 15 mentioned by Revans).

2. The project must be *monitored* regularly.

3. The participant should have a strong *interest* in the type of problem to be solved.

4. The client organization must *define its problem* clearly from the outset.

5. Before the project is started, adequate dialogue should take place between both parties to ensure there is a *common understanding* objective and interest.

   6. Solid *lines of communication* should be established.

   7. *Regular communication* between the client and participant is vital.

   8. The client should not allow the project to diverge from the *set course*, but the participant must be given freedom to approach the problem in the manner he/she sees fit.

Given this wide range of 'political' considerations, it is not surprising that Professor John Morris of Manchester Business School maintains:

> . . . the sympathetic and unobtrusive setting up and management of an action learning programme requires a high order of skill, intelligence and human understanding. It is a lack of this skill that prevents action learning spreading more widely (Morris, 1980).

I have already mentioned that whereas action learning has made great inroads in Belgium, its influence in this country has been sporadic, albeit widely spread. It has been largely up to individual management trainers and consultants in the Industrial Training Boards, Polytechnics, and a few companies, to spread word and action. Casey (1980), in commenting upon the 'Transfer of Learning' has commented upon his difficulties in disseminating action learning 'Programmes'. People clamour for something tangible that they can get hold of rather than a supposed cure-all that will develop the organization as a whole. The sponsors of the Action Learning Programme Consortium – involving a group of companies in the Midlands over a three-year period – have tried to overcome this obstacle by pointing towards some unique and yet tangible features of action learning.

   1. The manager is expected not just to write reports but to initiate action towards a *solution of the problem* he has been diagnosing.

   2. The participating companies can maintain a *healthy balance* between problem-solving and management development. The two are inextricably bound together in action learning.

   3. The project set (group of learners) can become a '*learning community* of peers' with similarly complex problems that require action – action which must be initiated through gaining the understanding and commitment of others.

To cope with the varied problems of implementation that accompany action learning, Revans has developed a formula:

> A decision has to be designed and then negotiated; the problem or the opportunity has first to be diagnosed and then treated. . . . All our work suggests that the guile of realistic diagnosis – what are we after? What stops us? What can we do? – demands just less than 50% of our total effort, and the artfulness of effective negotiation – *who knows? who cares? who can?* – most of the remainder (Revans, 1971).

The formula is in fact drawn from the 'three wise men of psychology' that I previously mentioned. Knowing goes with thinking and cognition; caring goes with feeling and affective processes; doing (being able to) goes with behaviour. In tapping the whole man we tap the whole organization, and vice versa. This

notion of tapping into resources or capacities to achieve objectives, of negotiating for position, is closely linked with the entrepreneurial process of generating commitment to action, or of doing the proverbial deal. We are at a point of transition here, from Vision to Action. The pertinent questions, therefore, are:
- What am I aiming for?
- What resources, risks, and returns are involved (the other three Rs)?
- How do I tap these resources, cope with the risk involved, and generate an acceptable return?

Action learning programmes aim to help managers and organizations develop the proactive skills and capacities required to deal with a changing environment. The resources required to achieve this are primarily management time and organizational co-operation; secondarily people, finance, and facilities. The risk is that the individual's 'predisposing mental set' or the organization's 'prevailing culture' will 'have a great fall', with no one able to 'put the pieces together again'. The expected economic return manifests itself as profits or productivity; the expected psychological return becomes an enhanced ability to cope with change; the expected spiritual return emerges as a resolution of inner conflicts and a gaining of moral conviction; the expected social return realizes itself as Toynbee's process of etherealization and as the healing of Mant's schizoid split in the nation. All these returns, in the final analysis, are based upon a theory, or process, of learning.

THE PROCESS: SCIENCE AND SYSTEM BETA

The theory of learning, whose inner logic is that of system beta, suggests that the recognition of one's own need to learn, the search for new knowledge, the test of that new knowledge in practical action, the critical evaluation of the results of that test, and the consolidation of the whole exercize in memory, are all essential to complete learning (Boddy, 1980).

After all this time and discussion, we still have not entered the heart of the action learning process. Now that we have crossed the threshold from thought (vision, harmonization, concept) into commitment to action, it is time to do so.

It all starts with the division between *action* and *reflection*. The actor changes the system; the reflector changes the self, though neither can operate effectively in isolation of one another. You can only learn from experience (action) if you reflect on it; conversely if you have no experience, you have nothing to base your learning upon (see Figure 1a). If we go a stage further, as Boddy does, our polarity becomes a triangle (see Figure 1b).

The model of the learning process that Revans puts forward is a particular application of scientific method. Faced with a problem, a manager uses his existing stock of *understanding* in general, and of the situation in particular, to decide on a strategy and a means of implementing it. He then goes into an action phase when he tries to put his ideas into practice. This is followed by a

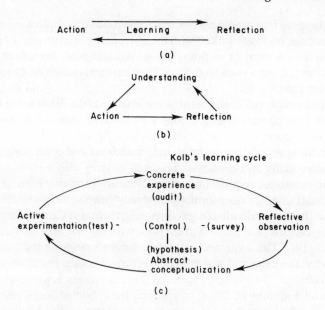

Figure 1

stage of reflection in which the results expected are compared with what has occurred.

From three we move to four, and further into scientific method. For Kolb's well-known learning cycle (Kolb, Rubin, and McIntyre, 1974) is an adaptation, consciously or otherwise, of Revans'. Where Kolb talks of reflective observation, abstract conceptualization, active experimentation, and concrete experience, Revans alludes to survey, hypothesis, practical test, and audit. This constitutes System Beta, the sequential cycle of learning that closely corresponds with scientific method (Figure 1c).

The *survey* activity involves observing, collecting data, investigating, fact-finding, becoming aware; *hypothesis*-making involves speculating, conjecturing, theorizing, design, invention, pattern formation; *testing* involves trial and experimentation; *audit* involves inquiry, inspection, scrutiny, verification; and, finally, there is an integrating *control* phase where an effect is made to improve general methods following the particular experiment. But the matter cannot rest there. For Revans is quick to point out that action learning is not founded on scientific method and rational decision alone. It is equally dependent upon the exchange between people and upon the learning of new behaviour.

We are reminded here of Botkin's innovative learning, involving anticipation and participation:

> Whereas anticipation encourages solidarity in time, participation creates solidarity in space. Anticipation is temporal, while participation is spatial. Where anticipation is a *mental* activity, participation is a *social* one (Botkin *et al.*, 1979).

For Revans learning is also just as much a social as an intellectual process. So where do we go from there?

We must return once more to our three wise men – thinking, feeling, doing. For Kolb's learning cycle allows for thought and action, but not for feeling. If we add this feeling dimension, and keep in mind the customary polarities, we come up with the three-dimensional model portrayed as Figure 2. These three dimensions tie in with Casey's (1976) views on the 'three elementary ideas' contained within action learning:

- There is a great power in an intelligent interloper asking idiot questions, i.e. the power of original *thought*.
- Comrades in adversity learn best with and from each other, i.e. through people with whom they *feel* identified.
- To get things *done* in an organization, one needs to find out who cares, who knows, and who can.

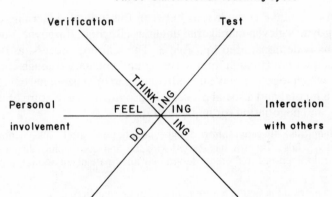

Three dimensional learning cycle

Figure 2. Three-dimensional learning cycle

The three wise men also crop up in what is perhaps the most significant of all Revans' statements:

> One cannot change the system of which one is in command [at least in any new sense] unless one is oneself changed in the process, since the logical structure of both are in correspondence. The change in the system we call action [behavioural]; that in the self we call learning [cognitive] . . . and learning consists much more in the reorganization of what was already [feels] familiar . . . than it consists in acquiring fresh knowledge (Revans, 1980). (The insertions in brackets are the authors.)

Because of common denominators (cognitive, affective, behavioural) the extended learning cycle and the model From Vision to Action are in correspondence. In Figure 3 this is made apparent.

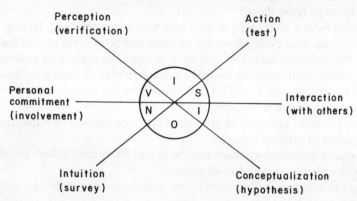

Figure 3. The cycle from vision to action

We can also make comparisons between this extended learning cycle and John Burgoyne's eleven managerial qualities (Boydell, Burgoyne, and Pedler, 1978). This is demonstrated in Table 3. The learning process, as described, contains sequential (though interactive) complementary (though contrasting) activities, which together make up individual and organizational development. It is both a mental and a social process. It also involves a mixture of design, or diagnosis, and negotiation (or implementation).

> After diagnosis, therapy; after design, negotiation, after talk, action. The dichotomy is false: therapy has started with the first questioning; diagnosis continues until the end of treatment; design may anticipate negotiation, but negotia-

Table 3 Management, action learning, and entrepreneurship

Management attributes	Action learning cycle	Entrepreneurship
Self-knowledge Creative imagination Proactivity Balanced learning skills	Control	Vision
Continuing sensitivity to events	Survey	Intuition
Professional knowledge	Hypothesis	Conceptualization
Decision-making skills Emotional resilience		Emotional Commitment
Command of the facts	Verification	Perception
Social skills		Interaction
Mental agility	Test	Action

tion may modify design; talk may prepare for action, but those who act learn to talk in a different tone for the future. But the dichotomy is also true: diagnosis, design and talk call only for intelligence; therapy negotiation and to act call also for courage, belief and commitment (Revans, 1980).

It is based on the whole man (thinking, feeling, doing), constitutes the whole manager (Burgoyne's eleven attributes), embraces the whole of entrepreneurship (From Vision to Action), and serves both the self and the system (Action Learning). All this is but a sketch, though; we still need to go into some more detail as to how people and activities are involved.

INTERACTION: INTRODUCING THE LEARNING SET

Action learning gives participants reasonable opportunities to think and take stock through the eyes of others. Inevitably some participants have limitations which cannot be remedied. And it is counterproductive to highlight characteristics which a participant cannot control or improve. But most individual talents and characteristics can be developed. So within a project set, in the process of seeking solutions to problems, we tried to improve our abilities to *listen*, *analyse* and learn, and to recognize and *improve* various personal inadequacies which impede effective management (Casey and Pearce, 1977). (Authors' italics.)

The 'set' is both route map and resting place for the action learner, even if the 'project' is the actual learning vehicle. It is a source of both challenge and support and a focal point for reflection upon action. It is through the set that the learning cycle is channelled. Action learning, for Revans, is a social process in which managers learn with and from each other by supportive attacks upon real and menacing problems.

A 'set' consists of some five individuals, and is convened by a 'set adviser'. In the course of a day's meeting, arranged perhaps fortnightly over a period of some six months, there will be:

● An exchange of *information* – ideas, advice, contacts, lunches, concepts.
● *Interaction* between set members, offering each other support and encouragement as well as challenge and critical appraisal.
● *Behavioural* change resulting more often from the re-interpretation of past experiences than from the acquisition of fresh knowledge.

Thus, within the set, learning takes place through the interplay of thought (information), feeling (interaction), and action (behaviour). A technologist and would-be entrepreneur, for example, who 'thought' that marketing was about 'bribery and lunches' would never be able to take in fresh information about it until he came to 'feel' differently about the subject. Only when he had re-interpreted his past experiences would he be able to think and subsequently 'act' differently.

Many people think and write about the learning set in psychological and sociological terms. In a very interesting recent article Burgoyne and Cunningham (1980) refer to Lippitt's trifocal perception:

● What is going on inside the person.
● What is going on between people.
● What is going on in terms of group phenomena.

This kind of orientation is exemplified by the comments of a technical manager at G.E.C.

> The project set quickly established a high degree of *group* cohesion. Within the framework of support a high level of *personal integrity* developed . . . support was counterbalanced by criticism. Eventually, however, the persistent pressure of the set on *each other* was effective in creating a definite awareness of personal short-comings (Casey and Pearce, 1977, p. 70) (Authors' italics.)

The 'set adviser' is similarly viewed in social-psychological terms:

The Role of Set Adviser

Burgoyne and Cunningham (1980) refer to the general characteristics of group leader effectiveness cited by Bolman (1976) as providing feedback, questioning participants, providing a behaviour model, giving psychological support, creating structured exercises, and providing conceptual frameworks. Casey adds, more specifically – tolerance for ambiguity, openness and frankness, patience, a desire to see others learn, and the ability to empathize – as required set adviser characteristics.

In contrast, if we take a more pragmatic look at 'group meetings', as Boddy (1980) does, we see the following kinds of things coming up:

(a) meetings provide an opportunity for members to *seek each other's help* in carrying out the project,

(b) meetings serve as an external *source of pressure* upon members to keep their individual work moving,

(c) they are a source of *progress planning and review*,

(d) sessions can lead to the provision of formal *inputs*,

(e) reflection leads to the gaining of *insights*, and

(f) meetings can provide for mutual encouragement and *support*.

We see, in this pragmatic approach, a balance of cognitive, affective, and behavioural influences and outcomes. This is borne out by Casey when he alludes to required set adviser skills:

● Skill in *timing interventions*: too early and the intervention is not understood, too late and the opportunity has passed.
● Skill in *asking good questions*, which make people think, but at the same time feel challenged and supported rather than criticized.
● Skill in using the language of *managers*; avoiding speaking down and intellectualizing.
● Selecting and applying the *appropriate model* to reflect *processes* taking place at a particular time.
● Skill in hearing two or three processes *simultaneously*.

Table 4   Set adviser roles

Role	Thinking	Feeling	Doing
1. Personal development tutor or friend	✔	✔	
2. Negotiator within and without the learning set	✔	✔	✔
3. Technical adviser	✔		
4. Process consultant	✔	✔	
5. Learning catalyst	✔		
6. Problem-solving adviser	✔		
7. Political adviser	✔	✔	

● Skill in *making statements truthfully*, while structuring them to be of maximum use.

Given the range of required skills, the set adviser role can be viewed from a number of perspectives. In Table 4 Casey's seven identified roles are grouped according to the cognitive, affective, or behavioural emphasis. Another way of looking at the set adviser's role is to reflect on how it might evolve over time. Many people believe that the 'adviser', so-called, should phase himself out of a job, and often this does happen. More specifically, Burgoyne and Cunningham (1980) see the role changing over the lifetime of the set. They first identify six kinds of task, and the accompanying role requirements of a set adviser. These are identified in Table 5. As the life of the set evolves, so the 'adviser' moves on down the table, from expert consultant to facilitator. He thus moves away from helping with knowledge acquisition, at the outset, and moves toward the development of skills and, finally, to facilitating personality change. Yet, as Casey suggests, the development of the role is unlikely to be as clear-cut as that. In my own experience, one is sowing seeds for personality change at the outset, and exhibiting expertise even toward the end.

The Action Learning Set

What about the set members themselves. Where do they come from? How do they learn? Where do they go to? Each individual is engaged on a single project

Table 5   The evolving role of set advisers

Process	Role
The task project	Expert consultant
The task process	Expert teacher/educator
Interpersonal processes	Interpersonal process consultant
The learning process	Learning process manager
Learning to learn process	Self-development facilitator

which involves design and implementation. The set is likely to be composed of people with very diverse project interests, but of roughly equal standing to each other. Earlier I referred to Revans' System Gamma and to each individual's 'predisposing mental set':

> ... all managers are branded (some for life) by their past experiences, particularly by those that seemed successful or disastrous at the time; in consequence, managers are often unable to see more in the present than still further confirmation of the unforgettable past; their vision of today's truth is obscured by the mists of yesterday's ghosts (Revans, 1978, p. 5).

Revans goes on to describe four typical responses to tasks that get in the way of learning:

(a) the idolization of past experience,
(b) the charismatic influence of successful managers,
(c) impulsion to instant activity, and
(d) belittlement of subordinates.

By implication, the set needs to deal with these blocks to learning. This is where the re-interpretation of past experience comes in, stimulated by other members' critical *challenges* and warm *support*. It is this particular alternating current which provides the action learning dynamic, but the exact way in which the current flows is very much open to interpretation.

In our model of Vision to Action, the 'Inter-Action' stage involves the following questions:

● Who are the key people involved in the enterprise?
● What are their strengths and motivations?
● How, when, and where can these best be deployed?

In our entrepreneurial programmes, next to the entrepreneurs themselves, it is the banks who are the most important of the interested parties. For this reason we involve a banker in each set, as a fellow learner rather than as an adviser. In other words, the enterprise that the bank manager is developing is his own branch. To check out the strengths and motivations of each entrepreneur, we employ the Strength Deployment Inventory. Based on Erich Fromm's original scheme in Man for Himself, people emerge as Caring/ Nurturing, Autonomous/Analytical, Assertive/Achieving, or Adaptive/ Innovative. Each of these types has his respective strengths and weaknesses (overployed strengths) which they bring into their learning. In the context of a set, the person with an analytical bent can be used in planning, and the person with a caring nature can be relied on to offer support. Conversely, the autonomous individual can resist learning from and through others, while the nurturer may lack the sharp edge required in being constructively critical. In a productive and adaptive learning set, individuals increasingly draw on their innate strengths and curtail their weaknesses. Often, the set adviser has to focus attention on such evident strengths to encourage individuals to make more use of them.

In the final analysis, individuals are making contact through their thoughts (analytical), feelings (caring), and behaviour (achieving) as well as through combinations of all three (adapting). The Strength Deployment Inventory helps to highlight this. The set adviser needs to consolidate upon those notions by reinforcing their application. In some cases, he will need to use structured exercises to achieve this. These we shall consider in the final section on Action or Activity.

ACTION: THE MISSION OF ACTION LEARNING

The fundamental of this educational method is action, as the essential task of the manager. Experts and analysts may advise, forecast, recommend and so forth, but it is the manager's characteristic responsibility that, having listened to his advisors and perhaps debated their advise, he must do something. To help him carry this singular burden effectively is one mission of action learning; a second is to help him learn from the very carrying out of it (Revans, 1977).

There is an essential paradox contained within action learning. As Casey (1978) has pointed out, the project is the vehicle for learning and, as such, it must be seen by the students to be exciting and worth while. Yet, at the same time, by virtue of being a vehicle, it is taking the individual someplace else. It is a means rather than an end. Maybe it is the journey rather than the destination that actually counts. Let us look, then, into the journey.

The 'project' is a journey of some six to nine months' duration, usually in a department or company other than the manager's own. It needs to involve both design and negotiation, problem defining and solution, survey and test, hypothesis and verification. Of course, in our own case the new business is the project. This raises some interesting implications in terms of means and ends. Is the business, in fact, not the end? Before answering this, let us look again into Revans' project-based learning:

● It is concerned with taking *specific action* as well as with talking about taking some general class of action.

● Because specific action must be taken by *specific persons*, those engaged in action learning gain insight not only into their problems, but also into their individual perceptions of, and personal responses to, such problems.

● The majority of time is given both to *diagnosing* in the field what the problem may be (so challenging the value systems of those caught up in it) and to *applying* any solutions to the problem that may be suggested (so challenging the validity of such proposals).

● It is vitally concerned with the *posing of effective questions* in working conditions of ignorance, confusion and uncertainty.

So we begin to form a picture of what needs to go on. But the picture is a bit fuzzy, a bit too general in outline. Let us take a further look at what Revans has to say:

● Learning implies the acquisition of the power to *perform* the action as well as to *specify* it.
● People learn, or change their behaviour, of their *own volition* and not at the will of others.
● In learning such new behaviour, people must attack *real problems* so as to be aware of their progress.
● These attacks must carry significant *risk* of penalty for failure.
● Continuous comparison between prediction of outcome and results will bring home to the person the nature of their *learning* processes and the factors upon which they depend.
● The deliberate analysis and modification of a real-life problem uses the *scientific method*, and thus reflects the learning process of those who take part.

(Cited in Casey and Pearce, 1977.)

Things begin to get clearer. But we are still not right there where it is happening. Thus, it helps to give some examples of actual dialogues of our entrepreneurs in the process of learning. But before we do that I want to say something about the actual goings on of a learning group.

The ideal learning set contains a diverse mix of equally motivated and capable participants. This cannot always be the case. To the extent that it is not, the call for structured exercises is that much the greater. Even in the best of cases, though, it is my belief that certain 'tricks of the trade' are very important when it comes to enlivening and enriching the group learning activity. Some of the most simple and important of these are identified below.

1. Fixing *space and time*, i.e. allowing each participant a fixed allocation of time. This is common practice in action learning sets.

2. Appointing each day an *organizer*, other than the set adviser, to monitor time and space and, ideally, to inject energy into the group when it lags.

3. Devising, on an *ad hoc* basis, *other roles*, such as a 'gamesman', a 'critic', an 'analyst', a 'supporter', and a 'judge'.

4. *Role-playing* past and prospective negotiations between key parties.

5. *Brainstorming*.

6. Deliberate use of *analogy*, for example if a 'support group' acts as a distribution agency for a publishing business, what is the equivalent for a computer bureau?

7. Problem *definition*, i.e. deliberately getting a person to stay with a definition of the problem before moving on.

8. *Decision trees*, as a qualitive tool to structure a person's thinking processes.

9. Turning *statements into questions*; specifying what is the key question being raised over a period of project activity.

10. *Painting pictures*, not literally but in the air, i.e. getting a person to intricately describe what is actually going on before his eyes.

11. *Fantasy pictures*, using imagination, to construct a desirable scenario for the future.

12. Putting *pen to paper*. This is the technique I have used by far the most often. Instead of dealing with an individual's situation off the cuff, we take five minutes to write individual responses.

13. *Composing a symphony*. This involves relating what is happening, or prospective action, to key themes in a person's life, and trying to determine how the symphony will unfold.

14. *Empathy exercise*, i.e. putting yourself into the other person's shoes, and doing or saying what befits your understanding of him.

These are the little exercises used most often in our learning sets. I find that the organizing role, occasional brainstorms, and the putting pen to paper are the most popular elements, besides the basic time structuring. Now let us take a look at a learning set in action.

Participants learn, as we recall, by processing information – past, present, and future; by interacting with others; and by turning words into action.

Learning to Deal with Information

Each week participants were urged to set objectives and to retrospectively review progress.

R: What's your business? What have you done so far? Where do you go from there?

J: (Looks down the list of typed objectives from last week.) I've been too busy to find premises, I'm working on my priorities. I've checked out a lawyer – falling asleep Brian?

B: What you need to set up is an agency arrangement with your supplier of drinks dispensers.

J: It needs delicate wording. Found out I needed a V.A.T. number.

R: What do we feel about Joe's progress?

M: For me, Joe is back to the beginning. I don't see much.

B: Can't you learn about administration as you sell?

J: Advice from the group is OK, but its up to me to make the final decision.

This particular dialogue is rich with information exchange and with a testing out of the different ways of processing it: asking relevant questions, seeking appropriate advisers, giving and taking advice to and from the group. Joe and the set are also checking out together which of his objectives or achievements are more realistic. In the final analysis, Joe takes in what he wants but ultimately asserts his control over his own destiny.

Learning to Turn Words into Action

One of the essential qualities of the entrepreneur is his ability to turn words or ideas into actions or activities. Many of the more academically qualified of our participants found difficulty in integrating their thoughts with a convincing plan of implementation. This was illustrated in one particular simulation, involving Gill (word processing) and a potential collaborator (Oliver's brother). At the end of the first session the set adviser made the comment: 'Gill, you give marvellous presentations, but your report backs here are incredibly low key. Take off a half hour and come back with a prepared case. . . . At this point Gill left the room and, after returning half an hour later, the session was resumed. At the end of it the following comments were made:

R: The whole thing came across more impressively this time. You need always to present this positive image.
G: I took off the half hour you gave me to prepare, by sitting down and closing my eyes.
M: You need to do that more often!

In the course of the simulation, Gill was able to rehearse a negotiating stance. The prospect of making an actual deal that evening obviously made for a sense of urgency. The change in behaviour from the first simulation to the second was induced by that urgency rather than by any from the set 'advisers'. Moreover, the next week Gill had the opportunity of describing the actions she had taken with Oliver's brother that evening.

R: The main thing in the role-play was portraying commitment. How did it come out in practice?
O: The basic conclusion is that, provided the technicalities can be sorted out, they have the basis for a deal. A decision will be made in 6 weeks.
R: What does this all imply for you, Gill?
G: I've got to be harder nosed.
O: My brother wants you to come up with a deal.

Learning From and Through Others

The following excerpt from a set meeting gives an indication of how learning through others take place:

G: One problem is when I answer the phone, trying to arrange for a demonstration, and they say: 'What firm?' I fall to the bottom of the priority list. I have no firm.
O: This raises the question of credibility that comes up with all of us. How much are you prepared to kite fly?

R: What do you think Joe?
J: You've got to incorporate a bit of duplicity. People like to deal with something.
G: I can convince, on the academic side.
B: You've no need to apologize. You're a potential customer.
G: I shall say I am engaged on a survey of word-processing systems.

In this excerpt, Gill, whose business is at a very early stage, is drawing on Joe's experience as a hustler, Brian's as a salesman, and Oliver's as somebody at the same stage of development as herself. She combines their advice to come up with her own solution – integrating her academic bent with their selling/hustling approach. In the process of so doing, moreover, she is also acknowledging her dependence on others, and is learning to respect their different values and viewpoints. Furthermore, she is taking advice, and even criticism, and assimilating it.

CONCLUSION

Action learning gets caught between three stools. On the one stool sits Mr Commonsense. He says he does it anyway, so what is all the fuss about. On the second stool sits Mr Conservative. He says that it all sounds like good stuff, but why should he rock his steady boat. On the third stool sits Mr Social Skills. He says that action learning is just one kind of interpersonal process. It has its merits, but so do a whole lot of other approaches. My object in this paper has been to explore the spaces between the stools, as well as the responses to the three caricatures sitting upon them. For there is much more to action learning than common sense, organization development, and social processes. It is in fact a vehicle for moving all the way through from vision to action. In between we have the need being served, the concept involved, the commitment required, the process undergone, and the people involved. These aspects should become more apparent as the paper unfolds.

Developing a Vision

Vision is not something we associate with common sense, conservatism, or behavioural science. In fact, the vision of action learning has by-passed even some of its disciples. Revans is passionately concerned that we be 'doers of the words' and 'not hearers only'. His numerous quotes from the Bible reveal an almost religious devotion to grounded learning, and to the 'spiritual barter' that fellow learners undergo in the process. In reflecting upon action, man faces up to himself, and in taking appropriate action he has the courage to do something about it.

Perceiving the Need

Because the pragmatist focuses only on the company, and the OD people on the individual and group, society at large gets left out in the cold. Yet not only does Revans believe that learning must be greater than the rate of change in society, but he also deplores the split between artisan and scribe. Like Alistair Mant, he declares that our particular nation's schizoid tendencies, to divorce head from hand, lie at the root of our economic and social needs. The dual need, therefore, is to bring together thought and action within the person, and scribe and artisan within society. The internal issue is totally intertwined with the external one. We ignore this relationship at our peril.

Forming the Concept

Underlying, if not central to action learning is a concept of management developed by Revans. This has been relegated to the 'P' corner – Programmed learning – as opposed to the fashionable 'Q' corner – Questioning or Discovery learning. In fact the subjective manager and the objective management technique can never be completely separated. The stuff of management in Revans' terms – values, systems, information, decisions, uncertainty, and learning – lend themselves to both subjective inference and objective analysis. By separating P from Q too rigidly, management science has become divorced from social science. This has served to reinforce the case of the pragmatic and human relations people, and to detract from the more rigorous, scientific analysts.

Generating Commitment

The 'politics' of organizations have loomed large for action learning. Because of the radical implications of the approach, companies have had to be approached with due care and not a little guile. The 'three wise men' of Revans' organizational world – those who 'know', those who 'care', and those who 'do' – need to be involved in any development programme. The political activity required to generate that commitment has been dealt with at length in the action learning literature. Strategies for infiltrating conservative and pragmatic as well as socially aware institutions have been developed.

Learning

At the core of action learning is a sequential process that Revans has termed System Beta, involving 'survey', 'hypothesis', 'test', and 'audit'. Kolb has used the more academic language of 'reflective observation', 'abstract conceptualization', 'active experimentation', and 'concrete experience'. This is, in fact, scientific method in action. It is the renowned learning cycle. What it does not allow for is the interactive process surrounding it, the comrades in adversity learning from and through each other. For this reason I have developed an extended three-dimensional cycle that incorporates feeling together with thinking and doing. This further cognitive step falls between the stools of common sense, conservatism, and social skills.

Learning in the Set

The learning set truly introduces the social dimension. It has been thoroughly analysed by the OD network. It has been duly scorned by the common sense traditionalists, who say it involves the blind leading the blind. In effect, the combined elements of warm support and critical challenge create an alternating current, which in turn generates a very powerful dynamic. The continual feedback and feedforward between the person and the project ensure that both self and system are ripe for change.

Making Things Happen

Action learning projects incorporate elements of both design and implementation. It is the process of questioning and negotiation of the 'means whereby', rather than the particular result achieved – the 'end game' – that counts. The role of the educator, or facilitator, or 'set adviser' in making things happen remains ambiguous. For some, the role is perceived as an active one; for others more passive. Revans, deliberately or otherwise, has offered few guidelines as to how the role should be played. What he has offered is an extremely rich understanding of both human behaviour and of the management process, which educators are able to draw on. In moving all the way through, from vision to action, thereby falling between the three confining stools, I have hopefully managed to convey the Gestalt of Action Learning.

REFERENCES

Boddy, N. (1980) Some issues in the design of action learning programmes, *Action Learning Newsletter*, **9**.

Bolman, L. (1976) Group leader effectiveness, in: *Developing Social Skills in Managers*, Edited by C. L. Cooper, Macmillan, London.

Botkin, J., *et al*. (1979) *The Limits to Learning*, Pergamon, London.

Boydell, T. A., Burgoyne, J. G., and Pedler, M. J. (1978) *A Manager's Guide to Self Development*, McGraw-Hill.

Burgoyne, J. and Cunningham, I. (1980) Facilitating behaviour in work centred management development programmes, in: *Advances in Management Education*, Edited by J. Beck and C. Cox, Wiley, Chichester.

Casey, D. (1976) The emerging role of the set advisor, *Journal of European Training*, **5**, 3.

Casey, D. (1978) Project training for managers – the underlying paradox, *Journal of European Industrial Training*, **2**, 5.

Casey, D. (1980) Transfer of learning – there are two separate problems, in: *Advances in Management Education*, Edited by J. Beck and C. Cox, Wiley, Chichester.

Casey, M. D. and Pearce, D. J. (1977) *More than Management Development*, Gower Press, London.

Kolb, D. A., Rubin, I. M., and McIntyre, J. M. (1974) *Organisational Psychology. An Experiential Approach*, Prentice-Hall, Englewood Cliffs, N.J.

Kopp, S. (1976) *If you Meet Buddha on the Road, Kill Him*, Bantam Books, New York.

Mant, A. (1977) *The Rise and Fall of the British Manager*, Macmillan, London.

Morris, J. (1980) Book review, *Management Today*, **October 1980**.

Powell, R. (1980) *Initiating Action Learning Programmes*, Training Services, London.

Revans, R. W. (1971) *Developing Effective Managers*, Longmans, London.

Revans, R. W. (1974) *The Theory and Practice of Management*, Macdonald, London.

Revans, R. W. (1977) An action learning trust, *Journal of European Industrial Training*, **1**, 1.

Revans, R. W. (1978) *The ABC of Action Learning*. The Action Learning Trust, Luton.

Revans, R. W. (1979) Belgium's action economy, *Management Today*, **1979**, 56–59, 94–96.

Revans, R. W. (1980) *Action Learning*, Blonde & Briggs, London.

Management Development: Advances in Practice and Theory
Edited by C. Cox and J. Beck
© 1984 John Wiley & Sons Ltd

CHAPTER 16

Gestalt for Managers

Tony Fraser

INTRODUCTION

Interpersonal relations have become an increasing concern for managers in most organizations. Dramatic social changes and technical advance create increasing demands for understanding and co-operation between people. Misunderstandings, conflict and 'bad feelings' incur huge costs in terms of wasted effort and resources.

As managers begin to examine the field of interpersonal relationships, hoping to find a way 'to put things right', they are faced with complexity and difficulty. The majority of useful frameworks like Transactional Analysis, Interaction Analysis, or the 'T'-group as well as Gestalt which have been evolving over the last 30 years are still only partially understood and do not produce consistent results. This is probably because they originate from the field of psychotherapy rather than industry or commerce (because it is therapists more than any other group who have been most directly concerned in interpersonal relations). Although psychotherapy provides a depth of experience and understanding not available from other sources, it does not easily find acceptance in the commercial and industrial world. Consequently, managers and trainers are coming to recognize the need to adapt and develop the frameworks taken from other fields such as psychotherapy, and rightly no longer expect to uncover a magic formula or simple answer.

Gestalt theory is neither magic nor simple, nor does it represent an advance in the sense of superseding other approaches. What it does is add depth to understanding in highlighting the process of relationships, allowing this process to be experienced, explored, and understood. In a sense Gestalt is a micro level approach, focusing on events moment by moment. Unlike many of the more familiar frameworks, the Gestalt method entails the awareness of feelings and

251

needs and their direct expression creatively and adaptively. The result of this approach is that people are more likely to express themselves as they are.

In this paper I hope to outline some of the applications of a Gestalt approach in management, to introduce the main concepts and assumptions, the implications of these, and finally to outline the learning methods used in Gestalt training with managers.

APPLICATIONS

The Gestalt approach used as a management training tool can help to unblock the defensive exchanges that become a part of the manager's relationship with subordinates and colleagues. The blocks are discussed again in more detail in the section on 'interruptions'. It is worth recognizing at this stage that many of the responses are based on false assumptions or perceptions. The Gestalt training aims at the individual being capable of full awareness of the realities of his world and the ability to adapt to them.

Specifically the skills in *handling conflict* are important. This would entail, for example, the manager's ability to confront his subordinates with their avoiding awkward issues. Once the avoidance has been acknowledged, the issue itself can be resolved. In doing so both parties will need to be willing to *take responsibility* for actions and make realistic contracts. To help this process the manager will need to be *aware of himself* so that the *communication remains clear and open*. In this context a clear understanding of mutual expectations and demands will be required.

Picking up an introductory illustration, it is clear that often the main orientation in attending meetings is defensive. The primary objective is to avoid being damaged or hurt in any way. The goals associated with the achievement of productive work or making decisions are secondary. Typical strategies in defence are deflection, deception, manipulation, pre-emptive strikes, counter-attack, and the making of alliances and treaties. Most of the energy of those participating in the manager's meeting are devoted to these types of activities and all to avoid being damaged or hurt!

Is it worth taking all that time and trouble to fend off the hostility of others? Under the prevailing culture, clearly the answer must be 'yes', since the income and security of the manager may well be at stake! The important question concerns how the culture can be changed so that each manager is willing to take responsibility for himself.

In this sense taking responsibility means:

    (a) expressing needs, demands, and conflicts to the other managers;
    (b) confronting or exposing defending behaviours; and
    (c) expressing feelings (e.g. anger, fear, sadness, pleasure).

The expression of needs, demands, and conflicts that might arise could lead to agreements about the sharing of information, team support in solving problems, levels of effort, and priorities for action. It is likely that some disagreements will remain, but once expressed and aired these need not take up the time and energy in the group.

Confronting or exposing defending behaviours is likely to lead the group into more open patterns of communication. Managers are likely to replace the complex defence strategies with much more straightforward self-expression!

'What have you done about . . .?' becomes 'I am angry that you have done nothing about . . . .!'

'We cannot accept the proposal concerning . . .' becomes 'I will not accept . . .'.

Expressing feelings would involve the managers' sharing their concerns in terms of their needs for security, the maintenance of a particular self-image and their responses to their experience of each other and the events at work. The meeting would therefore include questions about feelings:

'How do you feel about the allocation of responsibilities?'

'Are you upset about our turning down your idea?' And questions about the expression of feelings:

'I am afraid that this new system will reduce my influence as a manager.'

'I feel sad that I have not been supporting you recently.'

Taking responsibility, then, means being aware of oneself and taking the risk of expressing oneself openly and authentically. The consequence of introducing a Gestalt approach to a management group is likely to be the development of a management team who can work together effectively. They are able to devote much more energy to the work of managing an organization and less to protecting themselves from each other.

Coaching and Self-development

The Gestalt approach can provide practical methods for coaching and self-development. These methods focus attention on the blocks to learning so that the manager spends time removing the blocks rather than pushing harder against resistance.

In terms of coaching this might mean that the manager explores with the subordinate what gets in the way of his doing a particular job. The blocks might be in the form of rules about behaviour or the need to maintain his image, fears of approaching senior managers to ask questions, fears of making mistakes, etc. In partnership the manager and his subordinate can develop creative ways to test the reality on which these rules, fears, etc. are all based. Having done so, the ways of coping with the reality can be developed. The coaching relationship changes from being one in which targets are set and the manager urges, encourages, or pushes the subordinate, to one in which the manager assumes that there are blocks to learning. The partnership is then devoted to removing these blocks. The process changes from pulling the ends harder in order to untie the knot, to pulling carefully and gently at the point where the knot is held.

Blocks to learning in self-development may occur in the environment (e.g. restrictive organization rules, little information-sharing) or they may occur within the individual (e.g. over-dependence, poor perceptual skills).

The Gestalt approach would lead to the identification of these blocks as well as exploring creative ways of removing them. In doing so the individual would be encouraged to seek feedback, to explore feelings, test the reality of his perceptions and fantasies, and the relevance of his personal rules. Above all the person engaged in self-development would be encouraged to try things out and to experiment with new approaches. In this process of discovery the individual is likely to draw on techniques of self-support, starting from issues concerning breathing and physical stance, leading to emotional self-support to take the risks necessary for learning.

Assertiveness/Influencing

The real skills in assertion or influencing are rooted in self-confidence. At a behavioural level it is possible to develop some effective techniques for self-assertion. These behavioural skills alone are in themselves unlikely to generate the confidence needed for effectively implementing them.

The Gestalt method encourages self-awareness, from which develops first a recognition of personal needs and, secondly, an acknowledgement of the ability and value of oneself in pursuing the process of need fulfilment.

The emphasis on good contact helps to ensure that in both making demands and responding to them people are communicating in a clear, simple, and specific way. For example, the question 'Can you spare me a minute?' might be made more direct by, say, 'I want to discuss something with you' and 'I find that idea rather difficult to understand' would become 'I don't agree with you'.

A further contribution that the Gestalt approach makes to the area of assertiveness stems from the idea of retroflection, to be discussed below. Broadly speaking, this is the process of turning back energy on oneself that could better be used to achieve results. Using a Gestalt approach the person is encouraged to look outwards to the world for the satisfaction of needs. These needs are far more likely to be satisfied by initiating action than waiting 'passively' for the world to happen (see Table 1).

ORIGINS OF THE GESTALT APPROACH

The word 'Gestalt' comes from the German and has no exact English equivalent. An approximate translation is 'whole picture' or 'complete image' and refers to the result of integrating a series of detailed perceptions into a complete experience or meaningful image which is more than the sum of its parts.

An example of this would be the way in which a collection of notes played in sequence resolves into a melody; a few lines, drawn on paper, become a face.

The Gestalt phenomenon was studied by German psychologists in the nineteenth century. They explored the ways in which humans and other animals integrate their perceptions and make sense of the world (Kohler, 1929). During the late 1940s and 1950s a group of psychotherapists in America began to combine these ideas with existing knowledge of psychoanalysis and their understanding of phenomenology. One result was a new approach to psychotherapy (Perls, Hefferline, and Goodman, 1973), in which the processes of Gestalt formations and destructions were applied to the whole range of human experience. The idea that the fulfilment of all human needs required first the formation and subsequently the destruction of a well-formed Gestalt led to the development of new understanding and subsequently implied methods of therapy. The Esalen Institute in California, established in the early 1950s by Frederick Perls and others, became a centre for Gestalt therapy and other new approaches to personal growth.

Since that time Gestalt therapy has become widely known and used by therapists and many books are available on the subject (Fagan and Shepherd, 1972; Polster and Polster, 1973). There are a number of centres at which Gestalt training can be received, there being major European centres in Germany, Holland, Italy, England, and Scotland. Gestalt methods are now frequently and often successfully applied in management training programmes (Herman and Korenich, 1977).

GESTALT FORMATION AND DESTRUCTION

The basic idea of the Gestalt approach is that in maintaining a balanced state of well-being, human needs arise and are satisfied in a pattern of Gestalt formations and destructions.

For example, imagine it is late evening and you are sitting comfortably in an armchair reading an absorbing book in your centrally heated home. Although you are not aware of it the heating system switches off automatically and the room begins to cool. At this stage the book continues to hold your attention and forms a 'foreground', the cooling temperature is the background. At first you are not aware of the drop in temperature, but gradually as it becomes colder you begin to respond to the cold, although perhaps not consciously. You may tuck your legs underneath you or move slightly in order to sit more compactly in some way. Your conscious attention, however, is still entirely in the book whilst your body begins to respond to another need. The Gestalt in relation to your need for warmth is beginning to form although it has not yet become a foreground figure.

Gradually, as the temperature drops, your discomfort penetrates increasingly into your awareness. You may make increasing efforts to ignore the cold

Table 1 Confronting blocks to problem-solving. Reproduced from K. Phillips and T. Fraser, *Facing up to People*, Gower, 1982

Block	Example	Possible confrontation
Generalizing	This person uses generalizations as basis for believing that he/she cannot do anything differently. 'After all everybody has this problem.' 'One has to cope as best one can.'	'How specifically is this a problem for *you*?' 'Say "I" rather than "one".'.
Talking about	This person talks about a whole range of things rather than face up to his/her particular problem. 'This friend of mine had the same problem and she had a terrible time . . .'	'What does this mean for you?' Focus on 'what' and 'how' rather than 'why'.
Having rigid expectations of others	This person has rigid expectations of others and frequently uses them as the basis for subsequently being angry or disappointed. 'In the light of all the sacrifices I've made I think I have a right to expect some gratitude from all my clients.'	'How have you come to have this expectation?' 'How long are you prepared to wait for your clients to express gratitude?' 'What are the consequences for you of having this expectation?' 'You sound as if you're setting yourself up to be disappointed.'
Blocking out internal awareness	This person blocks out awareness of internal processes. 'Of course it doesn't worry me in the slightest.'	'Not the *slightest* little bit?' 'What you're saying doesn't match your tone of voice.' 'What are you feeling?'
Blocking out external awareness	This person blocks out awareness of other people's behaviour and attitudes. 'Jean looks perfectly happy to me.' (Jean is on the verge of tears.)	'What do you see when you look at Jean?' 'What are you aware of?'
Self-interrupting	This person has difficulty in maintaining concentration and interrupts himself/herself by jumping from one point to another, agitation or withdrawal. The agitation may be retroflection, e.g. anger turned against self rather than others.	'I notice that you haven't answered my question.' 'What are you doing?' 'Exaggerate your foot-tapping. Is there a message for yourself or somebody else?' 'Sit still and concentrate on what I'm saying.' Imagery work, e.g. drawing.

Catastrophizing	This person uses a catastrophic fantasy as an excuse for avoiding responsibility and not taking action. 'I couldn't possibly do that, she would never speak to me again!'	'Would it have to end up that way?' 'What is the worst thing which could happen to you?'
Imagining artificial constraints	This person imagines artificial constraints as a basis for believing that nothing can be done to solve the problem. 'I can't do that.' 'My boss would never agree to it.'	'Say ''won't'' rather than ''can't''.' 'How do you know?' 'How could you persuade her?'
Projecting	This person attributes to others qualities which are really in himself/herself. 'The trouble with you is that you are so damned aggressive!'	'Try saying that about yourself.' 'Does what you have said apply to you at all?'
Minimizing	This person minimizes their feelings or the extent of their problems as the basis for believing they do not have to be faced up to. 'It's so unimportant it is not really worth worrying about.'	'Is it really so unimportant? You've spent a long time talking about it.' 'Tell me of any feelings no matter how small, which you have when you think about this problem.'
Sticking to obsolete rules	This person uses old rules of behaviour even though they are not helpful in dealing with current problems and relationships. 'Of course I must always be polite to people.'	'That sounds like a rule for you.' 'What's the benefit for you of that rule?' 'Where did you learn that?' 'What does politeness mean for you?'
Getting into a vicious circle of top dog/ underdog conflict	This person is caught up in a conflict between personal 'oughts' and 'wants'. The 'oughts' may have been swallowed whole (introjects) in childhood on the basis that this was how life had to be.	'What do you want to do?' 'What do you think you ought to do?' 'Is there any way of reconciling your ''oughts'' and ''wants''?' Two-chair work.

and maintain your involvement with the book but there comes a point at which you can no longer sustain your interest in reading. At this point the existing need or interest is destroyed in favour of a new one – the need to maintain body comfort through warmth. The new Gestalt 'figure' emerges into and now occupies the foreground of your attention.

You leave the book and the chair and take some action designed to restore your comfort (turning the heating back on, covering yourself with a blanket, going to bed). Once you are warm again you can pick up the book and quickly the temperature, along with all other possible concerns, becomes part of the background and the book's contents once again absorb your attention.

Needs are present in a hierarchy, so priorities resulting from the relationship between the individual and the environment are fulfilled to drop away and be replaced by other needs (see Figure 1).

All but the mentally or physically sick and the poor and oppressed can orient and organize themselves sufficiently to satisfy their needs concerned with most physical functioning. We mostly find breathing, eating, drinking, excreting, and resting fairly straightforward and satisfying, although this is by no means as obvious as it perhaps sounds. People who eat too much, drink too much, suffer from constipation or insomnia are not thought of as sick, but for these people even basic physical functioning, let alone the more complex relationships, presents difficulties.

Other needs are more elusive, like the needs to give and receive approval, love, recognition, companionship, stimulation, interest, acceptance, and communication. In these circumstances a person is perhaps unable to perceive his need clearly or does not know how to get satisfaction. The result may be a sense of uneasiness or confusion, but at the same time nothing stands out clearly.

Figure 1. Gestalt formation and destruction

An example in management might be an uneasy feeling that your boss treats other members of his group of subordinates in a more relaxed and informal way: he may seem to talk with them frequently, freely, and with warmth; with you he is rather formal and abrupt. You perhaps feel a little hurt and isolated and find yourself pulling back from contact both with your boss and with colleagues. Your dissatisfaction leads to a sense of isolation, low motivation, and a drop in work output which in itself produces a vicious circle. You tell yourself there's nothing you can do; either you carry on as you are or go and find yourself another job!

Here the need for personal recognition and acceptance remains unsatisfied and being as it were 'unfinished business' disturbs the healthy pattern of emerging needs and their satisfaction. In this way collections of unfinished business clutter our lives so that we are less clear and less ready for the next experience. The alternatives of asking for what you want or expressing the feelings may well have been enough to complete the Gestalt or perhaps some more creative alternatives for satisfying the need could be found elsewhere leaving you free to give all your attention to what would then become a new situation.

AWARENESS AND EXPRESSION

Learning to complete each piece of business in life requires awareness, sensitivity, creativity, and courage.

Awareness is important in order to recognize the unsatisfied needs that arise during the conduct of tasks and relationships. The guide to these needs are the emotions and feelings that we experience. In simple uninhibited terms anger is a guide to the wish to destroy or fight; sadness is concerned with loss; fear with the need to take flight or escape; pleasure with the wish to get more or move closer. At their strongest these feelings are unmistakable. Quickly without thinking these emotions instruct our behaviour. We use our energy to destroy or change what makes us angry, are reconciled to loss, move away from what is frightening, and approach or stay with what is pleasing.

Weaker emotional signals within us are less easily attended to or may be ignored and the guidance system breaks down. Holding back anger, even a little of it, leaves some need unsatisfied; putting a brave face on sadness leaves us in need of comfort; ignoring fear results in insecurity; and neglecting pleasure leaves us unfulfilled. The effects are cumulative.

Lack of awareness of feelings in chronic form results in the collection of unfinished business and unsatisfied needs. Usually the emotional blind spots are in one or two particular areas, blocking perhaps anger or sadness or fear, etc. rather than all feelings. The loss of awareness of some feelings then means the loss of a fully functioning guidance system for action.

Being aware of our feelings gives us a sense of direction for action, but in itself it is not enough. We also need to know how to be creative and adaptive in expressing them. The small infant initially uses very simple ways of getting what he wants – crying, smiling, grabbing, smashing. In growing up he learns new patterns, and to control and postpone some immediate wants in order for them to be better satisfied. In this way the family acts as a kind of emotional gymnasium in which we develop some muscles but not others. Our emotional development is therefore limited by our early experiences. Even so, as we get older many of these abilities decline with lack of use. Physical fitness is created from frequent and vigorous exercise which, whilst often painful at the time (with aches in muscles we did not know we had), is recognized as being healthy.

The same process applies to feelings and the Gestalt method encourages the expression of emotions as a means for dealing with present needs and, in specific exercises, as a means for developing emotional fitness. Just as physical fitness does not imply physical violence, so emotional fitness does not lead to the excessive or inappropriate use of feelings, but to their sensitive and effective expression. The Gestalt training ground then acts as a continuation of the emotional gymnasium where, under supervision, people can undertake exercises which stretch and stimulate, bringing about flexibility, strength, and stamina.

It takes courage to try out and experiment with new ways of behaving and new kinds of relationships, without knowing in advance what the result of our actions will be. A common example is when we ask someone to be a friend and risk rejection. Many fear rejection so much that they never get around to asking! This quality of courage and trust in our personal ability to survive, adapt and be satisfied is developed in Gestalt training through experience.

The process of healthy, creative adaptation occurs moment by moment as we encounter the environment. It entails a sequence of events and experiences which begin with a sense of 'beneficial indifference' – a state of well-being and satisfaction in which you are ready for the next thing without any positive or negative interest in anything in particular. At this moment there is no foreground figure, the foreground becomes a fertile field in which some object of interest will grow.

In the next moment, from among a series of, until now, equally unimportant possibilities, some aspect begins to emerge as more significant. As you begin to recognize and endow this figure with interest, feeling, and energy, it forms more and more clearly. As the figure emerges and brightens until it stands out clearly, you begin to approach or explore the environment, seeking out the means or possibility of need fulfilment. This process of orientation gives way to further activity in which you make contact with the environment. In the course of this contact you change the environment by adding, taking, exchanging, destroying, creating, etc. As you do so you destroy the Gestalt. The bright figure of interest dies away leaving the foreground empty and you return to a state of benign indifference: you are ready for something new.

This entire process can take place in the space of less than one second or may require minutes, hours, days, or even years. At one level, turning down a car radio that is too loud or perhaps adjusting the heater. At another level, stopping the car to eat and drink, and at a third completing a project such as making something or writing and presenting this paper. In terms of communication or relationships, it might mean making eye contact with someone as you enter a room and exchanging smiles, it might mean asking for information from a colleague. It might mean confronting someone with their lack of consideration for you in the way in which they performed their job. Each of these involves awareness, orientation, action, contact, and completion.

GESTALT ASSUMPTIONS

The Gestalt approach has its roots in the humanist movement and shares with other humanistic approaches a set of assumptions and beliefs (Passons, 1975). The methods and training originate from and aim toward the realization of these.

1. Man is a whole being who *is*, rather than *has*, a body, emotions, thoughts, sensations, and perceptions, all of which function interrelatedly.

In conjunction with Reich and others, Gestaltists take the view that it makes no sense to divide the human into thoughts and feelings, mind and body, emotions and sensations. In the process of making contact, of moving toward and acting in the environment, the healthy individual integrates and directs his experience and attention toward the desired goal. The splitting of mind and body, thoughts and feelings, and their separation is taken as evidence of the interruption of the need–fulfilment cycle and of unfinished business interfering in the completion of a Gestalt.

Common examples of interruptions or breaking away from the possibility of contact are:
- Breathing irregularities such as catching breath, sighing, blowing out, holding breath, shallow breathing.
- Swallowing, clearing the throat, coughing, constricting the throat.
- Muscle tightening jaw or fist clenching, pressing or pushing down, curling up fingers or toes. Stretching or distorting face, fixed smile, frowning.
- Agitation, foot-, finger-, hand-tapping, holding a part of self.
- Blinking, closing eyes, looking away, up, down.
- Stroking or rubbing hands, legs, face, arms, or neck.

These interruptions are momentary and happen outside the awareness of the person doing them. Yet each serves to divert energy away from making contact in the environment and blocks the process of Gestalt destruction.

2. Man is part of his environment and cannot be understood outside of it.

In the main Gestalt text book, *Gestalt Therapy*, this assumption is presented in terms of the 'organism environment field'. It is argued from the phenomenological standpoint that the separation of the organism from its environment simply does not make sense. The individual is inevitably at every moment a part of some field and it is the nature of the relationship between him and his environment which determines his behaviour.

The physical sciences can and do abstract from the environment and study its elements in isolation. Since the qualities of inanimate elements are unaffected by observation and they can exist independently of one another, this study yields valid results. This does not hold for any attempt at understanding human beings. As human beings we are organisms adapted to and a part of the environment with which we make contact. It is in terms of the contact boundary that our behaviour becomes meaningful, or otherwise. Our thoughts, actions, behaviour, and feelings in combination are the means for experiencing and interacting with the changing world of our environment.

3. Man is proactive rather than reactive. He determines his own responses to external stimuli.

A manager who says 'I had no choice', is operating from the reactive position. The Gestalt approach assumes that, except for reflexes and the basic instincts, we have choices about how we respond to the environment. Regardless of what is done to us we are free to choose from a wide range of options. Nor do we have to wait passively to see what the world will provide for us. Man is capable of creating, adapting, seeking, and moving toward objects of interest in the environment. For the individual to remain passive at a time of need or want indicates some kind of block or interruption to the cycle of need fulfilment.

4. Man is capable of being aware of his experience.

As you sit reading you probably do not direct your attention to your breathing, the various points of stiffness or tension in shoulders, neck, forehead, or to any small aches and pains that you might now be aware of. By a simple willing you can discover what you do with hands and feet, where your thoughts go, rising and falling levels of interest or excitement. It is possible to follow your emotional state through anger, sadness, fear, and pleasure.

This kind of self-awareness is rarely the subject of much deliberate attention, particularly if everything is normal. Even familiar aches and pains lose your attention as they continue unchanging. Only during times of great stress, change, or dysfunction do we become aware of ourselves.

5. Man, through self-awareness, is capable of choice and is thus responsible for covert and overt behaviour.

'I didn't mean to' or 'You make me feel . . . angry, hurt, sad'. These statements do not make much sense when looked at closely. The intention that is denied in the first statement may not have been in awareness, but nevertheless all actions carry some kind of direction or intention; the difficulty is in discovering to what piece of unfinished business the energy or activity is related if not related to the current situation. Here, as with the second statement, it is the denial of responsibility which is misleading.

The second statement implies that by your behaviour you have control over my feelings. With the exception of pain inflicted physically, one person cannot make another person feel anything particular. The implication of a causal relationship is false. That is not to say that there is no relationship between your behaviour and my feelings, but the Gestalt approach insists that each person accepts responsibility for himself and his feelings, recognizing that they are not caused by *your* action but a guide to my needs in the context of your behaviour.

6. Man possesses the means and ability to be satisfied and restore himself through his own assets.

The Gestaltist would not accept that someone cannot do something because he simply 'hasn't got it in him!'. (With the obvious exceptions created by physical limitations.) The Gestalt assumption then is that in terms of relationships the human being has sufficient inherent possibilities to meet all his needs. The denial of this is assumed to reflect the existence either of some kind of block within the individual or that the person simply does not know how to learn.

An example might be the person who wants physical comforting but does not know how to get it. There are a number of problems:
    (a) recognizing and accepting his need or want;
    (b) finding out who might be willing to comfort him;
    (c) choosing a time, place, and means of asking that is most likely to be effective; and
    (d) being open to the comfort and getting satisfaction when it is provided.

In saying he 'can't' get what he wants or needs the individual is really saying 'I don't know how to . . .' or 'I refuse to . . .' because of risks or 'imagined consequences'.

7. Man can experience himself only in the present. The past and the future can only be experienced in 'the now' through remembering and anticipation.

'Here and now' has become a cliché; nevertheless many training methods, including Gestalt, insist that learning takes place in the present and not by reference to one's own or others' past experience.

The Gestalt assumption is tied in with the idea of unfinished business or unsatisfied needs and the importance of acting in the environment as the source of satisfaction. Preoccupation with the past or the future will inevitably leave present needs unattended. Memories and fantasies of the future can and do serve as guides to present needs and present actions. However, in remembering or fantasizing we withdraw from the possibility of contact and action *now* and energy available is used up on oneself. The result is the accumulation of further unfinished business.

Anxiety can be defined as awareness of the gap between 'now' and 'then'. It is different from fear in that fear is the experience resulting from some real threat in the environment. Anxiety is entirely an internally-based experience. In concentrating on what is here and now the interruptions which occur together with or result in anxiety, can be recognized and worked on, and blocks to behaviour can be removed.

INTERRUPTIONS

The healthy process of need fulfilment is interrupted frequently by internal processes which have become habitual patterns of behaviour. Like all habits their persistent repetition leads to their taking place outside of awareness. The result is that we lose sight of them and therefore the behaviour is no longer available for review or consideration. The interruption is a set pattern occurring frequently and automatically.

Let us look at how this might work. A manager, whilst effective in most aspects of his work, particularly the administrative parts, avoids issues concerning the control or direction of his staff. As a result his department is less productive than he would like and the relationship between manager and subordinates is awkward and uncomfortable. The manager is aware of the poor relationships and wants to tackle the problem but cannot bring himself to confront his staff nor does he know how to do so. As a result the relationships in the department become more distant and the manager feels increasingly insecure and blames himself. Whilst he is aware of what he would like to do, he is not clearly aware of his feelings of anger, or his fear, and the two become confused into a general sense of discomfort which he pushes aside in order to get on with the work. The possibility of effective action is blocked by a number of processes each of which take place, as it were, automatically. These are called 'interruptions'; the main ones will be discussed in the following sections.

Projecting

Projecting is imagining that our own unwanted feelings/or experience belong to someone else. Our manager becomes aware of the need to criticize but immediately feels very uncomfortable and after a moment's confusion diverts his attention to something else. Between the awareness and the discomfort the manager has a momentary picture (based on his own unfinished experience) of how it feels to be criticized. He puts himself in the subordinate's place and feels bad. This bad feeling is projected onto the subordinate. Now the manager believes his own bad feelings actually belong to the subordinate and holds back from criticising.

We are particularly prone to projecting onto authority figures and so bosses are often attributed with characteristics of the projecting subordinate. Concealed criticism, excessive expectations, manipulation, and deviousness are seen as properties of the boss (which they may well be) allowing the subordinate to feel oppressed or restricted. Having done so, the subordinate feels justified in engaging in activities or comments which might be seen as critical, demanding, and manipulative or devious.

Trainers are also prone to projecting their demands of themselves onto their trainees. Questions from interested students become challenges designed to test their ability; comments which express doubt or concern are taken as rejection; criticism of the ideas presented is taken as failure by the tutor. The extent to which these perceptions are true (and they always have some basis in reality) will vary. Whether or not the automatic defence processes of the trainer are engaged will depend on his ability to recognize the difference between the demands he makes on himself and those made on him by others; in other words his ability to know the difference between his and theirs.

Retroflection

Let us return to our manager who is stuck with his desire for more output from his staff which he cannot achieve. He has interrupted the possibility of criticizing by projecting his own bad feelings and holds back on account of these. He further interrupts by retroflecting or *turning back on himself feelings that are concerned with someone or something in the environment.*

Instead of using his energy in acting positively toward his environment and confronting his subordinates with his needs and standards, our manager blames himself. In a few punishing moments of internal dialogue he accuses himself of being 'spineless', lacking in courage, and not the man he ought to be. For a few moments he despises and rejects himself. This internal splitting process will be accompanied by increased tension in many parts of the body, frowning, and may include hitting something, even himself! Other examples of retroflected aggression are jaw clenching and nail-biting, while retroflected love or comforting can be observed in terms of self-stroking gestures.

Obviously, British society in general, and organizations in particular, encourage retroflection. The stiff upper lip is a deformity fostered by the educational system and fostered by many parts of 'the establishment'. Whilst there are some grounds for believing that not all responses need carry the full weight of emotion found in, say, encounter groups, the studied reserve of traditional management is also counter-productive. The Japanese with their effigies of senior directors available for castigation and beating find safe outlets for the release of these energies. Using that energy productively may prove even more beneficial.

Confluence

Our manager who is unwilling to confront or criticize is also confluent. He *fails to recognize some of the distinguishing elements of his environment or relationships*. He operates from a kind of emotional or perceptual colour-blindness. His own predisposition to projection and retroflection suggests that he will perceive them (instead of himself) as condemning him as ineffectual. In perceiving them and lumping his staff together he fails to recognize the differences between them. This process leads to selective or confused perception in which only the supporting evidence is noticed and acknowledged. Offers of support, encouragement, or even sympathy are ignored, whereas criticisms and implied put-downs stand out clearly.

Above all the manager does not distinguish between the different members of his staff and perceives his relationship with all of them as containing a few unchanging elements. Confluence creates blind spots and also blanks out the possible solutions to problems or means for the fulfilment of needs. Other examples of confluence can be found in those who 'go blank', 'get confused', or 'change the subject' at key moments or in response to important issues. For the trainer a frequent experience is that the trainee holds him responsible for what he learns, which allows the trainee to remain a passive partner in the learning process.

In this situation the trainer and trainee, both unaware, are confluent with their mutual expectations. They both agree that one should be responsible for both in terms of training. The result is likely to be a series of 'games' (Berne, 1964) in which the trainer ends up feeling inadequate and the trainee self-righteous. Confluence then is the experience that occurs when there is no discrimination of the points of difference or otherwise that distinguish between individuals. Without the distinction and boundary between me and each of you, there can be no development of a clear figure, no awareness, no engagement, therefore no completion. Confluence is not always unhealthy since it is the natural consequence at the end of a successful experience during the period of satisfaction and beneficial indifference.

Introjection

An introject is a *rule or judgement which has been 'swallowed whole' by someone*. The rule (as with parent tapes in Transactional Analysis) becomes an internal controlling force which operates automatically and without regard to any particular circumstances which may apply. The rule is accepted without consideration or reflection, probably because it is initially enforced by an authority figure. When first internalized, the rule will be associated with strong punishments or rewards.

Once the rule or judgement is introjected it is no longer normally available for review since it becomes an automatic control mechanism which inhibits the need fulfilment process at any stage in the cycle. By this means the emergence and awareness of the need itself can be stifled. For example, our manager who cannot bring himself to criticize his subordinates may reinforce his stuck position with the rule (learned in his early life) 'Don't criticize somebody unless you're sure you can do better'.

In hearing this rule you may think that it is a good rule for getting on with friends, colleagues, and family. Maybe that is true but you, unlike our manager, have considered the rule and can accept or reject it depending on the circumstances. For our manager, the rule operates automatically so that each time he is thinking about the problem of his staff, he finds himself wishing he could do their job better than them so that he could criticize them 'properly'. As it is, he shrugs and frowns (retroflection), feels stuck, and diverts the remainder of his attention to something he feels he can tackle.

Egotism

This interruption occurs at the moment before contacting the environment so that instead of wholehearted commitment to his actions the individual becomes rather detached or self-conscious. Like all the interruptions this process of itself can be helpful and positive, but as a repeating pattern it prevents an individual from achieving any real sense of satisfaction. Instead of putting his energy into fulfilling his need he diverts some of it to an internal commentary as if he were observing himself. Characteristic internal questions or comments would be: 'I wonder what he thinks of me?' 'I'm not doing this very well' or, more positively, 'There, that should give them something to think about!' Each of these comments to self is a deviation of energy from the current concern and prevents completion of the need–fulfilment pattern.

In summary, then, the processes by which we interrupt the pattern of need–fulfilment, of Gestalt formation, and destruction can be understood as follows. The introjector does as others expect of him, the projector does unto others what he accuses them of doing to him, the man in confluence does not know who is doing what to whom, and the retroflector does to himself what he would like to do to others, while the egotist watches himself in fascination.

It is important to recognize that these processes which we call interruptions are also part of the process of creative adaptation and need fulfilment. The difference between an interruption and adaptive behaviour is that the former is an automatic repeated pattern and the other a choice. The person who interrupts himself gains no satisfaction, the adaptive person does.

LEARNING METHODS

The normal setting for Gestalt-based training is a small group of, say, 6–12 participants under the direction of a trained leader. The group forms a social environment within which individuals become aware of themselves and others. The work arises out of the blocks that people place in the way of their need satisfaction as they arise from moment to moment. The learning event is likely to be based more or less explicitly on a set of ground rules.

Much of the initial learning of the programme is addressed to the development of awareness, since it is awareness which provides the raw material for self-development; learning to follow our awareness sensitively rather than forcing it in any particular direction. Most of us in response to the question 'What are you aware of?' will switch our energy into thinking, making an intellectual search; this very process blocks out the awareness of other important events: breathing, smells, tensions, self-stroking, avoiding contact, excitement, interest, memories, images, irritation, rejection, each of which provide us with valuable data about who we are and what we want. Most readers will be focused on the external world, the words, memories, or ideas linked with what is written. Some may be aware of body discomfort or the presence of nearby people. By now there may be for you a clearly-formed Gestalt concerning your need for movement and that mid-morning elixir, coffee. In the initial stages of a training course the trainee will be asked to notice where his attention takes him and as patterns emerge to notice how he stops himself. So I would say to you: Notice what you want and how you stop yourself!

This ground rule also serves to highlight confluence and projections in substituting 'I' for 'we' or 'people'. Each individual is encouraged to speak for himself, or at least to check with each member of the group about their experience.

A corollary of this is the ground rule: turn questions into statements. Most questions in conversation are an avoidance and a manipulation, in particular: 'Don't you think that . . .?', and 'What do you think of . . .?' type questions. They serve to avoid the individuals having to take the risk of expressing his own views and concerns against a background of uncertainty and they manipulate the other into doing just that; sometimes the question implies a particular view and invites confluence.

The value that the Gestalt approach places on action, exploration, and experiment results in a special view concerning thinking about or talking about on the one hand, and acting or making contact on the other. In that sense this whole presentation straddles the paradox in that we are engaged in talking about Gestalt, while the real learning takes place in doing. In a Gestalt training event the mental process is rejected in favour of outward action.

Let us take an example of someone who wants attention – the simple recognition of existence. In order to get it the person may need to begin the process of making contact, perhaps with eyes, perhaps by saying 'Hello!', perhaps by making a noise of some kind, or more directly by saying 'I want your attention!' Instead of taking action, our individual engages in mental activity. He holds a conversation with himself, on the one hand imagining what he might do, and on the other hand censuring, criticizing, squashing down the need, or imagining rejection and experiencing the concomitant bad feelings. The two conflicting forces within him absorb all his energy, contact and satisfaction are blocked.

Obviously, the intellectualizing process of thinking and talking about are essential means of solving problems, managing machines, understanding and predicting events, etc. They serve as functions for staying alive and saving ourselves a lot of unnecessary trouble and effort. In relationships and in our need for personal contact, however, thinking gets in our way. The problem is that if we take action without carefully working out the consequences beforehand, we experience this as taking a risk. It is safer to do nothing, safer to keep inside what we feel. One of the purposes of Gestalt training is to enable the individual to take the risk.

The discouraging of talking about also implies that explanations and interpretations are not considered particularly valuable. Knowing *why* is less important than knowing *how* someone interrupts themselves. Since only the latter sets up the possibility of not doing so or doing something different. This emphasis of Gestalt on learning by discovering, by direct experience, makes it exciting and sometimes confronting and painful.

As with all other forms of interpersonal skills training, a main learning method is through the exchange of feedback. In a Gestalt training event the feedback is likely to be direct from person to person, using 'I' and 'you', descriptive in the sense that the giver simply describes his own experience not attempting to interpret what the 'other' was doing. For example: 'When you started talking about your boss I started to feel angry and I began remembering how my subordinates talk to me; I also noticed my jaw getting tight; then, later on, I got bored and watched the others in the group so I wasn't listening to you.'

The receiver of the feedback is not encouraged to respond to feedback, to argue, explain, defend, or in any way discourage the giver.

The ground rules, together with appropriate accommodation and a timetable, are the main structural elements of a training event. There are few other constraints with work proceeding as needs arise and individuals come forward to meet these needs and find themselves unable to complete the Gestalt. The leader works with the individual to explore 'the blocks' or interruptions. The process is one of discovering unfinished business and building the self-support (through breathing and reality testing) necessary to let go of the block, integrate the split, making contact, and closing the cycle.

COMMON FEATURES OF THE GESTALT APPROACH

One feature is top dog:underdog dialogues or two-chair work in which an individual explores his internal splits by acting out a dialogue moving between two chairs between the conflicting elements, usually one part expressing a 'should' and the other a 'want'. With this process the individual clarifies and identifies projections, introjects, and expresses retroflections, exploring them and moving toward some new insight or creative adaptation which is likely to result in integration and completion.

Another feature is the use of dreams, imagery, and fantasy as a guide to Gestalt formation. In one sense dreams, etc. are a retroflection in that they exist as internal activity and yet are concerned with the person in his environment. Fantasy and dreams in Gestalt work are re-experienced and enacted in the present. A person who describes their dream as the experience of flying in an aeroplane is told 'Be the aeroplane – describe yourself as an aeroplane'. The results of such explorations are exciting, dramatic, and effective. Some accounts of dream-work can be found in Frederick Perls' *Gestalt Therapy Verbatim*.

THE RESULTS OF TRAINING

The simple purpose of Gestalt training is to develop awareness of what is happening inside and outside and increase the ability to deal with what *is* rather than what ought to be or might be. The task is not easy. The results can be disturbing and uncomfortable and the training requires the guidance of an experienced Gestaltist. As a training tool the Gestalt method is likely to be most effective for those individuals or organizations who see themselves as stuck with old patterns of behaviour which bring about unwanted consequences. To be a trainee and to learn does not require any understanding of the theory of Gestalt. On the contrary, since intellectualizing is discouraged, theory and abstraction are abandoned in favour of experience.

At worst, a trainee will become more entrenched in self-limiting patterns of behaviour and will continue to see others as the 'cause of his problems' or continue to blame himself for the difficulties that the environment presents. At best, the trainee may discover how he limits himself: he will be able to review the rules which govern his life; he will realize how he has been imagining things about others and reacting to unreal perceptions; he will understand how he has shied away from openness and directness with himself and others; he will be able to see the differences between himself and others; he will have a wider repertoire of behaviour, be more flexible, less manipulative, more willing to assert himself or engage in conflicts. He will be more creative and enthusiastic by looking for and finding ways of being satisfied rather than waiting for things to go wrong and saying 'I told you so'. In short a successful trainee will take responsibility for his own life and continue to discover ways of satisfying his needs by creative adaptation.

REFERENCES

Berne, E. (1964) *Games People Play*, Penguin, Harmondsworth.

Fagan, J. and Shepherd, C. (Eds.) (1972) *Gestalt Therapy Now*, Penguin, Harmondsworth.

Herman, S. and Korenich, M. (1977) *Authentic Management: A Gestalt Orientation to Organisations and their Development*, Addison Wesley.

Kohler, W. (1929) *Gestalt Psychology*, Liveright.

Passons, B. (1975) *Gestalt Approaches to Counselling*, Holt, Rinehart & Winston.

Perls, F., Hefferline, R., and Goodman, P. (1973) *Gestalt Therapy: Excitement and Growth in the Human Personality*, Penguin, Harmondsworth.

Polster, E. and Polster, M. (1973) *Gestalt Therapy Integrated*, Vintage Books.

Author Index

Subject Index